CONFESSIONS
OF A PROFESSIONAL

JOHN KELSO

Black Tie
BOOKS

Black Tie
BOOKS

Published by Black Tie Books

Austin, Texas

The Library of Congress has catalogued the trade paperback edition as follows:

Kelso, John

Confessions of a Professional Smart-Ass / by John Kelso

ISBN: 978-0-9888643-6-8

LCCN: 2013943647

Printed in the United States of America

First Edition

10 9 8 7 6 5 4 3 2 1

Acknowledgements:

A lot of people made this book possible, and only one of them was me. I'd like to thank my good friend Gary Rice, who used to enjoy professional wrestling, but is the best editor I've ever worked for. Gary is one of those guys who can actually make a story better with a couple of suggestions. Gary did the original edit on the book, and helped immensely with the organization. He figured out what parts should go where, something I couldn't master. Flowers to Janis Williams for doing a second edit and changing the style of the prose from newspaper to book form. Not sure what that means, because I couldn't tell the difference after she was finished. But that's the sign of a good editing job. Special kudos to all of the people in Austin who told me their funny stories over the last 37 years. Without them this book wouldn't be here, unless I made up a bunch of stuff off the top of my head. Thank you so much to Larry Brill, the Austin novelist who actually took the book on and published it when others turned me down. And a great big way-to-go to Kim Brill for the excellent cover. Until Kim came along I didn't realize typewriter keys could look quite so artistic. And special thanks to the *Austin American-Statesman*, for keeping me around all this time.

For Kay.

CONFESSIONS
OF A PROFESSIONAL

JOHN KELSO

Those Pesky Editors

I was never a violent person, so I've never wanted to kill anyone, not even an editor. And speaking of killing, the thing that always gave me a three-ZIP-code-wide case of the ticked-offs was when an editor would kill one of my columns. Didn't these people know who I am? Maybe that was the problem. Maybe they *did* know who I am: some wise guy trying to get another cheap laugh.

Once after one of my columns was killed, I did cause a rather large scene by punting a medium-sized wastebasket across the newsroom. This was in the mid-1980s. I got so cheesed off when the editor wouldn't run one of my columns that I kicked the wastebasket into the air. An instant three points. I think it got a couple feet off the carpet before it came down.

The column wasn't really that big of a deal. At least I didn't think so. We're not talking Watergate reportage here, sports fans. We were not at a Woodward and Bernstein level of uncovering bad shenanigans with this particular column that was axed. The story I had written was that Robert Barnstone, an Austin City Councilman and a well-off developer of downtown high rises, had spent hundreds of dollars of city money on pricey track-lighting for his City Hall office. I thought it was a bad time to be spending money on frills at City Hall. The city was going through a budget crunch. There had been talks about spending cutbacks among the Council members. So I interviewed Barnstone in his office, and decided to write something funny about his new yuppie lights. They seemed like a waste of money to me.

Barnstone didn't appear particularly upset to be asked about the lighting. In fact, he seemed to be looking forward to getting a laugh out of the column.

Next thing I knew, though, I got word from my friend, Gary Rice, one of the assistant city editors, that the column wasn't going to run. Maggie Balough, the editor at the time, had nixed it. Maggie was like that. If there was any possibility an article might ruffle some big shot's feathers, there was a good chance that Maggie would yank it, or at least sit on it until there was no longer a story. She was especially likely to sit on a story if it had anything to do with a developer, such as Barnstone.

Gary remembers what happened this way: "I told John the bad news and he was ticked, not at me but at the situation that we both understood," Gary wrote. "John went back to his desk and started slamming stuff around. I kept editing other copy. John did a slow burn. Then he exploded.

"I heard yelling and then I saw a small plastic wastebasket fly through the air after John kicked it. Then John, in his weight-lifter phase, unleashed his 16-inch guns, heaving a 1,000-count plastic bottle of liver pills toward the bank of elevators as he rampaged around the newsroom. The bottle hit the elevator doorframe about the time the elevator door opened. To make the story better, I would like to say the bottle exploded and liver pills went everywhere. However, the bottle stayed intact — plastic was tough in those days — but it made a loud thud as it hit the doorframe.

"John's timing was perfect. Inside the elevator was one of our part-time reporters, Tara Parker, who was bringing a guy into the newsroom. I recall he was the Ugandan Ambassador, or at least a big shot in the Uganda government. This was back when Idi Amin was a mover and shaker in Uganda, killing and eating people. I'm sure the Ugandan big shot thought his time had come, perhaps figuring he had been shot. Tara, sizing up the situation and showing the quick thinking that eventually would take her to the *Wall Street Journal* and the *New York Times*, calmly told the shaky Ugandan: 'Sometimes emotions run high in the newsroom.' Thankful that he wasn't bleeding, the Ugandan smiled and said he understood.

"The last I saw of John that day, he was heading toward the stairs and out of the newsroom. A company car in the parking lot had a door kicked in about that time, but John said he didn't do it, and I believe him."

Gary's right. I didn't kick in the door of a company car. I wasn't going to ruin a perfectly good pair of shoes on one of those hunks of metal the newspaper foisted upon its reporting staff. Nor did I know when I hurled those pills that some muckety-muck from Africa was about to step off the elevator.

I'm glad he was visiting that day, though, since it makes for a better story. That's what it's all about in the news business: getting a better story.

I began working at the *Austin American-Statesman* in 1976, and I started writing my humor column in April of 1977. I'm 67 and 68 years old as I write this in 2012-2013. So I have literally spent about half my life trying to get funny stuff in the newspaper past editors who can't always take a joke. It hasn't always been pretty.

There was the time in the '90s, for example, when President Bill Clinton pushed through his don't-ask-don't-tell policy in the U.S. military. I couldn't leave a fat pitch like that one alone. When I told people what I was fixing to write about, they would often respond, "That's shooting fish in a barrel." Like there was something wrong with shooting fish in a barrel. All the better to bag the fish, I always figured. So I wrote a column outlining the changes the don't-ask-don't-tell policy would bring to life in the U.S. Army.

For example, I pointed out that it would give a whole new meaning to the military command, "To the rear, march!"

Sorry.

There was soon a competition among the editors about who could kill the column the fastest. It was like they all were fighting over a plaque. Word spread across the newsroom about this tasteless piece, and people who weren't even involved figured they better read it now, because they wouldn't get a chance to read it later.

"The funniest part of this is that you actually think this is going to get in the newspaper," said Debbie Hiott, a young reporter at the time, as she peered into a computer screen to read the column. She was just sport reading.

I should have known right then she'd make it to editor, because she nailed it. The column was in pretty poor taste, and she recognized it. Debbie eventually made it all the way to editor of the *American-Statesman,* and I think she's the best editor we had during my days at the paper.

So "To the rear, march!" just marched on out of the newsroom and never made it into the *Austin American-Statesman.* In fact, many of my brilliant lines ended up on the cutting room floor, and. each time it happened, it ate a little piece of my butt.

A Lucky Man With a Wonderful Job

I've been in Austin for so long that there are only two things left in this city that were here when I arrived in 1976: me, and the Broken Spoke, that legendary honkytonk on South Lamar.

If I sound like I'm crabbing about my job at the *American-Statesman*, just tell me to shut up. The *Statesman* gave me an opportunity most people never get. I'm one of those fortunate people who actually spent his life getting paid for doing what he loves. And my job goal was pretty simple: to make people laugh, and occasionally to make a serious point. I wasn't trying to change the world. I was simply trying to get people to shoot their breakfast cereal out their nose. My task was to bring a little levity into an otherwise often gloomy world. And I was pretty successful at it. Whenever there was a readership survey, there was a good chance it would show my column as the most read column in the newspaper.

That's the big way I measure success in column writing. The more people who read a column, the better it is. When it comes to newspaper writing, in numbers there is strength. It's like what Red Auerbach, the Boston Celtics' legendary coach, said about basketball. "It's not a good pass — unless somebody catches the ball."

Well, it's not a good column unless somebody reads it. That's just the way it is. But lots of readers or not, along the way, I've had to deal with editors. Or should I say these poor schleps had to deal with my edgy ways. Either way, since I had to get my sometimes-gnarly observations past them, I learned their hang-ups. I say, "learned." All I had to do was watch. Most writers would judge their editors by their ability to spot a good news story, or take an awkward sentence and make it better.

I used those measuring sticks, too, but I also rated my editors on their innermost humor fears, their ha-ha hang-ups, if you will, their fun phobias. What was it that would make them run screaming from the room when they picked up the paper and saw it under my photo in the paper? I made a study of this phenomenon. The reason I studied this? Simple. I needed to know what jokes would cause me trouble.

For example, Rich Oppel, who brought hard news coverage back into the *American-Statesman* when he took over as editor in 1995, hated poop jokes. That was his little problem, as regards to me. I don't like poop humor that much, either. You can't win many Pulitzers writing poop jokes. During the fifteen years Rich was editor of the *Charlotte* (N.C.) *Observer*, the newspaper won two Pulitzers and shared a third. So it should come as no shocker that the man hated scatological humor worse than chicken flu.

If poop appeared in a story, he'd come unglued—that is, as

unglued as he ever got. Rich didn't lose his temper, at least not so you could see it. But he had the ability to cut you off at the knees with a scathing remark so subtle that you wouldn't notice you were bleeding until half a block later, when you saw your leg was missing.

And I still have the scabs to prove it.

I wrote a column in 2001 about the best place to bird watch in Austin, Texas: ironically, it's the sewage treatment plant at Hornsby Bend. "In a way, you could say it's the crappiest birding place in town, but it's also the best birding place in town," Rob Fergus told me. He had just become executive director of the Travis Audubon Society.

Birds, you see, appreciate the nutrients in poop. Bird watching/poop: I found the marriage amusing. So I spent part of the day with Fergus, traipsing about the sewage treatment facility, watching birds. I even expense-accounted the mileage. That's one piece of advice I'd give to any budding journalist. Always expense-account the mileage. It adds up. In fact, if you're a bit short of money, drive somewhere.

Anyway, during our bird-watching expedition, Fergus pointed out a variety of birds that had landed in poop at Hornsby Bend, among them the red-crested turd swallow.

I just made up that bird species, as if you didn't know.

So Oppel hated the column, and he made a point of saying so. He said it ruined his breakfast. That's one thing about editors: they're always having their breakfasts ruined. Also, they "wince." Whenever I'd write something that offended them, they'd tell me they winced. They also "cringed" now and again. Wincing is a little old-fashioned, isn't it? I think the only people on the planet who wince anymore are editors. Sure, the column wasn't fit for the Junior League's annual Christmas bulletin, but I thought I'd performed a public service by letting people in Austin know where to take their binoculars and go to see a lot of birds.

I could go on and on about editors and their hang-ups. So I will.

Ray Mariotti, the editor at the *Statesman* when I arrived in 1976, and a real old school seat-of-the-pants editor, had a hang-up about people not finishing their drinks. So at a party, he'd go around the room, picking up half-finished drinks people had left behind, and he'd finish drinking them. At least that's what he told me he did. I guess you could say he was a whiskey recycler.

Ray also had a brief crusade to get rid of the word "scumbag." You see, editors have notoriously dirty minds. Your average Joe sees "scumbag" and he thinks of some lowlife guy on the street. Mariotti, however, figured the term meant "used condom." Being an upstanding citizen and a former Cub Scout, it hadn't occurred to me that scumbag meant used condom.

So when the word "scumbag" appeared in a news story on the front page, Mariotti put out an edict banning "scumbag" from the doorstep of the *Austin American-Statesman*. This was odd, because Mariotti was far from a prude. He used to drive around with a briefcase that served as a wet bar on the seat of his car. It had everything you'd need for a drink, except for running water.

I first saw this briefcase in action in 1984 while Ray was riding around in his car during the Republican Convention in Dallas. I can't remember whether the briefcase/bar rode in the front seat or the back, but it was one or the other.

Ray went up to Dallas to cover the convention, and so did I. As I said, Ray was no prude. During the convention we spent a little time together at Pappy's Showland, a topless bar near the Loews Anatole Hotel, where the Republicans were staying. I remember Ray asked me specifically NOT to introduce him to the dancers as the editor of the *Austin American-Statesman*, so, of course, as soon as I saw him in Pappy's Showland, I introduced him to one or two of the dancers as my boss. I doubt that made him real happy.

I spent a lot more time at Pappy's Showland than at the Loews Anatole because Pappy's had a better class of people. And some of them were named Danniell, Brown Sugar, and Ree. I remember the dancers complaining about what lousy tippers the Republicans were. "I've been here four-and-a-half years and I've never seen anything like it," said Juanita Lee, the proprietor. "I think it's terrible. Like I said, they won't spend money. They just won't spend money." Sounds to me like Juanita Lee was forecasting the coming of the Tea Party.

Fred Zipp, another top-notch editor at the *Statesman*, kept a keen eye out for Aggie sheep jokes in my columns. I managed to sneak in a couple of Aggie sheep remarks while he was the editor. But Fred would not rest while there were sheep in the area, so he put a stop to the running of the sheep. Fred and I just didn't see eye to eye on sheep humor. Fred thought of sheep jokes as "bestiality." Meanwhile, I was thinking of these jokes as just, you know, sheep jokes.

Then there was Balough, the *Statesman*'s editor in the late

1980s and early 1990s. She had a hang-up about putting anything in the newspaper that might be offensive to any group you could name — up to and including Lithuanian banjo players.

Okay, so that last one is over the top, but only because while Balough was editor, there were, as far as I know, no Lithuanian banjo players in Austin. But if there had been, Maggie would have been concerned about their feelings, and she would have made sure we didn't offend them. Maggie was to sensitive what Donald Trump is to a bad hair day.

For example, there was the time I wrote a column making fun of Yasser Arafat, the late Palestinian leader. If you can't make fun of Yasser Arafat, who can you make fun of? I've always wondered whether, if Hitler was still around and I wrote a funny column about him, Maggie would kill it for being insensitive to Germans.

When the Arafat column came out, a local guy of Palestinian descent, a fella named Kahlil Sakakini, got his nose in a twist and called Balough to complain. I heard later that Maggie was using this guy as a source at the local high tech company where he worked at the time. So maybe she figured she should stick up for him—and to heck with me.

So she organized a meeting in her office between Sakakini, her, and me. During the course of the meeting, Sakakini leaned over and gave a little yank on my beard. In the column, if I remember right, I had joked about Arafat's beard. So this was Sakakini's way of insulting me, I guess. And no, not being an editor, I didn't "wince" when he did it. I pretended it was no big deal. It wasn't, and besides, I needed the job—so I didn't slap him. Meanwhile, Maggie said nothing about it. Maybe she didn't notice. Or, maybe it was okay with her if the guy wanted to grab my beard and give it a little tug.

But that's the way she was. The writers were wrong and the readers were right. If you expected her help in a dark alley, you were in a dark alley with the wrong person.

We've had all sorts of unusual personalities working at the *Statesman* over the years. We had an intern, for example, who was afraid of making left turns while driving. So you had to be careful about what reporting assignments you gave him, because it might take him three or four hours to get there, if there were any left turns involved.

We also had a guy who robbed a laundry and did prison time. He was an excellent copy editor, too.

Another time, we had a reporter who allegedly got hooked on crank and stole a TV set out of the newsroom, along with a lot of used books. People bring their old books from home into the newsroom all the time, and drop them off for other people, such as school kids, to read. I was told that this guy was lifting the books, then taking them and selling them.

But here's my favorite personal encounter of the startling kind. We had a fashion writer who came up to me on the steps of the building as she was returning to the office after lunch, and she said quietly, into my ear, "Do I smell like I've been f***ing?"

I am not making this up. I told her, um, no, she did not. Why she asked me that question I have no idea. I had no personal relationship with her except for chatting. Maybe she thought I was an expert on that particular scent, but if so, she would have been mistaken.

Then there was the newsroom clerk who looked like a serial killer, but who was fluent in about six different languages. The guy, who seemed somewhat antisocial, was really a good dude. He didn't speak to most of the reporters, but he spoke to me, because I spoke to him. He was very helpful. Whenever I needed help putting a Latin phrase in my column, I'd just ask him how to write it. And he'd tell me.

This guy was quite the eccentric. I think he had an IQ of about a hundred thousand. He'd take his lunch breaks at a desk in the newsroom, and for food he'd squirt those tiny to-go packets of mustard directly into his mouth. Squirt, squirt, squirt.

Yes, we had a fair number of eccentrics working at the newspaper. Then there was me.

How Come I'm Goofy

People often ask me where I got my sense of humor. Fact is, I've always enjoyed comedy, and I like hanging out with characters. Maybe it's because the paper mill town in Central Maine, a town called Winslow where I spent most of my growing-up years, was in the woods. People in Maine are not impressed by pretense. They admire individuality. And I picked up on this as a child.

A lot of comics and comedy writers say they got their funny bone from bad treatment when they were growing up. I can't make that claim. Life in the little Maine paper mill town wasn't idyllic, but it was close to it. We had a mailman who talked like Donald Duck. When I was a little kid, every time he'd come to the door, he'd do his Donald Duck voice, which I just thought was great.

My parents, Elmer and Dorothy Kelso, weren't rich, by any means. I recall that on the occasional Sunday night, dinner would consist of milk and bread in a bowl. And every Saturday night, here came that New England staple — baked beans and brown bread. On a good night, some hot dogs would be tossed into the mix. I'm surprised I can still look a baked bean in the eye without screaming.

My parents couldn't have treated me better. Yes, my father could be a bit tough on occasion. When I was in elementary school, he gave me a task I thought was impossible: shovel the driveway, and have it done by the next afternoon. Trouble was, the driveway was covered with four or five inches of concrete-hard ice. Just plain snow would have been a cakewalk. The iced-over driveway was a challenge.

I knew I couldn't do it myself. So I Tom Sawyered it. I talked a few of my friends from school (Boston Avenue Elementary, about a 30-second walk from our house) into helping me out, and we got after it. But we didn't finish the job. We tried, but we ran out of time. My father made note of the fact that the work hadn't been completed. Maybe he was testing me to see if I was smart enough to find a bag of sand. If so, I flunked.

But he was a kind man, never used bad language (he got a bit cross when my mother once used the expression "hot spit"), would have nothing to do with violence except to watch football, and only ever hit me once — a little slap on the fanny, when at the age of 3 I accused my mother of having a "fat bottom."

My parents were hard-working people. My father was a forester who worked in conjunction with the local paper mill, and my mother was raising two small children, although she taught home economics by the time I reached high school age, after we'd moved to New Hampshire.

My mother couldn't abide sloth. As a home economics teacher, one of her jobs was to visit the homes of her students who came from poor families. She did this make sure the kids were getting the right nutrition and treatment. On one such visit, she saw two men playing Monopoly in the broad light of day. Why were these guys lounging around the house when they should be working? Mother was appalled. She was a gentle soul, but she could level you with a few well-chosen words. I remember one of my wives complaining that my previous betrothed had taken the vacuum cleaner.

"Yes dear, but you got what she really wanted," my mother replied. Pow! Take that.

Then there was the time that an English teacher who taught in the same high school as my mother got on the case of one of her students, unjustly, my mother thought. She gave the English teacher a piece of her mind. Of course, she had to look up at him while doing it. She stood just five-foot-two, but she wouldn't stand for her students being messed with.

Dad's mother, my grandmother Florence, lived in in a farmhouse in Bar Mills, Maine, a wide place in the road outside Portland. I suspect when they had chicken dinner there, Florence wrung a chicken's neck in preparation. My dad took me back to his little hometown once when I was a teenager. A bunch of old men were sitting around a wood stove spitting into it. You could easily hear the sizzle when the spit hit the flames.

My parents should have realized early on that I would grow up to be a newshound, or some sort of professional snoop. When I was about five, my dad took me to a big outdoor show in Waterville, Maine, right across the Kennebec River from Winslow. There was country-western music by a singer in Western duds, along with a cotton candy stand. I wanted me some of that cotton candy, but when I asked my dad for it, he said no, because it was "dirty." So when the old man wasn't looking, I sneaked over to the cotton candy stand and asked the man selling the stuff if it was, indeed, "dirty." The guy said no, it certainly wasn't dirty.

So I went back to my dad and reported that the cotton candy man had said the cotton candy wasn't dirty. This chapped my father's behind. He gave me a dirty look to indicate he wasn't happy that I'd gone off and done my own investigation. I can't remember if I got the cotton candy, though. But I did show my father that I wasn't easily fooled. Or that I had some brat in me.

My dad loved baseball and just about every summer in the 1950s he'd drive my big sister, Joan, my mother, and me down to Fenway Park in Boston for a Red Sox game. My dad would get chapped when somebody cut in front of him in his seat to go get a beer. That's how serious he was about watching the game. He didn't want anyone disturbing his view for a 35-cent beer. He loved the game so much he even took the time to show my sister Joan how to keep score, which was pretty cool stuff for a 12-year-old girl sitting in the stands with her dad at Fenway Park.

Dad had a warm heart and a dry sense of humor. On the way back to Maine from Boston after the Red Sox games, he'd tell my sister and me that we could have an ice cream cone at every single Howard Johnson's restaurant we passed, if we were still awake. I think Joan used to shake herself to keep going. She usually made it through two cones; I was the baby brother and usually conked out in the back seat after the first one.

To someone outside of New England, my dad might have seemed cold. Complain about the meat being tough at the dinner table, and he'd say, "Tuffa' (read "tougher") where there's none." When he'd get me out of bed in the morning, he wasn't exactly warm about it. "SIGNS OF LIFE," he'd announce when he walked into the bedroom. He had a way of getting right to the point. One time I asked him if it was going to stop raining.

"Always has," he said, looking out the window.

But Dad liked kids, and since he was a forester who worked in the Maine woods, he could get his hands on all sorts of Smokey Bear posters and movies. When I was about 8, I knew the words to the Smokey Bear song: "Smokey the Bear, Smokey the Bear, prowlin' and a growlin' and 'a-sniffin' the air." There was nothing better in the whole wide world than dad's taking me over to his office to show me all the latest posters, films, and other Smokey Bear promotional materials.

Even as stern as he was, my dad knew how to laugh. He loved women, and held them up on a pedestal. He would have crawled through fire to help my mother. He used to read bedtime stories to me at night. But instead of using the real names of the characters, he'd stick in our neighbors' names.

That's those dry Mainers for you.

My father wasn't exactly David Letterman. His humor was so dry that you had to be from Maine to notice that anything funny was going on. One day when I was a little kid my dad walked across the street to visit Mr. Turbyne, one of our neighbors. Mr. Turbyne was in the living room having a drink, so he asked my dad if he wanted one. My father told Mr. Turbyne he'd have whatever he was having.

Turns out Mr. Turbyne was having an Alka-Seltzer. So that's what he brought my dad, who drank his Alka-Seltzer and never said a word about it. In Maine, that would be a real knee-slapper. If anybody in Maine ever slapped their knees.

One thing I particularly admired about my father was the way he dealt with racism. When he came back from World War II (he served as a lieutenant colonel in the Army and went to Germany toward the end of the war), it was obvious that he had picked up some racial ways from some of his fellow officers. Dad was an officer over black troops for a while. And some of his fellow officers were Southerners.

My dad didn't use the N word, but he did use a J word occasionally that had the same meaning. But as time went on and the world changed, Dad changed with it. I remember an evening when I was 16 or 17 and Eleanor Parker, one of my high school English teachers in Laconia, New Hampshire, came over to our house to give us a Christmas card. It was the season to be jolly.

The Christmas card showed a dove, and a black hand shaking hands with a white hand. Behind Ms. Parker's back, my father made a disparaging remark about the card. Then he thought better about what he'd said, and he got real sheepish.

"You don't suppose she heard that, do yah?" my father asked me, embarrassed. "No, Dad," I told him, "I don't think she heard you." He looked relieved. I was glad, and a little surprised, to see that he was concerned about the words he chose regarding race. It hadn't always been this way. I admire a man who can grow with the times. And he definitely did.

While my father was fairly no-nonsense, *his* father was a real character, a hunting guide and constable who worked in the north woods of Maine. A news story from 1915, with a Bangor, Maine, dateline, tells of the adventures of Skeffington Kelso when he had to retrieve a heifer as part of a civil law suit. I never met my grandfather on my father's side, since he died before I was born. But based on this story, I'm sure I would have followed him around like a puppy dog if I'd known him.

That loose heifer led Skeffington Kelso through four miles of swamp. He broke through the ice twice during the chase. He stepped into a mink trap and lost a jackknife. He tore his clothing and ruined his shoes. In a court case, a judge ruled that Skeffington Kelso was due extra pay to cover his losses.

But the coup de grace came when "he was held up to derision by a young woman, who wrote a funny poem about his chase and read it at a Grange meeting."

Decades later, I was holding other people up to derision as I wrote the same sorts of things.

Mom and dad never nudged me toward writing, or writing funny, but comedy was available around the house regularly, and I went for it, hammer and tongs. In the 1950s, our black-and-white TV set often as not was tuned to the latest comedians, and I loved them all: Jack Benny, Jackie Gleason, Groucho ("Fenneman, lower the duck") Marx, Herb Shriner, George Gobel, Lucille Ball, Steve Allen. By the time I was in high school, I loved me some Steve Allen.

My favorite of all the funny people? Groucho Marx, partly because he interviewed all of those screwballs on his game show

"You Bet Your Life." The show was based in Southern California; so even at the age of ten I realized the crazy people moved from east to west, to run away from problems back home. I noticed the same truth when I moved to Florida in my twenties, so it's got to be true. Lunacy is a regional condition. And the biggest loons live in parts of America — L.A., Miami — where people go to avoid an arrest warrant back home.

So I was in love with crackpots from an early age. If you want to know about one of my favorite TV comedy sketches of all time, just climb into the ol' time machine and go back about sixty years. So I'm a little kid and I'm watching that classic TV show, The Honeymooners, starring Jackie Gleason as New York bus driver Ralph Kramden, and Art Carney, as Ed Norton, Kramden's buddy who works in the sewer.

Kramden and Norton are talking golf in Ralph's dump of a living room, as if either one of them would be allowed out at the country club, or even own a set of clubs. Ed is showing Ralph how to "address" the ball.

Ed takes the golf club from Ralph, steps up to the ball, plants his feet and wiggles his club. Then, with a little bow and a friendly tip of his hat, Ed says, "Well, hellllooooo, ball."

I was always on the prowl for the goofy side. We lived in Winslow from the time I was five until I was twelve or so. Winslow was a blue-collar paper mill town. Just about every man in town worked at the mill. And even we kids in the neighborhood provided comedic material. Many of the dads, including mine, had just returned from World War II a few years earlier. So we kids sang a little ditty while we played hide and seek or kick the can: "Whistle while you work, Hitler is a jerk. Mussolini bit his weinie; now it doesn't work."

There's also a good chance I inherited my sense of humor from my grandfather, John Bradford. A master carpenter who built spars for clipper ships, he spent his later years driving around Maine, selling caskets to funeral homes. Gramp would come back from his funeral home road trips with little souvenirs just for me. My favorite was the King Tut magnet. The King Tut magnet, a promotional gadget from one of the funeral homes on Gramp's route, consisted of a tiny cream-colored plastic casket with a green plastic liner. Inside the casket was a magnet. The green plastic Tut, also magnetized, would pop out of his casket if you put him in backwards. This was fascinating to an 8-year-old with a warped mind, like me.

Sometimes at the dinner table, Gramp would, uh, entertain us with gory stories he'd picked up from morticians while making his rounds. And it wasn't pretty.

"Well, this fella down tah Rumford got his head run clean ovah (read "over") by the train…" That sort of thing. My parents would cringe a little, but they were Mainers, too, so I suspect this seemed fairly normal to them.

Then there was Gramp's prank rock. Gramp got his hands on a brown rock that looked just like a baked potato. I mean, it really did. You could set it today in a pile of baked potatoes at the to-go food counter at Central Market and somebody would buy it for dinner.

One of the funeral home directors loaned this rock to my grandfather, and did that ever make his day. Gramp brought it home one night and showed it off like it was the Hope Diamond. He liked to put it on your plate to see your reaction when you tried to stick your fork into it. And your fork went, "Clank."

I haven't said much about my sister Joan. This is because Joan is the normal, steady one in the family. A more loving and patient person you'd have a hard time finding. As a kid in high school she played three musical instruments — viola, clarinet, and piano — and she was talented enough to make it into several state high school orchestras. When I was a boy, my mother and my sister would sit at the piano together in the living room and play tunes from 1950s musicals.

Joan went on to marry her high school sweetheart, who had a lifelong career in the Army and retired as a colonel. They had two kids. Joan never got in trouble, never did anything goofy.

That, as it turned out, was my job.

How to Do a Group Sneeze

After graduating from high school in Laconia, N.H. in 1962, I went off to college at the University of Missouri. Leaving home and going to a part of the world I'd never set foot in was a grand adventure. This would be my first flight on a big commercial airliner. The Midwest looked different from New England out of the plane window. The land was cut up into neat squares. It certainly looked nothing like home. Where were the lakes and the winding roads?

Before I left, my mother showed me how to iron a shirt and write a check, so I could fend for myself. I was ready to roll.

At the time I had no idea I would end up writing a humor column. But even back then, lurking somewhere in the back of my head, was the notion that that was what I wanted to do with my life.

In preparation, I was always doing crazy things. For instance, when I was a high school senior I took part in something we called a group sneeze.

You don't know how to perform a group sneeze?

Well, first, you find four guys. You shouldn't recruit a woman for this stunt, trust me. You don't want to hang around with any woman who would take part in a group sneeze.

So you've got your four guys. In our group sneeze quartet at Laconia High that year, we had Jeff Lunn, my best friend; Newell Bacon, who became H. Newell Bacon after he went off to one of those snooty Eastern colleges, somebody else I can't remember, and me. I think that fourth guy was Ed Fitzgerald. But maybe that position changed from sneeze to sneeze.

Anyway, to accomplish the group sneeze, you assign a different sound to each guy. One guys says (for example) "hish," another guy says "hosh," a third guy says "hash," and the fourth guy says "rasp."

You say all four sounds — hish, hosh, hash and rasp — simultaneously, and distinctly. Put it all together and it sounds just like a sneeze. Honest. Give it a try.

Somebody asked me what kind of audience you get for a group sneeze, but you don't actually get any kind of audience. That is, unless you think of yourselves as the audience.

Whenever we'd perform a group sneeze in high school, we'd have four guys sitting there laughing at themselves, maybe while sitting in a car. This is not the sort of thing we attempted in an auditorium. And finding people who enjoy viewing a group sneeze in progress is next to impossible. You can't sell tickets to a group sneeze.

So, given that I enjoyed that kind of lowbrow humor, is it any surprise that I knew I wanted to be a humor columnist all along? I mean, guys who want to grow up to be president don't take part in group sneezes. And conversely, guys who take part in group sneezes and remember doing so fifty years later don't become president.

I was an average student at Laconia High. I was on the tennis team. We won two state championships, but not because of me. I wasn't one of the top guys on the team. I didn't have a backhand. I think my senior year I made it up to the number three man on the team. And just about every year I'd try out for the basketball team, but I never made the team.

I wasn't a complete cutup in high school. Also, I was an honest kid. One day in physics class when nobody was looking I stuck a pencil in one of those long-necked skinny water faucets you see in science labs. When our physics teacher, Mr. Davis (or, if you prefer, Porky Davis), turned on the water later, he got sprayed good. People laughed, except for Porky Davis, who thought my friend Freddie had put the pencil in the faucet.

So he gave Freddie hell.

I felt bad about this, so later on I went to see Mr. Davis and turned myself in. I, and not Freddie, was the one who monkeyed with the pencil and the water faucet, I told him. Mr. Davis looked befuddled. I guess he didn't give a hoot one way or the other, because he didn't say much. Basically his facial expression told me to get the heck out of there, that I was wasting his time.

I guess I wasn't much on science. When I was in junior high in Orono, Maine, we had to complete a science project. The student got to pick the subject. Up in Maine in winter, I had frequently seen fish swimming beneath the ice in a frozen lake. I'd be skating along on the lake, and I'd look down and see fish swimming around down there.

I wondered how fish could survive that way. To find out, I put a goldfish in a bowl of water and set the bowl outside overnight in hard-freeze temperatures. The next morning, I checked on the fish. Here are my scientific results: that bowl of water was one gigantic ice cube, the fish was frozen solid, and it was altogether dead. I think I got a B on that research project.

I was a crafty child, however. I spent a couple of months of my junior high years in a private school called St. Luke's for Boys, located in upscale New Canaan, Connecticut. My father had taken a job in nearby New York City, so we moved from Maine down to Connecticut. I hated it. The kids at St. Luke's for Boys were wealthy and snotty and you had to wear a tie and a sport coat to school. If I'd had any snap at the time I would have called it St. Puke's for Boys.

Our science teacher assigned us a fifty-page paper. This was daunting to me. I was thirteen at the time and I had hardly read fifty pages, let alone written them. So I devised a plan. A devious little plan, to be honest, but a plan nonetheless.

I knew we were moving back to northern New England in a few weeks. My father hated it in New York because the place was too sissified for a Maine guy. So I knew we were leaving. And I also knew that the deadline for the fifty-page science paper would land AFTER we were long gone from Connecticut.

The first part of the paper, though, the bibliography, was due shortly. So I hit the local library and wrote down the names of a whole lot of books I knew I'd never even open. Then I turned in this really long and impressive bibliography.

I got an A on the bibliography. Pretty smart, huh? A couple weeks later we moved to New Hampshire, meaning I didn't have to write the rest of the 50-page paper. Now you're wondering why I didn't grow up to run for office. But some of the skills I used in junior high were useful in high school and college, too.

My collegiate experience started out pretty well. My parents drove me down to Boston from Laconia and put me on the plane. Being shipped to the Midwest was a major cultural shift for a kid from Cow Hampshire. But it had to be and it was what I wanted. For one thing, I wanted to see the world beyond New England. I wanted to move somewhere where it might be warm enough for a motel to have a swimming pool. But just as important, as a kid, I'd always wanted to be a newspaper writer. So when it came time to pick a college, I decided on the University of Missouri, since it was affordable, and it had what many consider to be the best journalism school in the country.

Missouri's journalism school is different from many, in that it's basically a trade school. The school is light on theory and heavy on getting out the door and doing the work. If you're majoring in print journalism at the University of Missouri, you work for an actual newspaper, the *Columbia Missourian*, which is available for sale to the public.

The editors weren't students who were elected to their positions in popularity contests. They were professionals who had worked at other publications. One of my professors, for example, had worked as a reporter for *The Wall Street Journal*.

There were some early bumps in the road when I arrived in Columbia. I had to adjust to living outside New England. The first bump came when I learned that all incoming freshmen had to stand up in front of a classroom full of fellow freshmen and make a short speech — about two minutes.

As I later learned, the purpose was to find out whether a student had a speaking disorder. The experts weren't looking for Winston Churchill. They were looking for defects. After my presentation, the woman speech expert who was running the class pulled me aside. My little talk had been rambling and juvenile, but that wasn't the problem. She thought I had a speech impediment, and she was thinking of sticking me in some sort of remedial speaking course. I explained to her it wasn't a speech impediment, but my thick New England accent. As in, "Pahk your cah in Hah-vahd Yahd." She had an a-ha moment when I explained my accent, and she let me off the hook, figuring I didn't need help after all.

In my freshman year in the dorm, my roommate and I didn't even speak the same language, really. He was from a small Missouri farm town called Neosho, down near Arkansas, and he sounded like he was from Mayberry. I had the New England a-yup and no-sah thing going, and we didn't even use the same words. For example, my roommate called them rubber bands; I called them elastics.

Still, we got along just fine — in part, I think, because we couldn't always understand what we were saying to each other. You know how you just stand there and smile and nod when somebody says something and you have no clue?

That first year I did nothing but study, and I kept my head stuck in the books. I had a great fear of flunking out. I hadn't been a genius in high school, earning mostly B's and C's, but I ended up my first college semester with a 3.5 grade point average, including several A's.

My trouble started the second year. Because of my initial scholastic success, I now figured I was Albert Einstein, so I didn't study much at all. I took to whiskey and partying. They actually had a kind of liquor called Old Panther Piss on the shelves in Columbia's liquor stores. I never tried it, but it wasn't just because I was too young to buy it. We'd give the money to some wino in the liquor store parking lot, and he'd bring our booze out to us.

If I hadn't pulled such high grades my freshman year, I would have flunked out because of my lousy grades in my sophomore year. I flunked modern American poetry, for gosh sakes. I had no idea what they were talking about.

I had some funny friends in the dorm, no doubt about it. And I don't necessarily mean funny as in ha-ha. This big guy named Wayne who had a real high voice used to hand out Feen-a-mints to the other guys without explaining the chewing gum was a laxative. Wayne, who eventually joined the Marines, called me a Communist because I listened to a lot of Bob Dylan.

There was another guy in the dorm who was a Navy veteran. He was also big. On weekends, he'd get drunk, then come back to the dorm and terrorize other guys. One night he decided to toss me around the room, bouncing me off the walls like a laundry bag.

Living next door to me was a skinny, egghead journalism major whose room was so crammed with books that you could hardly walk from one end of the room to the other. He used to keep cigarettes in his room, and on weekends, when smokers would run out of smokes, he'd sell them cigarettes. If I remember right, he charged us a dime for each smoke.

In the dorm I made friends with several kids from Crystal City, a somewhat Hillbilly little town on the Mississippi River half an hour south of St. Louis. Most of these kids were politically conservative. I'd never been around this tribe before. New Englanders were conservative when it came to money, but socially? Not so much. Northern New England wasn't exactly loaded with Baptists back then, and the adults in Winslow, Maine, where I grew up, were pretty logical and down to earth. I was led to realize (by age five) that Sen. Joe McCarthy's communist scare routine was a political stunt, and that the man was stark raving mad. That was the opinion of the grown-ups in the neighborhood. And I bought into it, fortunately.

I found out about the assassination of President Kennedy while I was hitchhiking with a college buddy on Interstate 70 in Missouri. We were headed to my friend's home in Crystal City for the weekend. It was a Friday afternoon around 12:30 when a traveling salesman picked us up. When we got in his car, we heard on the radio that the President had been shot. At the time I didn't comprehend the enormity of the tragedy. It took time for me to realize the magnitude of this national disaster.

We arrived at my friend's house, and I was surprised to see that the people of the household didn't seem that upset about the assassination of the President. In fact, there was some harping because there was nothing on television except news about the assassination.

This seemed wrong to me. I hadn't grown the balls yet to tell these people how screwed up they were. So I just shut up and observed them, for the most part. (I still do that a lot.) The situation was a real eye-opener. Even my friend's mother didn't seem all that moved by this history-making moment. I mean, here was one of those times in your life — like Pearl Harbor — that is so important that you'll always remember where you were at the time, and what you were doing. And these people were worried about the TV schedule?

My friend and I spent the weekend on his living room floor, playing a baseball board game. The TV was on and we followed the tragic news. I can't say the other people in the house were glad the President had been killed, but it didn't seem to bother them as much as I thought it should have.

Leaving the dorm and joining a fraternity in my second year of college didn't help my grades much. It was a good choice in one way, though, because I finally started meeting girls. Girls liked fraternity boys back then, although in the case of our fraternity there was no logical reason for that. This fraternity was a particularly dorky gathering of human beings. There was this one older guy, probably in his late forties, a body builder who had been out of school for years. He came to visit the fraternity house on some weekends to give us social advice. His big line about women was this: "Do 'em a good job and they'll never forget ya."

We had one rather fat member whom everybody called Fat Hog. As you can see, this was not a particularly sophisticated bunch. Some of the guys living in the house weren't even members, just hangers-on living in the house. One of these guys was a fellow named Ernie Poppers, which is one of my favorite names ever. Ernie wanted to be a CIA agent, or a soldier of fortune. Ernie was sort of round and I don't think he was even enrolled in school at the time.

Another of these losers was a guy from St. Louis who went by the name of Griff. "Hey, let's go eat some beer," Griff would often suggest. Eating some beer was at the top of Griff's dance card. His running buddy went by the name of Ped. You rarely saw Griff without Ped. Ped used more soap than Griff, and had somewhat of a preppie appearance, but that was a facade.

Early one Sunday evening, Griff and Ped enlisted me in a prank. They decided that the thing for the three of us to do would be to drive over to a nearby men's dorm and steal the cigarette machine from the first floor. Apparently these two had been scoping out this particular cigarette machine for some time, as a source of income. It was at this point that I should have realized I needed to hang out with a better class of people. *I can't believe I'm holding onto the end of this cigarette machine*, was my thought as the three of us carried the cigarette machine out the dorm door, and loaded it into the trunk of Griff's beat-up old Plymouth, a car known as The Green Groper.

We took the cigarette machine back to the frat house, unloaded all the cigarettes, and pocketed the money. I think there was about $35 in the machine. I kept some of the cigarettes, since I was a smoker back then. Then we dumped the cigarette machine out in the country. I guess you could say that we helped improve the nation's health, since we got rid of quite a few Marlboros.

We never got caught, but the incident taught me one thing: don't hang out with people who may get you locked up in the joint.

One good thing about my college days is that I didn't watch a lot of television. As you can see, I had a busy schedule.

I suppose every guy remembers the name of the first gal he, um, scored with. Mine was named Dixie Maiden. I am not making this up. I might be spelling Dixie's maiden name wrong. But it was pronounced Maiden. I realized this wasn't true love when, about a week later, I walked into a bar and saw her sitting in some other guy's lap. Dixie was really nice, though. She even gave me a ring. (And that wasn't all she gave me.)

Some of the gals I dated were fairly classy. One icy winter day, I was opening the door of my car for one of the classier ones. She was from Illinois, and she was cute. Unfortunately, I slipped on the ice as I opened the car door for her. On the way to the ground, I tried to stop my fall by grabbing the car's radio antenna.

So there I was, sitting on my ass on a patch of ice, holding onto the radio antenna I had just snatched off the car. I'll bet my classy date was impressed. But for some reason, she dated me for a few months before dumping me for one of my fraternity brothers who had a Corvette. By contrast, I had an old Peugeot with a burned-up engine. And a missing radio antenna.

My fraternity experience didn't end well. During my second year in the frat, I was elected House President, which should give you an idea of the judgment of this bunch. The idea of me in a leadership position is completely ludicrous. In Army basic training, I was the only guy in my squad who was never named squad leader.

However, in the fraternity, I was the pick of the litter.

Around the time I was president, I started dating a gal the fraternity guys didn't like for some reason. She was an intelligent and attractive redhead from the Boston area, a debutante who turned out to be my first wife. (I married way too young, and it only lasted for about a year. She was a nice gal; it wasn't her fault.) Anyway, for whatever reason, some of the frat members decided I shouldn't be going out with this girl. So every time the two of us walked into the fraternity house together, some of the guys would make these whip motions toward us, the idea being that I was "P-whipped" by this young lady. I figured my dating choices were nobody's business but mine. So I solved the problem by walking out of the fraternity house, moving in with a friend at his apartment, and telling the fraternity to go to hell. The fraternity president has left the building. That was about 1966. In 1967, I underwent a major cultural switch. I started listening to Jimi Hendrix and soon I was popping Dexedrine, which led me to snorting crank. This made it fun to sit up all night, studying for finals.

About that time, I started my first year of journalism school at the university. At Missouri, you had to complete two years of other classes before you could get into journalism school. I'd finished those two years, and then spent a year dealing with Army basic training for my Army Reserves commitment.

To clarify how the J-School works:

My freshman year at the University of Missouri was 1962. In 1966, I earned my degree in English, and then I took a year off to satisfy my Army obligations, including basic training and

Advanced Infantry Training, or AIT. AIT is an extension of basic training. It's when troops are trained in their various jobs, and it doesn't necessarily have anything to do with infantry. My Military Occupational Specialty (MOS) was carpenter, and I couldn't build a doghouse. The Army complicated things, to say the least.

After that year of dealing with the military, I returned to the University of Missouri in 1968 for two years in the journalism program. During that first year of J-school, I moved into a grungy basement apartment with Smilin' Fred, who was really a smart guy, but like so many of us at the time, temporarily deluded.

We called him Smilin' Fred because he rarely smiled. Fred was a graduate student in sociology, and something of an intellectual. But he was a cranky guy who did every sort of dope he could get his hands on — and he was pretty good at getting his hands on it. Fred was dealing speed and pot, but customer service was not his forte. I remember one guy who came over to our basement apartment during the middle of the day and started banging on the door.

Fred opened the door and the guy apologized to Fred, who had been napping. "I'm sorry I got you up," the guy said.

"You're not getting me up, you're bringing me down," Fred snarled. No charmer, that one.

On another occasion we were all sitting around in the basement apartment's living room, which had concrete walls covered by colorful hanging fabric. It was your typical hippie rent house design.

We were passing around a joint, or a bong—something

that required fire. In the process, somebody set the extremely flammable lightweight fabric covering the walls on fire. So everybody had to stand up and flap out the flames. It was a close call there for about thirty seconds.

Meanwhile I was working as a sports reporter for the journalism school's newspaper, the *Columbia Missourian*. This was basically Reporting 101. One evening when I was on the desk, Fred called me up and announced, "I'd like to report a score."

He wasn't talking about a football game, either.

I wasn't the star of the sports department, by any means. One semester I covered Missouri baseball. The coach, John "Hi" Simmons, was a crusty old red-faced guy who coached Missouri baseball from 1937 to 1973. One day he asked why I hadn't been around for the opening of practice. He also wanted to know why I had such a good tan.

I explained that I had just returned to Columbia from Colorado in a convertible. What I didn't explain to him is that I had taken Smilin' Fred out to Colorado to leave him off since the police were looking for him. (Fred later turned himself in and paid a fine. He grew up, got a state job, and quit dope.)

On the sports desk, I was the odd man out. I had thought I would enjoy sports writing, but I found it pretty boring.

The sports editor, a perfectionist named John Walsh, wasn't particularly impressed by my work, and he didn't have much reason to be. I wasn't absolutely horrible, but I hadn't risen to the top of the class, either.

One evening, I covered the Missouri Class M state high school basketball championship game between the Dixon

Bulldogs and the Oran Eagles. It was a great game, one of the best basketball games I've seen live in my life. Dixon won a thriller, 76-74. I was stoked. I came back to the office, wrote up the story, and turned it in. I remember writing that one of Dixon's big men handled the ball like a bartender handling lemons.

A few minutes later I heard sports editor Walsh hollering across the newsroom. "Hey Kelso," he bellowed, "Did you write this?"

"Yes. Why?"

"Because it's good," Walsh said. He was a smart-ass. But later on he worked for *Long Island Newsday*, so he knew what he was talking about. In any case, it was the first time I remember an editor telling me my writing was good, and the first time I believed it.

While I was in Missouri I lived in a few trashy little apartments. My landlady at one point was a middle-aged, humorously red-necky woman named Maggie, who had a burly truck driver husband who would come over to collect the rent. He was scary looking, with a big head and a burr haircut, so he did a good job as a rent collector. Maggie was one of those women who had a living room that nobody was supposed to sit down in. You've seen those sitting rooms where you know nobody is supposed to sit, because everything is covered in clear plastic.

One day Maggie was complaining to me about some Asian students who were renting a place from her. The neighbors were crabbing about the aroma of their cooking.

"Maggie," I said, "Why don't you just tell them to stop cooking?"

That's when Maggie laid on me one of the most poignant philosophical observations I've ever heard. "John," she said, "sometimes the shit smells worse when it's stirred."

That was among the most valuable lessons I learned in college, and it didn't come from a professor.

I managed to get out of college with about a 2.8 grade point average. I got my B.A. in English, but I never did get my journalism degree, but not because I didn't pass all the requirements. I just never bothered to file for the degree. Back when I was an English major, I had my stuff together enough to actually apply for that degree. But by the time I was in journalism school, I was just raising so much hell that I didn't bother to take care of the paperwork necessary to get the degree. I could probably do it today, but why bother now?

It wasn't long after leaving Missouri in 1969 that I landed a reporting job at the *Portsmouth Herald* in New Hampshire. Also, it was about that time that I freaked out on acid in my apartment in the nearby town of Rye. I ran into the fire department next door, paranoid and convinced I was Jesus Christ.

Turns out I was wrong. But at least I didn't get busted. I'm not completely ashamed of my college years, but I probably should be.

After college, things went from bad to worse. They say marijuana is a gateway drug. Ha. I skipped the gateway and went right to the gate. My trouble was that I liked speed way too much—for about five years. It got me fired from my first job out of college as a reporter for the *Portsmouth Herald*. I don't blame them. I would have fired me, too.

It was 1971, and this was the low point of my work life. The *Herald* canned me. I took my $180 severance pay and immediately invested it in $180 worth of Robin Hood flour from the Hells Angels motorcycle gang. Rule of thumb: don't do business with the Hells Angels. I thought what I had purchased was speed, but every time I put it up my nose I made tiny biscuits in my nostrils.

Actually, I had bought the would-be dope through a local speed dealer who got it from the Hells Angels. This dealer was hooked on crank, and his brother was hooked on smack. The mom ran a pawnshop. This was not the Brady Bunch, if you catch my drift.

When the speed turned out to be bogus, I told the dealer I wanted my money back, and he said we'd have to get it from the Hells Angels. So we drove down to Massachusetts and went into a house where some of the Hells Angels lived.

They had a bar in the living room with three or four stools. How many living rooms have you ever seen with a bar in it? This was a unique design, I thought. A few scruffy lookin' guys were sitting there drinking. Above them was the chicken they had hanged until dead from the ceiling.

When I saw the hanged chicken, I decided not to ask for a refund.

Immediately after I was canned from my job, my boss, editor Ray Brighton, author of a Portsmouth history titled *They Came To Fish*, actually put his hand on the back of my neck and led me out the newsroom door. My problem was that instead of coming to fish, I had come to get spaced out. So I ended up with hepatitis. This time I had really fallen in with the wrong crowd. Two of my friends in Portsmouth were named Bat and Angel, which should give you an idea of my social life.

Fortunately for me, my parents came to my rescue; they put me in the hospital. I'll never forget what my father told me on one hospital visit. "Johnny," he said while I was lying there in bed. "It looks like you've found a way to die early."

Turns out he was wrong, though, because somehow I managed to recover. It must have been good genes. That's the only explanation I can come up with.

You're in the Army Now

I've always gravitated toward what some of you might refer to as weirdos, and I refer to as copy. Take Diesel and Cooder, two guys I met in the army.

When I was in college, I wanted to stay out of Vietnam. I didn't want to put my life on the line for a war I thought was wrong in the first place. It seemed highly unlikely to me that the day would ever come when North Vietnamese soldiers would be running up my street toting rifles. If that had happened, I'd be all over it. But I knew it wouldn't.

So to stay out of the jungle, in the middle Sixties I joined the U.S. Army Reserve unit in Laconia, where I'd gone to high school.

When you were in the Reserves back then, you had to go through basic training just like the regular Army guys did. I did my eight weeks of basic at Fort Leonard Wood, Missouri in 1967, the same year the Red Sox went to the World Series for the first time in my life (not counting 1946, when I was just two, or too young to know about it). I've been a Red Sox fan all my life, and it was just my luck to show up for basic training at Fort Lost in the

Woods about the same day the 1967 World Series started. That meant that instead of watching the Red Sox in a World Series for the first time ever, I'd be sucking in toxic gas without a gas mask, and crawling on the ground under machine gun fire. I'd be screamed at regularly by some drill sergeant who kept saying, in a loud tone, "I DON'T CARE IF YOU'RE JESUS H. CHRIST."

He never mentioned what the H stood for.

I realized that Army guys were just regular Joes like me, though, when a sergeant came up and asked if I wanted to buy in on a World Series numbers board. *Hey*, I thought, *these guys are betting on the game just like everybody else. They're normal.* Knowing that made me feel better about being in the Army.

Diesel and Cooder were perhaps the most worthless and equally evil characters I met during boot camp. They could be dangerous. On the other hand, they laughed a lot and they were great storytellers. Cooder was fairly well spoken, while Diesel spoke entirely in street jive, difficult for a white guy from New England to understand. But you did not want to mess with these guys. Both of them were pretty big and sturdy. Cooder had an oddly feminine countenance, even though he claimed he was a member of a deadly Chicago street gang called the Blackstone Rangers. Diesel, who hailed from Joliet, Illinois, a prison town, had a large head that looked like an enormous pool ball.

The first night I stayed in the barracks, the two of them were putting a knot on a white guy's head because he had looked at them funny, or had made some smart-ass remark. They were instantly on this guy like a cheap suit on a used car salesman. I thought to myself, keep your distance from these guys.

But, as usual, I didn't take my own advice and became a chatting buddy with Diesel and Cooder. These two could spin a yarn that would make you laugh. So I loved being around them. And for some reason, they liked me. I guess they never expected a honky college boy to care enough about them to listen to their stories.

They also had impeccable manners in front of a woman. When my first wife came to visit me on the family weekend during basic, I introduced her to Diesel and Cooder. They treated her like the Queen of the Nile. They couldn't have been more polite. It was "Yes, ma'am" this and "No, ma'am" that.

The trouble for Diesel and Cooder was that they had no inborn governor on their behavior. If you have the guts to act bad in the Army, you have the guts to act bad anywhere. One day these guys snuck off to the PX (the Army base store) and drank a couple of beers. This, even after the drill sergeants had emphasized that if we got caught at the PX, it would be a very bad day and the punishment wouldn't be pleasant.

When they got caught at the PX, the drill sergeants made Diesel and Cooder low-crawl across a long field with their gas masks on.

There may not be an exercise as exhausting as getting on your stomach on the ground and moving yourself forward with your arms and legs pulling you along. Get on the living room floor, and do that for about fifteen feet, and you'll see what I mean.

And these clowns were forced to do it across a long parade field, with gas masks inhibiting their breathing.

When they finally finished the course and took off their masks, they were choking, fighting for air. This exercise might have killed a man who wasn't in good shape. At least that's how it looked to me. I was taken aback when I saw them battling to get their wind. It was ugly to watch.

The guy in the bunk across from me in basic was named Karl. That was his last name; I don't remember his first. He was effeminate, fragile. Whenever his name came up, Diesel and Cooder would make little girlie noises. About three quarters of the way through basic training, I got a pass. So I went home to Columbia, a couple hours away, to spend the weekend with my new wife.

When I returned to the barracks for duty on Sunday night, Karl was gone. "Where's Karl?" I asked one of my bunkmates.

"He's in the infirmary."

"What for?"

Turns out Diesel and Cooder had raped him. I never saw Karl again. I figure the Army sent the poor guy home. I hope so. He just wasn't cut out for the military. And neither were Diesel and Cooder. The last time I saw them, they were in the supply room with the MPs, who had their hands handcuffed behind their backs.

"Ain't this a bitch," Cooder said, looking mournfully at Diesel. "Ain't this a mothah-fuckin' jive ass bitch."

Although I detested military regimentation, and I bristled at being told what to do by people I thought were kinda stupid, I did enjoy my time in the Army. I met a lot of fine and interesting people and I stumbled across some unusual situations that still make me curious. In other words, military life wasn't boring, a quality of life factor with me.

In the late 1960s or early 1970s, while I was in an Army Reserve unit, I spent two weeks at Fort Devens, Massachusetts, attending chemical warfare school. Recent talk of the threat of Syria's resorting to the use of deadly sarin gas on its own people brought back this memory.

Sarin is a colorless, odorless, and tasteless gas, one drop of which can kill in a second. It can come in through your eyeballs. If sarin gets on your clothes, it can kill the medic who's trying to help you. It attacks the central nervous system. It makes your lungs quit working.

To survive a sarin attack, a soldier has to jab a needle into his thigh within forty seconds. The device with the needle is called an atropine surette. Atropine is the antidote, and with luck it will save your life—if you act fast. Dawdlers die.

In chemical warfare school, we were taught how to use the atropine surette and we learned all about the effects of sarin. We saw a training film that featured goats twitching to death after being given the gas. But more fascinating to me then was the training film showing the Army surveying crew that had been dosed with a hallucinogen which, if it wasn't LSD, was certainly similar to LSD.

At the time, the Army was experimenting with the drug as a weapon. The experiments, I've read, were conducted on Army troops. If hippies all over the U.S. had known about this, they might have wished for the Army to invade every Saturday night.

This training film showed about a dozen extremely happy

soldiers gathered around a picnic table. Some of them were sitting on the table benches and others were sitting on the ground. Many were giggling and all appeared spaced out and they seemed to be having just a wonderful time.

The voiceover with the film explained that prior to being given the hallucinogen, the surveying crew had made, say, 400 attempts in its surveying work, with six errors. (I'm making up these figures because I can't remember them accurately after half a century. But I'm in the ballpark with accuracy here, all right?)

So next, the training film voiceover reported that after the agent had been administered, the same surveying crew made 400 attempts during its work, with around 436 errors.

That the surveyors made more mistakes than they made attempts while on the hallucinogen struck me as amusing. Also funny to me was watching Army guys waxed on dope, since I had been in that position back in that period of history in a civilian capacity.

That's why, right there in class, I laughed out loud. Some of the other troops in the class looked at me suspiciously.

The best part of the show, however, was the grizzled old sergeant who took the stage after the hallucinogen training film was finished. He talked about using this agent on civilian populations, and how the Army would deal with that. The only way to control people who had been dosed with this hallucinogen, the sergeant said, would be to "chain 'em to a tree."

I lost it on that one. This was better than Johnny Carson.

Then there was the sergeant in basic training at Fort Leonard Wood, who talked to us in an hour-long training session about how to handle a nuclear attack. He said he'd undergone training on that particular predicament, and that the training involved troops being left off in the desert and ordered to dig a hole. Then they were to jump in the hole, and cover the hole with their Army ponchos.

After the troops made those arrangements, the sergeant explained, a nuclear bomb was set off nearby. How near? I have no idea. But nearby enough that this sergeant was about the most nervous person I've ever seen in my life. While giving this class, he spent the entire time pacing.

I guess an atomic bomb going off in the general vicinity will do that to a fellow. I wonder what ever happened to that poor bastard.

In and around my Army experience, I was going to college and taking summer jobs in the newspaper business.

My first boss in newspapering, Earl Anderson, was a wonderful, kind-hearted man and a real character. While I was in college at Missouri, I had a summer job working in the Laconia bureau of the *Manchester Union-Leader*, perhaps the most conservative newspaper in the United States at the time.

Earl was the Union Leader's Laconia bureau chief. It was just Earl and me working out of a tiny office inside the Laconia Chamber of Commerce building, which had once been the town's train station.

Ours was a small-time operation. When Earl and I had photos we wanted to send to the main *Union-Leader* office an hour away in Manchester, we'd put them on the Trailways bus that came around once a day.

Earl was a bundle of quirks. He had his own special language.

He used the royal we. Really. As in, "we is" going to do this and "we is" going to do that. It was as if Earl thought he was the Queen of England or something. He was a kind, gentle soul and a good guy to work for, but he had all sorts of idiosyncrasies.

Earl worked himself to the bone. I think he was around fifty years old at the time, but he looked more like eighty. He'd keep a little piece of scratch paper with a list of things to do scribbled in pencil. Each day he'd have thirty-five or forty items on his to-do list. A fast typist, Earl banged out I'm betting 80-100 words a minute, using only two fingers.

As a journalistic role model, though, Earl flunked on one particular occasion. I had written a fairly major feature story on the boat police who worked on Lake Winnipesaukee, a big tourist lake near Laconia. I led off the story with an incident involving a man who was attacked by his houseboy at the man's home on an island in the middle of the lake.

Nobody was hurt, but the houseboy allegedly had gone after his boss with a knife.

Earl thought my story needed a little more pizazz, so he told me we should create a quote for the man who'd been attacked. In that moment of terror, if that were the case, what would he have said? Earl wondered.

It didn't take long for Earl to come up with a quote. It was lame, something like, "Oh my God." I figured if you were going to the trouble to cheat and make up quotes, you ought to at least make up a good one.

Anyway, Earl stuck the fake quote in the story and as best as I can remember it ran that way in the *Manchester Union-Leader*.

I knew that what Earl had done was wrong. And I knew that my standing there when he suggested it and not putting up a fight was wrong, too. But Earl was the boss, and I was young. I should have told him to knock it off. We managed to get away with it, since nobody noticed the fake quote. But it made me uneasy as hell. It also made me wonder how often Earl just made stuff up.

Not that I was without my own little flaws while working for the *Union-Leader*. Part of my job was to go next door to the cop shop every morning and check the police blotter for crimes. The only day I forgot to check the police blotter coincided with Laconia's first armed robbery, which occurred at the downtown jewelry store. So I blew the story, although it did run — just a bit late.

I'm sure that if I hadn't been a cub reporter, I would have gotten canned. And I would have deserved it. My time there was a learning experience, that's for sure. Never again did I forget to check the police blotter.

New Guy in Town

I knew from an early age that I wanted to be a humor writer, but when I arrived at the *Austin American-Statesman* in November 1976, I didn't know how to write humor, and I didn't have a clue about what I was getting into. I didn't move to Austin because I loved the place, although I did grow to love it. When I arrived, I didn't know anything about the city, or even much about Texas. People talk about what a wonderful place Austin is to live, but I didn't know that at the time.

When I moved here, I only knew three things about Austin, and two of them were wrong. I knew the Oklahoma-Texas football game was played here. (Since 1932, the game has been held at the Cotton Bowl in Dallas, during the State Fair of Texas) I knew the population of Austin was about 220,000. (In 1976 it was actually closer to 325,000) And I knew there were some things in town called "moon towers." At least I had that one right, although I didn't know what they were. They're towers placed around Austin that have lights at the top that replicate the light of the moon. I'd also heard of the Armadillo World Headquarters, the world-renowned rock 'n roll hall in the old National Guard Armory.

See, the reason I came to Austin was to escape Racine, Wisconsin, where I worked at the *Racine Journal Times* as the outdoor writer — for one month. That's right. I spent October 1976 on that job, and that was it. I didn't like the job, and I didn't like the town. The only stories of any significance of the outdoor sort involved catching salmon out of the Root River, and the salmon were headed upstream to die.

Here's the biggest outdoor story I did during my brief stay in Racine: One of the local high schools had a course that taught students to fish. We ran a photo in the newspaper of a high school kid dragging his salmon down the hall, on the floor.

The rest of the story is that the locals in Racine caught salmon by putting cheese on snag hooks. So these people weren't even tricking the fish into biting. They were being caught by complete treachery. Worse still, being the new guy on the sports desk, I was the low man on the scrotum pole. So I got stuck doing a lot of bowling agate.

Let me explain bowling agate to you. Agate is a tiny type size, and bowling agate amounts to a list of bowlers' names, set in agate type, next to their bowling scores. At the *Racine Journal Times*, the guy who got stuck with bowling agate duty (often me) had to type up hundreds of Polish and German names, along with their bowling scores. This was not exactly fascinating work. But even though this task was mind numbing, the bowling agate was important since it was perhaps the best-read item in the *Racine Journal Times*. Everybody in town who could stand up and put their fingers in the right holes was in a bowling league, and they took their bowling scores about as seriously as their own obituaries.

Okay, so let's say you're doing the bowling agate, and you leave off Koslovsky's 299 game, which is one heckuva game for Koslovsky. Koslovsky is all worked up about seeing his name in the newspaper next to his fantastic score, but his name doesn't make it into the paper over the weekend. What does this mean?

It means that on Monday morning, here'd come Koslovsky and his buddies into the *Journal Times* newsroom, a bunch of bowlers all cheesed off and ready to kick somebody's behind because the newspaper hadn't mentioned Koslovsky's nearly perfect game.

One Monday, in fact, I watched as some bowlers charged into the newsroom, wanting a piece of somebody because a bowling score had been left out.

I realized that I hadn't attended the journalism school at the University of Missouri for this. So after a few weeks of this version of hell, I called up Ray Mariotti, the new editor of the *Austin American-Statesman.*

Ray had been my boss at the *Palm Beach Post* in Florida, where I'd worked as his outdoor writer for three-and-a-half years. I'd done some funny work in West Palm Beach, so I decided I'd hit him up for a job. When I called Ray up from Racine and asked him for a job in Austin, he said, "Sure, come on down, and maybe we'll give you a column."

I couldn't pack my old orange VW Bug fast enough.

Ray had liked my work in Florida. I'd volunteered as the

outdoor writer on the *Palm Beach Post*'s sports desk, but not because I was a fishing expert or intrigued by trout. When I took that gig, I hadn't gone fishing since I was in seventh grade in Orono, Maine, catching eels and other trash fish out of the Penobscot River.

No, the reason I volunteered for outdoor writer in West Palm Beach is that I thought covering a bunch of geezers in Jupiter, Florida, catching Spanish mackerel would be more interesting than covering the West Palm Beach Expos, the local minor league baseball team.

If you worked for the *Palm Beach Post* sports department, you ended up writing about West Palm Beach Expos baseball games. We all took turns with the minor league beat. This had just one perk. The team owner, a surfer dude named Fred Whitacre, used to keep the ball park press box fridge full of cheap Genesee beer. But even free beer couldn't make the Florida State League games all that fascinating.

Probably my most memorable moment covering the South Florida baseball scene occurred when Minnie Minoso came to town. At the time, Minoso was in West Palm for a spring training game. Minoso in his day had been a big star and a solid hitter for the Chicago White Sox. He had a 17-year major league career, batted .298 and hit 186 homers. He's been mentioned often as Hall of Fame material.

Tom Kelly, editor of the *Post* at the time, heard I was headed out to cover the spring training game the day Minoso was in town. So he mentioned to me that, how do I put this delicately, they didn't call him Minnie for nothing.

I swear to God, when I saw that man nekkid in the locker

room, it was like he was dragging a baseball bat between his knees. I'm surprised he didn't trip over the thing.

Not that I particularly care about that sort of stuff. I just thought I'd mention it since it would explain to you how dull the beat was, if that was the big moment.

But I digress.

Since I didn't know much about fishing, I covered fishing differently from most outdoor writers, who are usually guys who can tie flies and make their own stink bait in the garage. So my outdoor articles were different from most.

I had an undercover source I referred to as "Deep Trout." He was sort of like Deep Throat in the Watergate investigation, but instead of our meeting in a parking garage, we met next to the minnow tank in a Riviera Beach bait shop.

Deep Trout was actually this guy named Ray from North Carolina. Ray and I went fishing together every so often.

Anyway, Deep Trout gave me tips. Okay, so he only ever gave me one tip as Deep Trout. He revealed to me the location of a small canal in the middle of West Palm where you could catch a lot of panfish. What's a panfish? Simple. It's a fish small enough to fit in a pan. That's the kind of explanatory outdoor writing I did, whatever kind of outdoor writing that is.

My hottest story on the South Florida outdoor beat had to be about the fly-fishing trip to Lion Country Safari, a tourist attraction a few miles west of West Palm Beach. Lion Country Safari was one of those places you could drive through and see exotic animals—with the windows rolled up, unless you were in the mood to be eaten by a lion that day.

Anyway, Lion Country Safari's PR director wanted to teach me how to fly fish. So we spent the day fly-fishing in some of the Lion Country Safari ponds. It was unusual fishing out there. What I thought was a large rock, for example, turned out to be a hippo. When my fly landed on the hippo's back, the hippo rose up and startled me. Fortunately, the hippos weren't biting that day, or I would have lost the PR director's fly rod.

A gaggle of chimpanzees was an integral part of this story. The chimps were kept on a little island so they'd be separated from the mainland. They were free to roam around the island and do chimp things, but chimps don't like getting in water. So they were stuck on the island, and they were protective of their territory.

These chimps were about a hundred feet from where we were fishing, but they apparently thought it was too close for comfort. So the chimps began picking up big rocks and hurling them, underhanded, in our direction. These rocks were about the size of bowling balls. Soon the rocks started coming in fairly close to taking us out. So I wrote about that, and it was a pretty funny story.

Of course, it would have been a lot funnier if I'd been nailed by one of the rocks. I can see the headline now: "Lion Country Safari chimp nails writer, picks up spare."

Then there was the day I spent fishing with Doug Rader, the former Houston Astros star third baseman, who lived about an hour north of West Palm Beach, near Stuart, Florida. Doug was one of those guys who would do stuff just for a laugh. While we were getting ready to take off in his little outboard motor boat, he tossed the anchor overboard. The trouble was, the anchor wasn't attached to a rope or anything else.

Doug acted as if he'd done it by mistake. I think he threw the anchor overboard on purpose as a joke. But he never said.

After we'd finished fishing, Doug and I went into a tiny three-barstool, one-pool table beer joint for a beer. This was Doug's favorite local hangout. After we'd been there a few minutes, the old lady tending bar asked Doug if she could have a word with him in private for a moment. Doug said sure, no problem. (Of course, I eavesdropped.)

"Doug," the lady bartender said. "I've been having trouble with my pick up lately. Could you put in a word for me?" Doug told her he could do that, no big deal. Out of earshot of the barkeep, I asked Doug what this "pick up" she had mentioned was all about.

"I tell everybody in here I'm a garbage man, because I don't want them knowing I'm a major league baseball player," he said.

In the end, what I learned as the outdoor writer at the *Palm Beach Post* is what a fishing report actually is: it's when you call up the local bait and tackle shop owners and charter boat captains and they lie to you about where the fish are biting. Fishermen, you see, are supposed to lie. It's part of their DNA. One of my favorite fishing stories came about when I busted one of the local charter boats for exaggerating their catch one day. This led one of the *Post*'s editorial writers to write a tongue-in-cheek piece making fun of me for expecting honesty out of a fisherman. He was right. I was expecting far too much.

Some of My Best Friends Are Weirdos

Doug Rader would have fit right in with some of the eccentrics I fell in with when I started writing for the *American-Statesman* in 1976. Some might say I immediately fell in with the wrong crowd.

That's by your standards. By my standards, it was the right crowd to fall in with, since these characters would give me plenty to write about. Not that I could always write about the stuff these people were doing—that is, without sending some of them to jail. But let's just say that Thomas B. and Jimmy Carter were a couple of real flamboyant outlaws, and they were never boring.

In his younger days, Carter had been known around town as a street fighter. A friend of mine told me that in the old days, if Jimmy and his friends were on one side of town, you wanted to be on the other side. Word was, he could dead-lift five hundred pounds when he was in shape, even though he probably weighed only 165 pounds.

Ironically, Jimmy had the courtly manners of a Southern gentleman, and he always called women "ma'am." Also, he loved dogs. He said if you scratched a dog's chest just so, you had a friend for life.

Jimmy Carter stayed on my couch for months, and while he was in residence in my little South Austin home he stayed glued to my dog, Bubba, whom he called Bubbles.

Thomas B., or Thomas B. Thomas, depending on which day it was, was less polished than Jimmy Carter. Thomas B.'s legal advice was always to tell the law, "It wasn't me. It was somebody else."

He wore one of those high-topped Tom Mix-looking cowboy hats, and a bandana. Austin singer/songwriter Michele "Mike" Murphy, in 2012 the mayor of Liberty Hill (a small Hill Country town of about a thousand people located thirty-five miles northwest of Austin) tells the story about the hat. She bought the hat for Thomas B. back in the day at McGill's, a dry goods store in Bertram. The hat was a find. It came in a fancy box and only cost $29. Apparently it had been in the store a while. A hat like this one today would set you back $300-$500.

Anyway, Mike gave Thomas the hat. "Whoa," he said as he pulled it out of the box, turning it over in his hands and examining it. Then he took the hat, and slammed it over his leg, breaking the crown.

Mike shuddered and gaped at Thomas as if to say, "What the hell are you doing to that hat? Why are you beating it up?"

Thomas replied, in his basso profondo voice, "Well, is this your hat, or is this *MY* hat?"

It was definitely his hat. I don't think he slept in it. Because of the shape of the crown, it wouldn't have worked. But if he could have, he would have.

Mike recalls going over to Thomas's flophouse room one morning. A bunch of guys, including Thomas, had been sleeping on the floor, and they were just getting up. Thomas seemed perturbed over his hat, and Michele asked what the problem was.

"Oh, there's nothing wrong with the hat," Thomas said. "It's just that somebody got drunk and used it as an ashtray."

Thomas had a strong sense of decency. On occasion back in the '70s, when Mike would play gigs at clubs in Austin, Thomas would walk her to her car after the show to make sure nobody messed with her.

One evening, Mike was concerned about a guy who was walking behind them, and she told Thomas about it. Thomas reassured her that everything was under control, saying, "Well, little miss, that's just one of your fans."

I first met Thomas B. and Jimmy Carter while hanging out at a beer joint called Don Politico's Tavern. It was on East Sixth Street across from the old, iconic Driskill Hotel in downtown Austin. All sorts of people wandered into Don Politico's. Tony Proffitt, an advisor to Bob Bullock, Texas' legendary lieutenant governor and comptroller, was a nearly daily visitor. Tony hung out toward the back of the bar and played the pinball machine.

Tony had the best collection of jokes I've ever run across. Any time you'd call him up, there was a good chance he'd lay a new one on you.

Here's a sample: Guy speeding up Interstate 35 at a hundred thousand miles an hour got pulled over by a state trooper. "Listen," the cop told him. "My shift ends in half an hour and I want to go home. If you can come up with an excuse I've never heard before, I'll let you go."

"Well," the guy said, "a couple of years ago a state trooper ran off with my wife. And I thought maybe it was you, bringing her back."

That's the kind of joke Proffitt liked to tell.

I also remember an Austin Community College student who hung out at the bar, smiling crazy all the time for reasons nobody could figure out. Everybody called him Smiley. He was just about tall enough to lean on the bar. So you'd look over, and about all you'd see was this head, poking over the bar, with a crazy smile on its face.

There were state employees, businessmen, a retired Air Force colonel who read a ton and was quite the intellectual. There was a retired newspaperman who had worked for a paper in San Diego and who was the world's foremost authority on journalism. Or at least he thought he was. He'd always crab because the bar didn't carry Anchor Steam beer.

Pat Conway, the owner, says that one time a guy showed up and ordered every kind of beer he had on hand. The guy explained he'd just gotten out of prison after being locked up for years, so he wanted to try out every beer there was.

Yes, indeed. All kinds wandered in.

Conway, an old newspaperman himself, collected political bumper stickers and signs and covered his place with this stuff. Everybody called him Pops. Pops was a wise guy. A friend of mine said that one time when he attended a funeral, Pops had gotten there early and was standing under the funeral tent.

Pops greeted my friend with a bow. "Welcome to the Big Top," he said.

Pops had a sign on his bar for the "Dinner Theater Special." For about $5, you got a can of sardines and a couple of quarters for the peep show around the corner. That was the "Dinner Theater Special."

Pops had worked for United Press International as a reporter, and he hated chicken, because while covering some ongoing event in Dallas all they had to eat every day for several days was chicken. I remember Pops claimed to have invented the expression "cool," in its hip context. He also took credit for coining the term "grassy knoll" while covering the Kennedy assassination in Dallas. Every Kennedy assassination story you've ever read mentions a "grassy knoll." Pops says he's the man responsible for that.

He was also proud of the news story he wrote about the demise of the Wabash Cannonball—the train, not the song.

Pops' bar was nothing fancy. No ferns in this place, folks. But he did have an electronic baseball game on the wall of his bar. It came with a little black box with a button on top. The box sat by itself on the bar, unattached to the baseball game display hanging on the wall.

Push the button on the little black box, and the batter shown on the wall display would swing. If you hit six home runs in a game, you got a free game.

I got so good at the game that we eventually decided that I should try to beat the machine out on the sidewalk through the window in the front door. That turned out to be too easy, so I tried beating it behind my back with a hand mirror. That was a tough stunt, but I did manage to pull it off.

Eventually we decided to up the ante and try to beat the game over the phone. To accomplish this, Pops asked one of the managers at the Driskill Hotel across the street if we could borrow one of their rooms for a few minutes to try to beat the baseball game over the telephone.

The manager gave us her okay, so Pops and I went up to a hotel room, little black box in hand, and gave it a shot. We phoned the bar and Jim Walls, Pop's business partner, would tell me when it was time to swing. Then I'd hit the button.

Trouble was, the game's signal wouldn't make it across the street from the hotel to the bar. So we took the electronic box into OK Records, the little store next door to the bar, and tried to beat the game over the phone from the record store.

"Swing," Walls would say. I'd punch the button. I won a free game on the second or third try.

We thought about trying to beat the game from a pick-up truck while driving around the block with the little black box on the front seat, but we never got around to it.

Jimmy Carter and Thomas B. were regular customers at Don Politico's, and they were constantly on a search for beer money. One day the two of them came into the bar with a medicine cabinet they'd picked up somewhere, maybe an apartment complex. They showed the medicine cabinet to the bartender and traded the medicine cabinet for some beer.

They'd do whatever it took to find a way to finance beer. The story was that Thomas had pawned his false teeth for beer money. Then one day, he showed up at the bar with his teeth back in place. He'd bought them back from the pawnshop.

Did I mention that Thomas and Jimmy liked dogfighting? I didn't think so.

Once in the late 1970s, they asked me if I wanted to see a dogfight "roll" and I said, "What's that?" A roll, they explained, was when you took a pit bulldog that had never fought, and tested it with a veteran fighting dog, to see how it would react.

This is going to be ugly, I thought. But I was curious, so I went along. We drove out Spicewood Springs Road to Northwest Austin. Back in those days Spicewood Springs Road was out in the country. We pulled up to one of the few houses out there at the time, and there were about a dozen pit bulldogs chained to trees, barking.

The guy who owned the house and the dogs was a local small businessman and overt redneck. He had an easy sense of humor, though.

We walked into the woods down behind the house, where there was a makeshift dogfighting ring. We're talking about a rambling enclosure, probably two feet high, about twenty feet on each side. It had been slapped together on a low budget, obviously.

The veteran dog selected for the roll was named Gyro, because when he wagged his tail it went around in circles instead of back and forth. Gyro liked to fight, but he would be no problem to the newcomer dog he was about to fight, because Gyro had no teeth.

I don't recall the name of the female dog whose fighting

skills these guys were testing, but it soon became obvious that she didn't understand the drill. While Gyro lit into her, she just stood there looking like, "What the heck's his problem?"

For some reason this attitude set Thomas B. off, and he started screaming at this female dog who declined to fight. She didn't put up much resistance as, for about five minutes, Gyro gummed her. Neither dog was hurt, and the whole thing looked pretty stupid to me.

Afterward, Thomas B., Carter, the dogfight ring owner and I were standing around a picnic table, chatting. "I'm bored," Thomas B. said. "Let's go down to San Antonio and feed reds to the monkeys."

I learned that on occasion they would go to the San Antonio Zoo and toss barbiturates into the monkey pen. Thomas B. said it made the monkeys go crazy. This was his idea of fun.

A few years later Jimmy Carter tried to talk me into getting the newspaper to pay him a couple thousand bucks to take me to see a real dogfight for a story. The request was absurd. I wasn't interested in even seeing a real dogfight, let alone writing about one. Dogs are for petting, not for messing with. And I knew the newspaper wouldn't be remotely interested, especially at those rates, and anyway, the newspaper didn't pay for stories. So I told him no, but thanks for thinking of me.

I hung around these guys off and on for years. You wouldn't call them formal. One day Thomas B. stopped by the newspaper to visit me. On his way out, he stopped by the elevator, pulled a flask out of his back pocket, and took a big slug before disappearing behind elevator doors and leaving the building.

For a while Thomas B. and Jimmy Carter worked as cooks at Hut's burger joint on West Sixth Street. They were real proud of the cream gravy they put together in a huge pot early every morning, and actually, they *did* make some pretty darned good cream gravy.

Other than that I don't recall either of them ever holding a job. Carter worked the couch circuit. In other words, he stayed for free at friends' houses and slept on their couches. He stayed on my couch for several weeks. I couldn't get him to leave. One night his attorney drove by to visit, and I thought maybe that meant he'd actually be vacating our living room. Wrong. The attorney came in and got drunk with Jimmy—and Jimmy stayed on.

Eventually, I just put all Jimmy's stuff out on the lawn. And I guess he got the hint because the next time I went to use the couch there was actually a place for me to sit down.

A while later, Thomas B. died of cancer. He'd come around to my house unannounced every once in a while during his cancer treatments and spend the night. I don't know how he made it, considering the condition he was in and the pain he must have been feeling. He'd come driving up in his ratty old pickup truck with his feeding tube hanging out of his shirt.

Carter died, too, at the age of 44, though I'm not sure what from, although I imagine it had something to do with the consumption of drugs and alcohol. I remember the last time I ever saw Carter. He drove up to the newspaper in one of the big old cars he always drove, one of those nasty American models that got about nine miles to the gallon. On this particular day he'd come around to pick up a newspaper out of the machine in front of the newspaper building on South Congress Avenue. It was around nine in the morning. Carter had a cold beer — his breakfast beer, what he called "a can of Kellogg's" — wrapped in a coozie. On the coozie *Coca Cola* was printed in Spanish. I guess Carter figured the Coca Cola in Spanish trick would fool the cops, because he looked at the coozie and said, "You know, the Mexicans finally did something right." And those were the last words I ever heard out of him.

The Days of Ray

Things were really crazy at the Statesman when I got there in the 1970s, and a lot of the reason was that our editor was a nut. Ray Mariotti knew a news story when he saw one. He also liked to tip a few. Actually, more than a few.

My friend, Ed Crowell, who worked as city editor for Ray back in the day, says the drunkest weekend he ever spent was when Ray brought him to Austin from Florida for a job interview.

Ed recalls that when he got here, Ray had several cases of beer piled up on the back seat of his car. He took Ed and Jim Trotter, another reporter being interviewed for a job, on a tour of the city. Part of the tour consisted of visiting a trailer owned by one of Ray's friends. The guy had parked his trailer downtown, right outside the bar at the iconic Driskill Hotel on Sixth Street. Ray's friend had positioned the trailer there to pick up girls as they came out of the Driskill bar.

In Ed Crowell and Jim Trotter's cases, visiting the trailer was one of the highlights of the job recruitment tour of Austin. Sadly, executives don't recruit new hires that way anymore.

As part of the tour, Ray took Ed over to Austin's East Side, where Ed recalls a bunch of hookers were hanging out on the street, flashing Ray's car as he drove by. Ed says Ray circled the block a couple of times so he and his passengers could get another look.

While Ray was editor at the *Statesman*, you never knew what kind of stories were going to pop up in the paper. One of Ray's best was an investigative series on the city's massage parlors. Today we would call them brothels, but back in the late Seventies, the euphemism was "massage parlor."

Ray picked one of his best reporters, Linda Anthony, to do the hands-on massage parlor investigation. There was a ticklish aspect to that selection. Linda is an heir to the Cox family fortune. The Cox family owned the *Statesman*, a number of other newspapers in the country, and some cable TV interests, among other things.

So you had an heiress to the company working as the receptionist at the Magic Touch of Venus right here in Austin, Texas. That was the name of the massage parlor where Linda worked to get the story.

To gather the facts for the series, Linda worked answering the phone, taking care of the books, and making appointments. "I got to explain the specials," she recalled about thirty-five years later. "There was the Around the World, which I'll leave to your imagination. That was my favorite. And there was Cotton Candy."

Linda had a hard time remembering many of the names of the specials, but Tickle My Fancy finally popped into her mind. "Everything comes to me while I'm walking the dog or pulling weeds," she said.

The weeklong series that ran in the newspaper did not set well with everybody. Many readers simply didn't expect a dignified publication like the *American-Statesman* to publish this sort of exposé.

We got more protests than you can imagine," Linda said. "People thought we were printing smut. They were horrified. Stuff like that did not get printed in a family newspaper. This was back when the *Statesman* was still writing stories about bake sales."

I wrote a few paragraphs back that Linda was doing a hands-on investigation, but I didn't mean it THAT way. Did the guys who called the Magic Touch of Venus ever ask Linda to, you know . . .?

"Yes, they did," Linda said.

Did she, you know . . .?

"No, I didn't," Linda added quickly.

Ed Crowell, who became city editor after his wild job interview weekend, recalls Mariotti approaching him about the massage parlor series. Ray explained to Ed that he had an heiress to the company jewels doing investigative work at a massage parlor in town.

"Just don't get me in trouble," Ray said. Ray probably said that a lot to his editors. Plenty of his story ideas were on the edge. The guy knew how to assign stories that people would read.

Take *Statesman* reporter Pete Szilagyi's trip to Grenada, for instance. Pete Szilagyi says he was chosen to write that story for a bizarre reason. The reporter who had been covering Texas Supreme Court Justice Don Yarbrough's legal problems was too wide to fly in those itty-bitty plane seats.

Yarbrough ran for the Texas Supreme Court in 1976 because he said God told him to. He won the Democratic primary partly because voters confused him with Sen. Ralph Yarborough, or Don Yarborough, who had run for Texas governor. Don Yarbrough fled to Grenada in 1981, three years after he was convicted of lying to a grand jury about forging an auto registration. Yarbrough enrolled in Grenada's medical school as a dodge. So Mariotti wanted one of his reporters to head to Grenada and track him down.

Originally the story was being covered by Larry BeSaw, another *Statesman* reporter. However, when you fly to a Caribbean island way off the coast of Venezuela, you have to fly on puddle jumpers with tiny seats. And BeSaw, who did a column about his public diet to lose a lot of his 360 or so pounds, didn't have a tiny seat. He couldn't fit in small planes.

To promote BeSaw's public diet, the *Statesman* had even printed up T-shirts that read "Don't Take Larry to Lunch."

So Pete, who is kind of skinny, got the job of trying to track down Yarbrough in Grenada.

Grenada's medical school, Pete said, was "famous for being a half-baked institution where Americans could go to medical school and not learn very much. It was just a filthy, nasty place. They had a building where they dissected cadavers, and you could smell it from five miles away."

But the stink was the least of the problems Pete faced after he arrived in Grenada. Complications arose because he hadn't done much international traveling before.

"The only other places I'd been outside of the United States were Mexico and Canada," Pete said. So he didn't understand the concept of needing a visa. He didn't know you had to have one to go to foreign countries such as Grenada, which at the time was a communist country run by an anti-U.S., pro-Castro dictator.

So guess who got detained at the airport in Grenada for at least five hours, to answer a lot of questions?

The locals were quite suspicious. "It was typical bullshit with people coming in and interrogating me," Pete said. "But I had such an innocent story that maybe they believed me."

His "innocent story," by the way, was an age-old one used by many throughout history: he didn't know what the heck he was doing. Hey, nobody told him he needed a visa, right?

Then again, maybe the Grenadians didn't completely believe Pete's story. The island, Pete recalls, was littered with hammer and sickle designs on every building. "The place made Mexico look like Monte Carlo," Pete said. So it's not surprising that the Grenadian government sent a goon to follow Pete everywhere he went.

"This guy who was following me was very subtle about it. He'd sit up in a tree outside my (hotel) room," Pete said. Pete tried to break the ice with the guy, but that didn't work. "He sat out there in the tree, but he wouldn't talk to me. He would just jump down out of the tree and run off in the other direction. Or, if I saw him on the street, he'd run off."

The other person who wouldn't talk to Pete was Yarbrough. Pete finally found Yarbrough's house on Grenada and went to the door, but Yarbrough would only give Pete one word: "Nope." Pete finally gave up and came back to the U.S. I doubt if he'll be going to Grenada again any time soon. Even the plane trip down there, hopping from one island to the next, was a bit dreary.

Pete reports that the plane sat on the runway in Barbados for hours before it took off. And it was hot and sweaty inside that cabin. "Everybody on the plane was wondering what was going on. Finally this hearse shows up and they pull out a casket with a body in it and load it on to the plane. Then we took off."

You gotta wonder if the smell Pete noticed coming from the Grenada medical school came from the body in that casket.

One thing is for sure, though. Pete's not going to become the Grenadan Ambassador, or the director of the Chamber of Commerce.

"The country was just an unbelievable wreck," Pete said. "Nobody had a job. Every tree that had shade had a bunch of guys sitting under it either drinking beer or playing cards or smoking pot."

Sounds kind of like South Austin in the early Eighties, but what do I know?

Pete does see one piece of irony connected with his visit. He says one night, while he was at his hotel, he heard all these big noises off in the distance. "I could hear explosions all night long, and I asked the woman at the desk what that was. She said the army was training, because the U.S. was going to invade."

So Pete told the woman, "Oh come on, the United States doesn't care about you." He says he thought it was complete nonsense. Wrong. A couple years later Ronald Reagan invaded Grenada.

It was just one crazy thing after the next during Mariotti's time as editor of the *American-Statesman*. There was the time when Joe Froelick and Glenn Garvin, a couple of reporters

(Garvin is now a columnist with the *Miami Herald*), were assigned to go spend the night in the Rainbow House, a hippie flophouse on Guadalupe Street, aka the Drag. Goings-on on the Drag have been of interest to Austinites for years, since the Drag sits right across the street from the University of Texas campus, and since the Drag attracts a lot of street weirdos.

Around midnight one night, Ed got a call from the reporters. Some character named the Space Teddy Bear, staying in the next room over from the reporters in the Rainbow House, had shot and killed a guy.

Ed raced up to the Rainbow House in the middle of the night to get his reporters out of there. "I can't believe you people have reporters staying in this place," Ed says the cops told him in so many words. "Now get them the hell out of here. "

So he did. Ed, Froelick and Garvin went back to the paper and stayed up all night writing about the murder. Ed says it wouldn't have been nearly such a big story if the newspaper hadn't had a couple of reporters living in a flophouse next door to the murder.

Reporters seemed more adventurous back in Mariotti's day. There was a Hispanic reporter on the staff who was dating Austin's Playboy Bunny, Janet Quist. Janet was a hot ticket in town. Folks considered her somewhat of a celebrity, apparently, since somebody got her to put her handprint along with her name in the sidewalk in front of the old Rackley Hardware, in the 200 block of Congress Avenue. It was there for years.

This particular reporter was quite the lady's man. He told Crowell that there wasn't a woman in the newsroom who could resist him. And here he was, going out with this hottie Playboy chick. Where the reporter screwed up was in leaving evidence behind. He wrote about an evening with the bunny in lurid detail, and then left the story where everybody in the newsroom could see it.

You see, in the newsroom back in those days we had a printout machine that had a quirk. When you'd hit the button, sometimes it wouldn't make the printout — until, say, the next morning.

Well, the next morning came, and there, on the printout machine, was this long, torrid, steaming, heaving, screaming piece written by the Hispanic reporter about his marvelous evening with the Playboy bunny. It even mentioned the color of her underwear. I think it was purple.

That would make it purple prose, right?

The reporter was quite taken with Janet Quist, apparently, because when she invited him to leave town with her and go to Hawaii, he asked Ed if he could have a leave of absence.

Ed said no. What a killjoy. Ed eventually fired the guy, but for a different reason. Ed says the guy kept calling up saying he couldn't make it to work because he had a flat tire.

The newspaper covered all sorts of funky little stories in the old days that might go ignored today. See, we didn't suffer from the budget problems newspapers face today, since we weren't facing annihilation by Internet.

There was the Neillsville, Wisconsin, story in 1984, for example. You're wondering why a newspaper in Central Texas would be covering a story about a small town in the middle of

Wisconsin that nobody hanging out in the Horseshoe Lounge in South Austin had even heard of.

Easy. This travel story had a funny twist.

This adventure was born when one of the major airlines erroneously posted an extremely cheap fare for round trip tickets from La Crosse, Wisconsin, to Austin, Texas. The ticket price was $25-$30, recalled Joe Vargo, the *American-Statesman* reporter who flew to Wisconsin with photographer Bob Daemmerich to cover the story. (You've probably seen Bob's photos in the newspaper. He's been taking pictures around Austin and the State Capitol for decades.)

Joe says a travel agent in Neillsville saw the price misprint, then arranged for a whole bunch of locals to buy tickets at the cheap price to go see Austin, Texas. "The airline had to honor the cut-rate fare," Joe said. "And folks took advantage of it. By the time the airline had figured it out, about half the population of Neillsville had come to Austin to visit."

Joe and Daemmerich covered the story by going to Neillsville, then flying back to Austin with a planeload of Wisconsinites who had bought the cheap tickets. "We flew back with the first group of people who were coming back," Joe told me. "And I remember two of them were these really fat teenage girls. I mean *really* fat. These were kinda like corn-fed heifers."

That's Wisconsin for you, the home of the barstool butt.

Reporting as a profession has its perks. While in Neillsville, Joe camped out in a neighborhood bar and talked to the locals over cheap beer. "We sat in a bar drinking beer for about fifty cents a glass," said Joe, who was the *American-Statesman's* cop reporter at the time.

Joe says there was only one cop in Neillsville and his name was Bunny, which gave Neillsville a Mayberry RFD feel, he said. "He told me to call him Bunny, and he had a listed phone number. So I guess he took calls from home."

Joe didn't come back to Austin empty-handed, either. Wisconsin is a prime spot to find inexpensive local beers. So Joe returned to Texas with five twelve-packs — some of it Point Beer from Stevens Point, Wisconsin (in a steel blue can with the word "Point" on it), and some of it Leinenkugel's.

"I couldn't carry them on, so I checked them," Joe said.

Because of financial considerations, a goofy story like this would be less likely to see the light of day in our newspaper today. But back in 1984, this wasn't a problem.

"If we could make a pitch for a story, we could go pretty much anywhere," Joe said.

Especially if Ray Mariotti was listening to the pitch. And he figured a lot of people would read the story.

Learning the Ropes

When I started doing my column at the *American-Statesman* on April Fool's Day, 1977, I didn't know what I was doing.

I had done some columns before, on a small-time basis. While I was in the Army and stationed in Frankfurt, Germany, in the early 1970s, I worked for a troop newspaper, the *V Corps Guardian*, which was basically a house organ for the Army. I wrote a column every two weeks called "Inside the Corps". It was supposed to be funny. I guess my favorite was the one about how they were selling C-rations at the Post Exchange.

I wondered why anyone in his right mind would pay money to eat canned meat from World War II, and that question was the gist of the column.

I also did some fairly serious news stories while working for the troop newspaper in Germany. Oh, I blew it big time when I didn't bother to do a story when I happened to be in Munich for the Olympics on the very day that the Israeli team got attacked by terrorists. I'd been sent to the Olympics by my sergeant major on temporary duty. Not that he expected me to do any work. It was a gift from the sergeant major because I made his coffee every morning.

On a Sunday morning in 1972 in Munich, I just happened to be walking by a big field enclosed by a fence. Inside the fence were all sorts of big military vehicles, an unusually large array of major fighting hardware. It looked like a war was about to start.

What's this all about? I wondered. It was a Forest Gump kind of deal. I just happened to be there. I had no idea what was up, so I stopped a stranger who spoke English, and asked.

He told me the Israeli Olympic team had been taken hostage. I didn't write about it for the troop paper. Stupid. Like I said, it was a house organ. And I was being lazy. And I wasn't expected to write anything at the Olympics, since our troop newspaper didn't cover real news. So I took the day off. Or, as they used to say in the Army back in those days, "Never volunteer for anything."

But I did do some fairly decent stuff in the Army. I wrote one story on a group of soldiers who went around to various Army bases performing plays. One play was about drug abuse, another about racism. They were basically morality plays designed to help make the troops behave correctly.

From talking to the soldier/actors, I found out that the Army had been giving them trouble for allegedly smoking hash. And I use the term allegedly here because back in those days almost all the troops in Germany were smoking hash. There was a park in Frankfurt the troops called Shit Park, because that's where they went to score their hash.

These troops in the V Corps road show felt like they were being singled out. They complained about how often their bus had been searched for drugs.

So, like an idiot, I wrote a story about that and turned it in. A red-faced major who worked in the commanding general's office nearly screamed at me for writing the story, asking me where I'd gotten that information. Then he drew red lines all over the story, and it never ran. But at least I didn't get busted in rank. All I got was a tongue-lashing. I should have seen that one coming. Brother, was I naive. I had more guts than brains back then.

But the column thing? Color me a rookie, but I was somewhat in the dark about writing this thing called a column when I first landed at the *American-Statesman*. Before they'd give me the column, they tried me out as a general assignment reporter. And I wrote some good stuff on that beat.

One day in 1977, for example, while working on a story about Meals on Wheels, I stumbled across Willie Wells, a black shortstop from the old Negro Leagues of the 1930s, who happened to live on Newton Street in South Austin. I had been following around a friend of mine who worked for Meals on Wheels, going door to door to find old folks who might need some food delivered to their homes.

That's how I ran into Wells, who was seventy at the time, and trying to get into the Baseball Hall of Fame in Cooperstown, New York. He didn't make it in when I was writing about him. But years later, he got into the Hall of Fame's section for Negro League players — and he deserved it. Wells had a career batting average well over .300 in Negro League play, as well as a .392 batting average in thirty-three exhibition games against major league competition. I wrote a long feature on him that ran on the front page.

However, I soon saw that column writing was going to take some learning for this beginner. Making matters worse was the pressure. Much fanfare accompanied the introduction of my column. The newspaper took a picture of me standing in front of a big piece of road machinery that had large gears on it. This was in Northeast Austin. They turned the picture into an ad: "John Kelso: He Writes Like He Has a Gear Loose," read the ad. The ad campaign also came with similar plywood billboards — probably four by six feet, and yellow with big blue letters — placed on the sides of the paper's delivery trucks.

I was so taken by this sudden patch of fame that I decided I needed one of those billboards. So one night after dark, I drove my VW bug down to the newspaper with some of my friends and we stole one. This was way before Osama Bin Laden, so security in those days was pretty loose. The security guard just waved us through the gate.

We loaded the billboard onto the roof of the VW, and the folks in the car reached out the windows and held it down. Then we took off. If I remember right, I was driving, and along for the ride were my wife at the time, Sharon, and Patrick Taggart, the newspaper's movie critic.

For years the billboard sat unceremoniously in the garage of my little South Austin house in a neighborhood near Crockett High School.

But back then I knew that if management had gone to all this trouble to promote me with a billboard and an ad campaign, they expected some hot results. I did three columns a week for the front of the local/state news section, and on the other four days the same space was filled up by Mike Kelley, who also wrote a humor column.

Trouble was that Mike Kelley was really, really good. He's one of the best writers I've ever read. I couldn't carry his pens, and I was worried that my boss, Ray Mariotti, thought the same thing. In fact, I knew that's what he was thinking.

Plus I had no street cred. Zip. Zero. Nobody knew who I was. How could they? I mean, most people in Austin never read the *Palm Beach Post* or the *V Corps Guardian*.

I remember the first time I ever visited the Broken Spoke, on South Lamar, the last true honky-tonk in Austin. I'd been assigned to do a story on where the State Legislature went to drink. And this place, I'd heard, was one of 'em. In fact, our elected officials would gather and hoist a few at the Spoke each week for "Speaker's Night."

So I walked in and talked to the guy running the Spoke at the time, a good ol' boy named Joe Balon. He was the father-in-law of James White, who currently owns the Spoke with his wife, Annetta.

So I asked Joe if this was indeed one of the spots where the legislators gathered to drink. Joe immediately got chapped. He said something about how if I wanted to talk like a man he'd be glad to sit down and talk to me, whatever the heck that was supposed to mean.

I think what that was supposed to mean was mind your own business.

Defeated, I slumped on over to the bar where Nat Henderson, a longtime columnist at the *Statesman*, was enjoying a few toddies. Nat had his whiskey bottle on the bar in a brown paper bag. People used to bring whiskey into beer joints in brown bags back in the day. Then they'd order "set-ups," mixers like Coke and club soda. Nat asked me if I wanted a drink, so I told him what I was doing and what had just happened. We sat there and chatted for about two minutes before Joe Balon came over to see me again. He'd seen me talking to Nat, so now I was okay. If I knew Nat, I must be a good guy. Now Balon walked over to me smiling and said, "Son, let me introduce you to Senator Peyton McKnight." At that point, we walked a few feet from the bar and I met the state senator, from East Texas, who just happened to be in the Spoke that evening.

When I started working at the *Statesman* I was pretty darned clueless, and I made some clumsy writing mistakes. One of the first stories I ever did for the paper had to do with the Electoral College. There had just been a presidential election, and Jimmy Carter had been elected. Select citizens from around the state had come to Austin to cast their Electoral College votes. I interviewed them and made fun of their small town ways. But even worse, I started the story off with a quote from a fictional character named Captain Skinny. At my job as an outdoor writer in Florida, I had created a charter boat captain character named Captain Skinny.

So like an idiot, I began a Texas story with a quote from a fictional character from Florida. Like that fits, right? And the quote was, "There was so much going on at the depot, I didn't get a chance to see the village." I had lifted the quote from a comedy record album.

So Jim Fain, the *Statesman's* publisher at the time (meaning he was the big boss), saw the Captain Skinny quote and apparently thought it was completely stupid. From his office upstairs, he sent a marked-up copy of the front page down to the newsroom. He had highlighted the name Captain Skinny and written the following message: "Who he?" That was it. "Who he?"

The story was so damning that Ben Sargent, our political cartoonist and now one of my friends, wrote a nasty note about it to Jim Baker, the city editor at the time. I wasn't supposed to see the note, but Baker left it in plain sight on his desk. I said to myself, *this job may not last very long.*

Even the readers were on my tail. One of the first columns I ever wrote for the *Statesman* had to do with belly dancers. I talked to a group of Austin belly dancers and wrote about how guys were always gawking at them. As if they were, you know, pole dancers. That column chapped the belly dancers something fierce. If you follow horse racing, you know that there used to be a famous thoroughbred named Kelso. So one of the belly dancers wrote a letter to the editor that said she preferred Kelso the gelding to Kelso the stud.

Ouch.

But I was so far in the dark at the time that I didn't even realize it was a good thing for a column to tick people off. That's how ignorant I was about my new job.

It came to my attention, however, in the fall of 1977, that a good way to get people to read a column is to make them screaming mad. You know, get them up out of their chairs and make 'em come down to the building looking for you.

It was at this point that I had my a-HA! moment. And for this epiphany, I'd like to thank the Texas Aggies.

Here's what happened. The Texas A&M-University of Texas football game was being played at Kyle Field, and this was back in the days when all-world running back Earl Campbell was running over other teams' linebackers for the Texas Longhorns.

On the particular day I was writing about, the people Earl was running over were Aggies. Before the game began, U.T.'s Alpha Phi Omega coed service fraternity ran onto Kyle Field in College Station with a huge Lone Star flag, as is traditional with Alpha Phi Omega.

A&M's Cadet Corps didn't appreciate this. A&M has a tradition that the first people on the field are supposed to be the A&M players, not a bunch of Tea-sips with a big Lone Star flag. So words were exchanged, insults were hurled, sabers were rattled, and there was heckling and taunting.

Well, I wrote about the incident in a wise guy way. I'd tell a little bit about the Aggies rattling their sabers, and then I'd slip in an Aggie joke. Then I'd tell a little bit more about the proceedings, and I'd sneak in another Aggie joke. I'd release still more details about the fracas, then throw in yet another Aggie joke. I repeated this pattern all the way through the column.

Come to think of it, the column began with an Aggie joke and ended with an Aggie joke. The final joke was the one about the Aggies who were deer hunting, mistook their buddy for a deer, and shot him dead.

The joke ended with the doctor saying, "Well, we might have saved him. But when you gutted and skinned him, that was all she wrote."

I also threw in the one about the Aggie who was arrested for being naked in downtown Austin. The cop asked him why he didn't have his pants on and the Aggie explained he'd been on a date with a young lady who had told him to take off his clothes. Then she took off her own clothes and told the Aggie, "Let's go to town."

The Aggie told the cop, "I must have beat her here, 'cause I haven't seen her since."

Those weren't the best jokes ever told. But they must have done the trick, because on the morning the column showed up in the newspaper, here they came — a small group of live Aggies, into the newspaper office, looking for my happy butt.

As it turned out, I wasn't there. I've learned over the years that if you want to avoid Aggies, sleep late, because they get up early to tend to the herd.

This also taught me another important lesson. If you want to get people to read your columns, poke 'em with a stick. In other words, that column got a lot of reaction. And it was the first column of mine that had.

Of course, it helps if you have a good reason to poke your readers with a stick. Just pokin' to attract readers doesn't cut it. You've got to have a reason. Or at least it helps.

There were instances when a smart-ass approach to a subject brought out the worst in people. In 2003, Alabama's Chief Justice Roy Moore was removed from office for defying a federal judge's order to remove his Ten Commandments monument from the state Supreme Court building.

I tackled the issue by writing my own Ten Alabama

Commandments, such as: Thou shalt honor thy mamma and thy daddy, as soon as thee figure out who they are.

This scorched the undershorts of an e-mailer who went by the name of Black Wolf. (Festive name, huh?) "Be advised that your address at home is known to us," Black Wolf wrote. "We also know where you work. You will be killed shortly. No matter what you do, you cannot escape this. You will die for your crimes, and if we kill others in the process... so be it. See you in hell."

I've had several I'm-going-to-kick-your-keister threats over the course of my career. But this was my only straight up bang-you're-dead death threat.

I turned the e-mail over to the newspaper's head of security. The newspaper decided it would be best to hire an armed security guard in street clothes and station him in an unmarked car for a couple of nights on the street in front of my house in South Austin.

I lived in one of those neighborhoods where everybody knew everybody else's business. So when one neighbor saw a stranger sitting in a car after dark in front of my house, she just had to walk up and ask the guy what he was doing. The security guard tried to blow her off, but it wasn't easy.

After I mentioned the e-mail to our security guy at the paper, the police were called. They started an investigation to track the guy down. It took the cops about three weeks, if I remember right, to find Black Wolf. I learned he was the son of a paper company executive in northern Alabama. The cops decided not to arrest the guy since he had mental problems and was bipolar.

So it wouldn't have been a fair fight anyway, since it would have been two against one.

No column I ever wrote got as much angry response as one about the Dallas Cowboys in the early 1990s. The column wasn't even all that great. I'd give it a B- or maybe a C+. All it said, really, is that I didn't like the Cowboys, and that I hoped on Sunday the San Francisco 49ers would stomp the Cowboys in the play-off game.

The reason I don't like the Cowboys is simple: I grew up in New England. Over the years I've mellowed, though, and I enjoy watching the Cowboys — lose.

Anyway, I wrote the column on a Friday for the Saturday paper. Immediately, our city editor said he didn't want to run it for a practical reason. Seems that particular weekend the KKK was coming to the State Capitol in Austin to promote their racist cause. The newspaper had to cover it, and the city editor didn't want to have to spend all day Saturday with the phones tied up by cheesed off Cowboys football fans.

At the time, we had just gotten this newfangled thing called voice mail. Callers could call up and leave recorded messages. So I told the city editor, "I know what. Why don't we just put the voice mail phone number at the bottom of the column?"

That way, folks could call up and bitch all they wanted, and the paper's reporters working the KKK story wouldn't be bothered by them.

The city editor said okay, and that's exactly what we did.

When I came to work the following Monday, I had more than three hundred messages on my voice mail machine. The first message set the tone for the day when the caller, sounding like a rodeo announcer, said in a boisterous voice: "WHY DON'T YOU GO BACK TO SAN FRANSISSYCO WHERE YOU BELONG?"

There are some lines you just never forget. For me, that's one of them.

Hail to the Chief

In 1979, I ran for President of the United States. Obviously, it was a spoof campaign. I couldn't lead a bunch of Cub Scouts to a hot dog cook-off. So it's always been my rule never to run for anything I could possibly win. I vowed from the beginning not to take my presidential campaign too seriously. Partly that was because I had a columnist friend in South Florida named Steve Mitchell who once ran for Congress. He did much better than anybody expected, which was the problem. When it became apparent to him that he wasn't going to win, he killed himself. I never came close to falling into the same trap. Although I'll admit that, toward the end of my campaign, when I realized I wasn't going to get my name on the Texas primary ballot, I was ticked off.

You ask why I didn't make it? I still contend the Republican Party of Texas hosed me out of the deal because they simply didn't want some smarty-pants humor columnist on their ballot. Could you blame them? Well, I did. Even though me running as a Republican was part of the joke. I've been a yellow dog

Democrat since the age of about 8.

If I were to run for President today, I would handle it entirely differently. I would have an actual platform. I would take stands on issues. I would say that I was against spending billions of dollars on invading countries that have done nothing to harm us. I would come out in favor of health insurance for everyone, and for spending as much money on education as we spend on defense. I would support affordable college education so that kids from poor families could get a degree without having to deal with a massive bill as soon as they get out of school. Things like that.

Back when I ran in 1979, though, I was of a different mindset. About the only party I was interested in at the time was the Keg Party.

My foray into politics started when "Pops" Conway told me about a story he'd read in the newspaper. This story explained how easy it was to get your name on the New Hampshire Presidential primary ballot. All you needed was a $500 filing fee and the signatures of a thousand registered voters. Since I had gone to high school in New Hampshire, Pops pointed out that I could run as a native son.

I decided to do it. I thought the effort would make for a funny (and easy) column. I'd just write that I was running for President, and that would be the end of it. I recently re-read that column, and I suspect that I had it in the back of my mind that I really did have a chance to make it onto the New Hampshire primary ballot.

I mentioned in the column that I had an old high school buddy whose dad, Pappy Whitum, ran a gas station in Laconia.

Pappy had been the president of Laconia's one and only Chowder and Marching Society. I figured Pappy could get me several hundred signatures, surely. My journalistic digging revealed, though, that the Chowder and Marching Society was just a bunch of old guys who sat around the back room at the gas station chewing the fat.

I pointed out in the column that my record was clean, that I'd only had one speeding ticket, and another ticket for backing into an intersection, but I'd never been caught doing any of the really nasty stuff.

"Isn't not getting caught doing all the really rotten stuff a prerequisite for being a decent president?" I wrote. Yes, if you're going to get caught in the Oval Office with a cigar and an intern, it's better if it happens after you leave office.

In any case, my campaign was off and running. I announced in my column that my campaign slogan was "Who Else But Kels?" My boss Ray loved the idea. He thought it would be a good way to show people the nuts and bolts of a grassroots campaign, how much it costs to have a bunch of T-shirts made up, what kind of paperwork you have to file with the Federal Election Commission — that kind of stuff.

The fact that Ray liked the idea became a problem for me later on. We'll get to that. To raise the filing fee, I said in that first column that I would hold garage sales, car washes, and "whatever it takes." The paper couldn't finance me, except to pay my salary. It would have been a conflict of interest, even though the campaign was a lark.

Shortly after the first column about the campaign came out,

I received $3.26 from readers in pennies, nickels, dimes, and quarters taped to the back of post cards. I called Pops and told him about it.

"We have to open you a campaign fund," he said. So the two of us got in my 1974 Super Beetle and drove down to the San Jacinto branch of the Austin National Bank, at Fifth and Brazos Streets, to open an account. The branch was a one-room operation. When we walked in, there was just one woman working inside, sitting at a desk.

"This is John Garfield Kelso," Conway said, introducing me with great flourish. "He's running for President of the United States."

I don't usually use my middle name, except for especially formal occasions, such as when I'm being sued, or running for President.

The woman looked up at us suspiciously; I could see she thought we were fixing to rob the place. "No, really," Pops assured her. "He is running for President. And we need to open a campaign fund for him. The trouble is we only have $3.26."

"Well, for a savings account, we usually require a minimum deposit of $25," the woman said. "But since we do it for little kids, I guess we can do it for you."

We deposited the money, and then we started having a few fundraisers. I don't remember much about the fundraisers, except that they usually involved beer. Soon I had a campaign committee to organize the petition drive I'd need to gather the signatures. A few crazy college kids got involved. We set up a table on the West Mall at the University of Texas campus. I still have an

8" x 10" black-and-white photo on my bookcase at home, showing a mob of college students gathered around a guy with no shirt on.

The guy had the words "Kelso T-shirt" painted on his chest. The excitement was building. The guy standing next to the shirtless guy had his arms folded, and had a look on his face that said, "Are you out of your mind?"

We had one actual Republican helping with the campaign as an advisor. Like I said, part of the prank was me pretending to be at one with the GOP. I've never owned a riding lawnmower and here I was running as a Republican. I'm not going to tell you the name of the only Republican we had helping us out, though. I will say that he worked for a high-ranking elected official, and that one night, my Republican buddy stopped at a massage parlor and used his credit card to get some, um, bodywork done. That's what he told me, anyway.

Who knew Republicans went to massage parlors? I sure didn't.

So as time went on, I raised enough money to actually take a couple of plane trips up to New Hampshire to try to get signatures. On one trip, I took two assistants: my long and loyal friend David Arnsberger, who used to perform with a popular and funny Austin band called The Uranium Savages (one of their hits was "Idi Amin Is My Yard Man"), and this middle-aged character named Liam Sullivan.

We got a rental car to drive around New Hampshire. I even went out and bought a new sport coat and a white shirt. Not as much business was conducted during our trip as I might have liked. I soon saw that bringing Liam along had been a big mistake.

Liam mostly drank during the trip. Actually, Liam mostly drank for any occasion. He even brought a flask onto the plane, and David and Liam passed it back and forth.

They also drank in the rent car. "There wasn't a day that went by that we didn't have a half gallon of Haig and Haig in the back seat on the floorboard," recalled David in 2012, when I spoke to him about our presidential adventure. "I don't remember you drinking that much, but I know Liam and I did."

Ordinarily I would have joined them in the drinking department. But I wanted to get those signatures, so I stuck to business. I was a nervous wreck over the situation. For one thing, I worried that Liam would get us busted for drinking in the car.

"You were really fidgety back then," David said. He said I had a nervous tick during our trip that consisted of my tugging on my moustache. "I think the moustache on the left side of your face was half the size of the moustache on the right side of your face," he told me.

He added that I wore the same new white shirt and blue blazer every day of our trip. "I don't know if you ever changed clothes," he said. "In fact, you might have worn the same shirt and jacket every day." So obviously the weight of the presidency was already chewing on my brain.

This was David's first trip to New England, and he had a noticeable Texas accent under normal circumstances. But the further north we went, the thicker his accent got. Before we left New Hampshire to come home he was starting to sound like Roy Acuff.

I'm not sure if David's Texas drawl helped or hurt our door-to-door signature collection drive in New Hampshire, but

I remember we were having trouble getting people to sign my petition. Either people didn't know who I was, so they wouldn't sign. Or maybe they remembered me from high school and wouldn't sign because they *did* know me.

While Liam sat on his butt, David gave my candidacy his best shot. He banged on doors, trying to round up signatures for our petition. He was met with rejection, however. People kept telling him, he said, "I'm voting for Reagan, I'm voting for Reagan." Still, I did manage to get my photo on the front page of the *Manchester Union-Leader*, the biggest newspaper in the state of New Hampshire.

That was the good news. Here was the bad news. My picture was right next to a photo of the Ayatollah Khomeini. "It was like, *Hey, Kelso made the front page, right next to the Ayatollah*," David recalled.

As for Liam, I should have known even before we got on the plane that he wouldn't be of much assistance. Back in Austin, Liam was publishing a small newspaper full of his own nonsense. He funded this rag by putting ads for businesses in without asking the businesses if they wanted an ad. Then he'd take the publication to the business and try to charge them for the ad.

If that wasn't bad enough, he ran an ad for Rooster Andrews' sporting goods stores that was of questionable taste, without telling Rooster Andrews. This ad had four panels: three showed black kids bouncing a basketball, and one showed a white kid bouncing a basketball. The message with the ad read something like, "Guess who's not going to make it to the NBA?" Or maybe it was three white kids and one black kid, with the question being, "Guess who's going to make it into the NBA?" It has been a long time, so I'm not sure. But it had racist overtones, no doubt about it.

Rooster Andrews had been a kicker for the University of Texas Longhorns back in the 1940s, in star quarterback Bobby Layne's day. Rooster was not amused by this ad, and he threatened to sue Liam, who apologized and managed to worm his way out of the suit.

Liam acted with the same kind of grace and élan up in New Hampshire. One night when we were trying to get some schoolteachers to sign my petition, Liam told one of them that schoolteachers were nothing more than glorified babysitters. This was not helpful. It didn't tend to win the teachers over.

Things weren't going well, so I decided my campaign needed to do something big. We needed a famous person to sign my petition, a big shot who would give our campaign some street cred.

So I got in the car with David (by now, fortunately, Liam had returned to Texas) and I headed over to Sherman Adam's office in Lincoln. Mr. Adams had been President Eisenhower's White House Chief of Staff back in the 1950s. He was a man of power and wealth who owned a ski area in Lincoln. I thought he seemed like a decent gentleman, so I wore my new white shirt and sport coat to impress him. I also wore a tie. Usually somebody has to pass away before I'll put on a tie.

During that meeting, Sherman Adams was cordial, polite, and gracious. He sat down with us in his office at the ski area and chatted for about twenty minutes. However, he told us he couldn't sign my petition, since he wasn't signing any of the other candidates' petitions. I'm sure he was thinking he couldn't sign my petition because David and I were a couple of loons.

After he turned us down, we got back in the rent car and drove off down the highway. We were pretty hangdog and depressed. I reached up to scratch my neck, and I realized I hadn't taken that cardboard thingy out of the collar of that brand-new white shirt. David remembered this. "Not only was it the same shirt you'd been wearing for a week," he said, "but also it had never been washed. It still had the cardboard in it from when you bought it at the store."

Maybe if I'd removed that cardboard, I'd have been elected President.

While we were driving back to Logan Airport in Boston to catch our flight back to Austin, David had to find a john, the quicker the better. As bad luck would have it, we couldn't find an exit on the highway to get to a service station. So David was suffering. "I had to pee like a racehorse," David said. "I'd had a Bloody Eddy (David's name for a beer and tomato juice drink), and then I had to pee, but there was no exit."

Finally, with him turning yellow, we found a service station in Massachusetts. But there was one problem. "It was a pay toilet," David said. "You had to put a quarter in a slot to pee and I just went 'f&*# that s^@#' and peed in the sink." (I wonder if the Romney campaign ever had an advisor who peed in the sink.) Anyway, after a few months of banging our heads against the wall it became apparent to me and the rest of my campaign staff that I was not going to get the thousand signatures I needed in order to get on the New Hampshire primary ballot. I think we gathered a total of about 120 names up in New Hampshire.

By this time, my boss was getting antsy. For the last few months I'd been writing about this joke campaign, and it was looking like the joke wouldn't come with a punch line. At least not the punch line Ray Mariotti was hoping for. But I pressed on. I decided to try to get the five thousand signatures I'd need to get my name on the Texas Presidential Primary ballot. I figured this would be easier, because at least in Austin people would know who I was and get the joke. I'd been the local columnist for three years, so I was becoming fairly well known by that time.

We stationed a construction guy named Kirk "Captain Kirk" Opyt at the Armadillo Christmas Bazaar over the holidays to get signatures. The annual Armadillo Christmas Bazaar gathers lots of Christmas shoppers, so it seemed like a good spot to look for signatures. You had your old Armadillo music hall hippies coming by in droves.

And Kirk, who became one of my best friends, liked the job because the signature table wasn't very far from the beer counter. Kirk was a loyal trooper. For a while he was the only guy I could depend on to show up and gather names. We also fanned out to other bars around town to chase down signatures. We didn't have any trouble getting people to sign the petition. The trouble we had was getting people's voter registration card numbers. That was a prerequisite. You had to include those numbers on the petition.

But I found out most people don't carry their voter registration cards with them. Therefore, we had all these names without the required numbers. At last count we had right at 5,600 names, about 600 more than I needed to get on the ballot. But I hired a gal anyway, to look up the voter registration card numbers that we were missing. She parked herself at the courthouse and looked them up. Trouble was, we ran out of time. So when we turned the names in to the Republican Party of Texas, a lot of the registration card numbers weren't included. Who knows how many were missing.

I don't think the Republican Party knew the number, that's for sure. A few days after I turned the petitions in, they said I didn't have enough names to make the cut. To this day, I don't think they had enough time to really check the pile of petitions I had given them, to know for sure that I didn't have enough names to qualify. I figured they just kept me off the ballot because they didn't want somebody who was making fun of the GOP on there. Imagine that.

Here's your little irony. In 1988, a company named Southern Political Consulting was indicted by a Harris County grand jury for forging names of registered voters to fill up the petitions of GOP Primary candidate Pete DuPont. The story was that college students were taken to a room, fed beer, and told to start signing names, since they hadn't been able to come up with names the honest way. The consultant firm's vice president was named Rocky Mountain.

Sounds like the college kids might have made up that one, too. Still, George Strake, head of the Republican Party of Texas at the time, ruled that all of the candidates who had turned in petitions would be on the primary ballot. He wasn't going to let these little technicalities get in the way. I'm still not exactly giddy about that one. I mean, what's better? A petition filled with names invented by college kids drinking Bud, or a petition that's short of voter registration numbers?

I'm not bitter about this turn of events, but it did open my eyes a little wider about politics. See, a lot of people went to some trouble to help me get those signatures. Like I said, I even lined up a group of college kids from the University of Texas to help with the signature drive. It was a pretty loosey-goosey group. So loosey-goosey, in fact, I'm surprised some of them didn't wind up in the state pen.

I recall the Easter Sunday morning when the U.T. student who was the head of my Who Else But Kels campus delegation decided to take a bunch of his hippie friends fishing at a catfish pond near the town of Garfield. Bright and early, he called me at home and asked if I wanted to tag along. I told him I'd meet them out there.

The place they'd picked to fish was a set of commercial catfish tanks located off Texas 71 east of town, and run by a nice old gentleman named Mr. Washington.

It was around mid-morning when I showed up at Washington's catfish business, looking for my college crew. Up walked Mr. Washington, who was obviously quite perturbed about something. He was pacing and he wasn't smiling. I asked whether he'd seen a bunch of college kids. He had. "You tell them to stop tearing down my fences and swimmin' nekkid in my ponds," he told me.

Uh-oh. Sensing trouble, I decided to not look for my student helpers, and to fish solo instead. I picked what looked like a likely pond, set down my tackle box, baited the hook, and tossed a worm into the water. Pretty soon I'd landed a pretty good-sized catfish, probably a pound or two. Shortly afterward I caught another one. My smile quickly turned to a look that said, "Holy smokes!"

"You better put those back, or Mister Washington will shoot over your head," said a guy who was standing nearby, watching me. Huh? Turns out I was fishing in Mr. Washington's stock pond, where no one was supposed to fish except for Mr. Washington. I hadn't known that, so I quickly took the caught fish down to the pond, put them in the water and dragged them around in the water to revive them.

Then I jumped into my VW Bug and got the heck out of there.

Later I learned that the head of my college team had borrowed his best friend's clunky old van that morning to take his pals fishing. Trouble was, he hadn't asked his friend's permission to borrow the van.

On the way back into town, I was told, all the hippies in the van, who were higher than Mt. Bonnell, were singing the words to "Follow the Yellow Brick Road" at full volume out the windows, all the way down the highway back into town. Unknown to them, in the van with them was a large quantity of pot that the van owner had stashed out of sight somewhere in the vehicle. The folks in the van didn't find out they had dope riding in the van with them until they returned the vehicle to the owner. How much pot are we talking about? "I think it was about a half," one of the hippies in the van told me recently, some thirty-two years after the fact.

"Half of what?" I asked.

"A half pound," he told me. "It was enough to get in trouble with." This guy owned a food trailer in South Austin the last time I talked to him, and he didn't want his real name used with this story.

Lucky for the impromptu choral group in the van, they didn't get pulled over that day.

Another amusing incident took place while we were chasing signatures in Austin. On a day when I was a judge in a chitlin' cook-off at Manor Downs, a horserace track east of Austin, David Arnsberger and his friend Dick Terry decided to work as my Secret Service agents.

They were so secret they didn't bother to inform the Secret Service. David and Dick dressed the part. They even carried an AM-FM radio with a wire and an earplug. It was pretty authentic. That is, if you're an idiot.

"We were talking into the cuffs of our sleeves, wearing Wayfarer sunglasses and coats and ties, and acting like Secret Service agents, which was a blast," David said. "After all, you were running for President."

Somebody called the FBI and reported that a couple of guys were impersonating the Secret Service out at Manor Downs, I later heard. But nothing came of it. It would have been a better story if my Secret Service crew had been interrogated by the Feds, but in this case I'd settle for a lesser yarn just to avoid the aggravation.

I did learn one important lesson from my Presidential campaign, though. After spending hundreds of hours working on this campaign, it became apparent to me that a person can never get elected president unless he or she has got a gigantic pile of money.

That didn't mean we didn't have to account for the piddling money we did raise, though. During the campaign, Ben Sargent, the *American-Statesman*'s political cartoonist, served as my treasurer. That job was a full-blown pain in the rear. Even though the campaign was a joke, Ben still had to keep filling out reports and sending information in to the Federal Election Commission to keep us out of jail.

Ben still remembers those days with some fondness apparently, because when I retired he gave me one of his cartoons as a going-away present. The drawing shows me talking to Texas Governor Rick Perry, who at the time was running a serious but equally unsuccessful campaign for U.S. President. In the cartoon, I'm telling Perry, "Seriously, dude — I hope you get twice as many votes as I did."

I never even got close to the White House. Oh, I've been there as a guest. I was doing a column there on the day Bill Clinton got in a helicopter and flew off into the sky on his last day on the job. And I did get a peek at the Oval Office, though I never got to sit at the desk.

I never got much national attention out of my campaign, although I did manage to get my name on the front page of *The New York Times*. The *Times* had done a story on the wacky presidential candidates who had filed with the Federal Election Commission for the 1980 run. The trouble was, they misspelled my name. In fact, they didn't even come close. The reporter apparently assumed my name was Kels, since my bumper stickers said, "Who Else But Kels." Making matters worse, she didn't even spell Kels correctly. In the story I was Presidential candidate John Keis. I called up the *Times* reporter to complain about it. She was very apologetic over the mistake, so I never pushed the issue. I was afraid if I took it upstairs that she might get canned, and it wasn't worth that kind of trouble. The real sad part of the campaign, though, is that after it was over, my boss went sour on me because I didn't get on the ballot. Here I'd been writing about this stupid campaign for the better part of a year, and it had gone nowhere. This did not set well with him. He made some remark about how I'd laid an egg.

So after the campaign, he took me in his office and told me my columns had gotten weak, and that he didn't really want to fire me. (But obviously he was thinking about it.)

Two Different Cities

Seriously, Austin really has changed about a hundred percent over the years. During my years at the newspaper, I've actually lived in two different cities — the easy-going one that was here when I showed up, and the big, frantic, stand-in-line, high-toney, high-rise, high-dollar condo, valet-parking city that's Austin today.

Really. If I'd been blasted into the future from the day in 1976 when I arrived in Austin to today, I wouldn't recognize the city. I'd probably have to ask somebody where I was. The trouble is, in the new version, the person I asked might not have time to tell me.

In 1976, Austin was a laid back, pass-the-joint college and state government town, where a traffic jam was an odd occurrence. You know how the Austin TV news guys these days make a big show out of pointing out where the traffic is piled up in the morning? You know how they show those little cartoon wreck depictions on your TV screen, so you won't have to sit behind two guys swapping insurance information at the corner of, say, Sixth and Lamar?

Well, the TV news guys didn't do that bit in 1976 because they didn't need to. There wasn't enough traffic for the news guys to bother warning us about it. In 1976 I could drive to work in the morning on Interstate 35 without having to brake.

Not so today. Nowadays when people set out to work in Austin, they know they'll be stuck in traffic for so long that when they finally make it home that evening, their dogs will attack them because they don't recognize them anymore.

When traffic studies are conducted these days, Austin generally ranks at or near the top of American cities for most hours stuck in traffic. Austinites jokingly call Mo-Pac, one of the city's main north-south routes, SlowPac, because of the congestion.

The main reason for this gridlock is Austin's tremendous growth, and the city's inability to keep up with road improvements. In the late 1970s, the signs around Austin said the population was around 325,000. Today, the Metroplex population number is 1.78 million. In 1976, Austin didn't even have a Metroplex. Instead, it had Pflugerville.

Speaking of Pflugerville, the first time I drove through that town, probably in 1977, I stopped in a beer joint. Here's how laid back we were back then: the beer joint didn't have its beer license when I walked in. So under the law they couldn't sell me a beer.

However, they could give me one without breaking the law. So the bartender handed me a beer, then explained that if I wanted to help out, I could leave some money in the tip jar. I did.

That exchange would not occur in the Austin of the New Millennium.

Around 1974, an old hippie/computer geek friend of mine named Rich Mann actually took a nap on 620, which was a country road back then. Today 620 is a busy highway in the northwest part of the Metroplex. When he was fifteen, Rich and a couple of buddies from Round Rock High School had walked all the way from a house in Round Rock out to the Balcones Country Club to party early one evening. They didn't have a car, so they made the nine-mile hike to the country club.

On the hike back, around 4:00 in the morning, the three boys were so tired they decided to sack out right there on the road for more than half an hour. Hey, the road was clean, and it was flat, and there was usually no traffic that time of night. There was no shoulder to sleep on, and besides, there might be scorpions or centipedes in the grass off the side of the road. The road, by contrast, was warm. "We were also stoned and not very smart," Rich added.

At the time, there was a flashing yellow light near where these kids caught a little shut-eye. "Now it's a big giant flyover," Rich said. These days, you'll find a tollbooth for Texas 45 near where they nodded out. "We were so tired that we laid down right on the road on 620, and the road was nice and warm and we all kind of fell asleep for thirty or forty-five minutes," Rich recalls. "I was more worried about rattlesnakes and tarantulas than cars coming by."

What do you think would happen today if they pulled that stunt? "In about ten seconds we'd get run over by eighteen cars," Rich said. "They'd just think we were some armadillo. They wouldn't even slow down."

When I arrived in Austin in 1976, we didn't even have horn honking here. In fact, Austin was so easy in those days that it was considered the mark of a Yankee to honk your horn. Really. You honked your horn and the guy you were honking at figured you were some jerkwad who just blew in from New Jersey. If you wanted to get the attention of some fool in front of you sitting through a green light, instead of honking you'd step on the gas and race your engine. And you would do this in a subtle way, without leaning on the horn.

That was considered proper driving etiquette in Austin in those days. Today, if you can get through the day without a driver giving you the finger or somebody running into your car causing $1,200 worth of damage, you're not getting out of the house enough.

Here's a yarn that'll show you how little traffic we had back in the Seventies. One day I got a call from a stock car fan who wanted to start up a car racetrack in Manchaca, a small town south of Austin. The caller was one of those guys who looked like he ought to roll up his Marlboro cigarette pack in his T-shirt sleeve. He drove a muscle car that got about eight miles a gallon, and went from zero to 125 in three seconds. He wanted me to write about Austin's need for a stock car track. To show me what he was talking about, he took me for a ride in his suped-up [*souped*] machine — straight down Manchaca Road. It was around 8:00 at night, and I'll bet we hit 120 mph zipping down that road which, back then, was out in the country.

Today the intersection at Slaughter Lane and Manchaca Road has an HEB, a bank branch, a Walgreen's, and a Stop 'n

Rob store. It's one of the most exasperating intersections in town. The traffic is so thick at this intersection that if you pull into one of those businesses, you'll have a hard time pulling out of the parking lot and back onto the street.

Really. A fella couldn't make that hot rod run today on Manchaca Road without causing a nine-car pileup.

The sort of people who live here has changed, too. Today, as you drive around Austin, you can't go but a few blocks without bumping into a coffee house filled with young hipsters peering into their laptops or checking their iPhones for Facebook alerts.

Back when I landed in Austin, the phones came with phone booths, instead of laptops we had lap dances, and I'm not sure there was a single place in town that even sold cappuccino. Now you've got more cappuccino around these parts than col'beer. Come to think of it, in 2012 Austin, I may be the only person left using the expression "these parts."

Maybe it's the caffeine, but the fact is, Austinites aren't as loosey-goosey as they used to be. Before 1980, you couldn't stop at Barton Springs Pool, the city's legendary spring-fed swimming spot, without seeing some hippie chick topless. Those days are over. Not that I go down there every day and check now. But the mindset in, say, 1977, was completely different.

We even had a story in the newspaper back in the day about some gal who was stopped by the cops for running topless on the track at the University of Texas football stadium. The cops couldn't charge her because she wasn't breaking the law. And they wouldn't charge her today, either, because she'd probably be wearing a shirt.

Another thing that's changed about Austin? A character shortage. Oh, in recent times we've still had our share of eccentrics (see the chapter on Leslie). But the sheer number of colorful goofballs in the 1970s and 1980s was impressive.

For example, we had two different "Dogs" running around town. Summer Dog worked at the Continental Club on South Congress. Summer Dog, a long-haired guy, said he got his name from lying around in the summer under some trees back in North Carolina. Then there was another guy named just plain Dog. I don't recall Dog's bar of choice. But he was out there.

And there was the bald drummer named Curley, who would take the stage uninvited at the Aus-Tex Lounge and the Continental Club, a couple of popular music clubs on South Congress. Curley would perform the 1963 song "Surfin' Bird" by a group called the Trashmen. This was truly The Arts. Curley was also known for doing his drum solo, "Let There Be Drums."

Wait, there's more. Curley worked as a doorman at Joe's Generic Bar on Sixth Street, where he was the club mascot. On Halloween he would draw hair on his head as a costume.

In many cities, management would have run Curley out the door. In Austin, his act was a welcome addition. Back then if you didn't find the eccentrics, they would come and find you. In 1978 a woman walked into the newspaper looking for me. This was back when the newspaper was at an old building on Guadalupe, around Fourth Street, across from the Bradford Paint Company. This lady wore an Army helmet shell over a blonde wig. The wig tried to conceal her real hair, which was dark, but it didn't quite get the job done. She was also wearing combat boots, and she told somebody she wanted to see me.

When I saw her coming, I disappeared and hid out back in the photo department, waiting for her to leave. But she parked herself on the office couch and started reading a really large book. It was obvious she was here for the long haul. I'm surprised she didn't set up a tent in the lobby.

Well, I finally gave up, came out of the back of the newsroom, introduced myself, and took her to Gordo's, a relatively fancy pool hall on Sixth Street, for a drink. We discussed Ferlinghetti's poetry, and had a couple drinks. When I left, she was still there. Later I got a call from Gordo's, saying the silly woman had run up a small tab, about $15, and could I pay it? I did. For a humor writer, that's the cost of doing business. I don't think she really wanted anything from me except someone to talk to. Here's my theory: She'd read my columns and figured I was as screwy as she was. And she may have been right.

Over at the Soap Creek Saloon you had two bouncers: Billy Bob and Big Arm Jerry. If you were a regular at Soap Creek, you were familiar with these guys. They were as much a part of the place as the rocky parking lot. Both of them were so menacing to look at that trouble rarely broke out, but I doubt whether either one of them would start a fight. Last I knew, Big Arm Jerry had gotten out of the bouncer game and was selling real estate over in the Hill Country. And I heard that Billy Bob had become a monk. By the way, Big Arm Jerry really did have big arms. And Billy Bob had a really big beard.

There used to be a guy named Fiddlin' Billy who hung out

playing fiddle outside the Travis County Courthouse — that is, until the authorities told him to stop. Fiddlin' Billy once called me from the bus station in Brackettville, asking for $100. I'd made the mistake of writing about him, which explains why he was hitting me up. I told him I didn't have that kind of money.

"Well, then, how about $10?" Fiddlin' Billy said. Fiddlin' Billy never played with the symphony.

You never knew what crazy stuff was going to break out right in front of you back in the old days. One evening in the late '70s or early '80s while I was eating at a restaurant on I-35 in South Austin, I noticed a man and a woman bumping into tables and staggering around across the room. Turns out, it was Shorty Fry, who had worked as a rodeo clown, and her friend, Ken Morgan, a retired airline pilot.

And they were pretending to be drunk. As they stumbled around the room, they laughed uproariously, much to the chagrin of other patrons of this establishment.

At first, I just figured Shorty and Ken were hammered. I knew Shorty, so I knew this was a possibility. Then they came over to my table, sat down and explained they hadn't had a thing to drink. They were just faking being loaded for their own amusement.

Management, however, was not amused. So Shorty and Ken were asked to leave. And they did, stumbling and smiling all the way out the door.

The music scene today is a lot pricier than it was in the 70s and 80s. Bring your major credit cards, folks. These days, music fans from all over the world flock to Austin for the South by

Southwest Music Festival every March, and they pay hundreds of dollars to buy a badge in hopes of seeing their favorite bands. And even buying the badge won't always get them in. Sometimes the clubs around town are so packed that even people who have paid up have to listen from the sidewalk.

By contrast, in the 70s I paid a three-dollar cover to see guitar legend Stevie Ray Vaughan play at the Rome Inn, on 29th Street near the University of Texas campus. And there wasn't even a line to get in.

Institutions that used to be one thing became something else altogether. In the 80s I spent a week out at Friday Mountain Day Camp, a kids' camp out in the country west of town, near Driftwood. I wrote a series on the camp. The location was idyllic. There was a swimming hole with a rope you could swing on and drop yourself into the water. I remember there was one little kid who was constantly in trouble. I did one entire article on this kid's cutting up. The kid is probably the chairman of the board somewhere by now. I think his name was Danny. To plug the series, the newspaper printed up promotional cards for the newspaper racks. The photo showed me riding a horse.

The camp is no longer with us. In 1990 it became the site of Barsana Dham, an enormous Hindu temple. Sadly, the place switched from a place where kids have fun to a place where some children were abused. The Swami Prakashanand Saraswati was convicted in 2011 of twenty counts of abusing two girls who grew up at the temple. The Swami is still on the lamb. Authorities think the old man (he was 82 in 2011) is hiding out across the border in Mexico.

On a lighter note, it seems ludicrous today that in December of 1984 I wrote an entire column carping about the Stephen F. Austin Hotel on Congress Avenue charging the outrageous sum of $1.31 for a cup of coffee. That'll get you about 40 percent of a cappuccino these days. But $1.31 was pricey for a cup of coffee back then. You could get a cup of coffee at Jake's on West Fifth for 47 cents and, unlike the Stephen F. Austin, Jake's had a shuffleboard table.

Even the food has changed. Today, Austin has cuisine. In 1976, Austin had groceries. Today Austinites can choose from internationally acclaimed restaurants, such as Uchi on South Lamar. We didn't have fancy restaurants like that when I arrived on the scene. We didn't have, say, stuffed Portobello mushrooms. Back then there were just two food groups: barbecue and Mexican. We still like our barbecue and Mexican food today. Just about every day out front of Franklin's Barbecue on East 11th Street, you'll see hundreds of people lined up for lunch as if they're waiting to get tickets to a Bruce Springsteen concert.

In 1976, your choices for dinner out were limited. Today, we've got more Chinese food joints in North Austin than we have Chinese people. With an Asian eatery on just about every block north of the river, why would Austin need a Chinatown? North Austin already is one.

It was not always so diverse around here, culinarily speaking. We didn't have dim sum in 1976. Dim Sum is that array of tasty Oriental bite-size yummies with shrimp, pork, or chicken feet — you name it. If you'd said dim sum to some good ol' boy back in 1976, he probably would have thought you said, "Dip some," and he'd reach for the Copenhagen tin in the back pocket of his Levis. And there was no sushi, although there was bait.

Near where Long John Silvers is today on Ben White Boulevard near Manchaca Road, there used to be a bait shop that had live crickets for sale. You'd go in there and the chirping from the cricket tanks sounded like the score from a Tarzan movie.

Back in the day, the main seafood place in town, Christie's, on the shores of Town Lake, served fried fish with quarters of iceberg lettuce doused in Thousand Island dressing, while the waitresses went from table to table in cute little sailor outfits.

Today on the shores of Town Lake you'll find the Shoreline Grill, with flash-fried calamari, lemon caper aioli, avocado puree, grilled Texas quail, Gulf shrimp nachos, ancho emulsion, steamed mussels, jalapeño white wine broth, an assortment of Antonelli's cheeses, haricots vert, caramelized Brussels sprouts, and hazelnut olive tapenade. In 1977, Austinites would have looked at that menu and said, "Do you have any ketchup?"

Austin restaurants in the 1970s and 1980s may have been short on gourmet, but they were long on character. Take Virginia's Cafe on South First Street, a home-cooking place that served the best chicken-fried steak in Austin. You could tell it was the real thing because it came with a bone in it.

Virginia's was a tiny place, maybe big enough for thirty people, but that would be pushing it. Just two people worked there: Virginia, the crusty old woman who ran the place, and Virginia's sister, the waitress. She'd hand you a small piece of paper and you'd write down your order. Then she'd hand the order to Virginia.

For whatever reason, crustiness was a trait that Austinites admired back in those days, so Virginia was much loved by her customers. I wrote a mostly favorable review of the place, but I did describe Virginia as "cranky," and I added that the vegetables tasted canned. On the other hand, I praised the chicken-fried steak and some of the other food, probably the meat loaf.

A friend of mine was having lunch there after my article came out. While my friend was in there, he overheard another customer telling Virginia that she seemed out of sorts. "You'd be cranky too if somebody called your fresh vegetables canned," Virginia spat.

Virginia might just get on your case if you didn't clean your plate. She didn't like for customers not to finish their food. This presented a challenge for the diner, because we're talking 18-wheeler driver-size servings.

One day Kenneth Sims, the two-time All-American for the University of Texas football team, was sitting at the counter, which seated about four. Sims was about the size of a truck, so with him at the counter, it would have seated about three. Sims, a defensive end, was well known around Austin, and the nation, too. He was the first pick in the 1982 NFL draft, and went on to an NFL career with the New England Patriots.

After Sims left the restaurant, Virginia's sister, the waitress, told Virginia the big guy who'd been sitting at the counter was that famous football player, Kenneth Sims. "I don't know much about football, but did he eat his lunch?" Virginia groused. She probably would have chewed him up if he hadn't. Even a 320-pound lineman wouldn't stand a chance against Virginia.

Virginia did things her way, and if you didn't like it, too bad. Her hours of operation were explained on a sign posted on the front door. "Closed 'til open, open 'til closed," the sign said. Actually, Virginia's was open from about 11 a.m. to 2 p.m. Monday through Friday, and that was it.

Virginia's points of reference were old school. When she thought of an Austin mall, an early Austin mall named Capital Plaza came into her mind.

I was in her restaurant one day when a hot summer wind was blowing dust around outside. Virginia blamed it on "all that dust blowin' in from Capital Plaza." I don't think Virginia appreciated Austin growth.

Virginia cooked over an enormous black gas stove that looked like something out of a Pittsburgh steel plant. Impressive blue flames shot out the top. Now that I think about it, Virginia's temperament may have stemmed from the heat the stove put out.

If you wanted to use the bathroom, tough luck, because Virginia wouldn't let you use hers. Instead, she'd send you next door to the plumbing supply store. The plumbing supply store guys didn't seem to mind.

If you were in a rush, and you were eating at Virginia's, you were in the wrong spot. Virginia had another sign posted that said that if you were in hurry, you might as well leave because this could take a while. Or something to that effect.

You may be thinking these touches of grumpiness were held in disregard by Austinites. Far from it. Virginia's cantankerous ways were considered precious local color, and she and her restaurant were much beloved. But Virginia hated publicity. I tried to interview her once and she said no. She explained she had to work too hard as it was, and she didn't want any more customers.

A British film crew working on a documentary in Austin asked me if I could get Virginia to speak with them. I called Virginia on their behalf, and she turned them down flat. I doubt she would have talked to Walter Cronkite — even if he'd finished his lunch.

We were more meat-oriented in the old days. We were less concerned with how the animal felt about the deal than we are today. In the Seventies, at the Bastrop Meat Company, a barbecue place in Bastrop, about half an hour east of Austin, they ran a slaughtering operation at the restaurant. Lunch lived in a pen behind the place. Can you imagine the stink that would cause today? Today we'd rescue the cows, give them names, and find them homes. In fact, when a turkey truck wrecked in Austin in the Eighties and the turkeys got loose, that's exactly what happened, although I'm not sure how many of the people who took the turkeys home gave them names.

But I'll bet some of them did.

We used to play with our food back in the old days more than we do now. In fact, some Austin hotspots held jalapeno-eating contests. These were largely disgusting yet entertaining displays to see who could eat the most jalapenos without throwing up. If you tossed, you got tossed from the competition. First prize was usually a stomach pump. Just kidding. The amount of time allocated to down the peppers varied from one event to the next. I attended an hour-long contest at Scholz Garten that the Geneva

Convention might have designated as torture. Still, these people seemed to be enjoying themselves.

Then there was Spamarama, a cook-off featuring dishes that included Spam. That was the only rule. Cooks had to put Spam in the dishes they were preparing. Austinites being a creative people, entries included Spamalama Ding Dongs, Spam Flautas, Spamwurst, Spamchiladas, Spamagator Gumbo, Spambrosia, Piggy Pate, Spamalini, Croissant de Fromage avec Spam, Creamy Spamapeño dip, Spamstickers, Spajitas, Spamiyaki, Spamish Fly, Spamales, El Rey de la Tierra Mojada's Spamales, chicken-fried Spam, Spam Foo Yung, Spamaghetti, and Spamtinis. The event attracted various local celebrities as judges, including City Council Members Jackie Goodman and Brigid Shea, columnist Molly Ivins and Texas Comptroller John Sharp. The idea was to see who could come up with the most revolting dish. The only year I ever entered I did something with Moon Pies.

One time when I was attending, somebody dropped a bit of one Spam concoction on the ground next to a wiener dog. The dog turned up his nose and kept walking.

Spamarama went on for years, but the venue kept changing. One year it would be on the shores of Town Lake, another year at the Soap Creek Saloon, while another year it would be at a popular bar called the Cedar Door. Spamarama moved around more than somebody enrolled in the witness protection program.

But even back in the day, Austin wasn't all fun and games. For sure, we weren't always big on women's rights. Back in the Seventies, a young guy named Joey Fuller (nicknamed "The White Boy") took over a beer joint on Austin's Sixth Street called

Benny's Tavern. One of the first moves Joey made was to allow women inside. The old cranks who had inhabited the beer joint before Joey showed up didn't want women around. A redneck friend of mine walked into Benny's one day with his girlfriend. "They told us it was a stag bar and she got all irate," my friend said. "They said, 'We won't serve you,' and she said, '#$%&*,' or something like that."

Benny's wasn't alone. Up in Round Rock, a few miles north of Austin, a bar called The Tap had a sign on the front door that said women weren't allowed. And this was just a modest pickled-eggs-on-the-bar beer joint. We're not talking Augusta National here.

As the area changed, though, an ironic thing happened to The Tap. A woman became the owner. And everybody at the bar seemed happy with the arrangement. Imagine that.

Austin doesn't look the same as in the old days, that's for sure. Now they're building high-dollar apartments in places you wouldn't think they would fit. More than 350 posh apartments are being built next door to the Broken Spoke, the last real honky-tonk in Austin proper. What are they going to call these units? One Col'beer Place?

When you think of high rents, you usually think of Central Park, or a mountain vista. But those amenities aren't necessary for Austin developers. Drive downhill on South Lamar from the Spoke and you'll see even more fancy apartments going in — across the road from the Goodwill Store. Great. A spectacular view of the stuff Austinites are throwing out.

In 1976, the town was yet to have a skyline. The tallest building in town, at twenty-two stories, was the Austin National

Bank building on Congress at Sixth Street. Now the tallest building in Austin, the Austonian, a swank condominium joint on Congress Avenue at Second Street, goes up to fifty-six stories. The city has 121 high rises these days. One of those high rises takes up the northwest corner of Cesar Chavez (formerly First Street) and Congress Avenue. In 1976, that spot was the home of the Tamale House, a low-slung shack where people walked up for Mexican food to go.

Moses Vasquez, the owner, became rich overnight in the early Eighties when the Lincoln Property Co. gave him $1.6 million so it could put up 100 Congress, the high-rise there today.

"This makes me madder than a toothless dog in a steak-eating contest," I wrote at the time. Even that long ago, I was crabbing about all the new buildings going up.

A regular kind of guy, Vasquez used to keep a bunch of junked cars in his yard in South Austin. In the new Austin, a city inspector would come by and write him a ticket.

When I moved here, the place had lots of real bars, but no sushi bars. Now you've got almost as many California rolls in town as you have Californians. These people have moved here for high tech jobs and comparatively low real estate prices. In the process they've transformed neighborhoods that used to be affordable into places where only the well-heeled can move in.

The transition has left us with a new and unflattering architectural term — the McMansion. A McMansion, a regular feature in South Austin's Bouldin Creek neighborhood, is a large, blocky, out-of-place new home that clashes with the easygoing wood bungalows built in another era. The McMansions clash with the laid-back atmosphere and the look and feel of the neighborhood. The Bouldin Creek neighborhood is still a great place to live, but a guy whose main source of income is his garage band can no longer afford to live there.

As prices have gone up, the city's goofiness quotient has gone down. Take the way Soap Creek Saloon owner George Majewski was honored by his hippie patrons back in the Seventies. George was not what you would call a looker. In fact, with his scraggly long hair, he sort of favored Mad Magazine's Alfred E. Newman. So when Kerry Awn, an Austin artist/musician/comedian, drew a cartoon of George's face on the side of a paper bag, it wasn't pretty. But it was funny.

And it was even funnier when loads of these paper bags with George's mug on the front were handed out to the crowd at the Soup Creek Saloon one evening. Each bag had eyeholes in the front. So you had row after row of Soap Creek music fans sitting in chairs wearing bags over their heads that looked like George Majewski.

The look was so spectacular that a photo of the bag-headed crowd showed up on a front page of the American-Statesman. It was a spectacular shot, although I'm not sure George thought it was all that great. When I called him in 2012 to ask him about it, he didn't want to talk.

Austin was a rockin' good-time place back in the 1970s. You never knew what you'd see when you went to a rock concert — and sometimes the audience out-performed the band.

This is a story about peaking too early.

John Dodson, 61, is an actor who has lived in Austin since 1969. For years he performed with an Austin band/theatrical troupe called the Asylum Street Spankers, under the stage name of Mysterious John. In 1974, John went to the Palmer Auditorium near the south shores of Town Lake to take in a performance of the Electric Light Orchestra, a nationally known band that was popular in those years.

John got to the auditorium early that night. The audience had yet to file in. "I was going to my seat. They hadn't even turned the lights down, and there was some frat boy, I think he was on acid or something," John recalled. "He was dressed up like the Hawaiian Punch boy. He had on a Hawaiian shirt and a ridiculously big straw hat."

Suddenly, the straw hat guy went off like a happy bottle rocket. He was having his own personal party in his own personal head. "I was taking my seat and the guy kept rocking back in his seat, hollering, 'I'M READY, I'M READY, I'M READY, MY GOD, I'M READY'," John recalls.

The guy kept it up. The "I'm readys" became louder, and attracted attention.

"As he was screaming 'I'M READY,' four cops came down one aisle and four other cops came down the other aisle, and they picked him up," John said, "carrying him over their heads like you'd carry a log."

Even while hoisted aloft by law enforcement officers, the guy kept up his raucous one-man celebration. Maybe the ceiling looked pretty. Heck, who knows?

"He continued to scream, 'I'M READY, I'M READY, OH,

GOD, I'M READY'," John said. The guy may have been ready, but he was so ready that he missed the show.

"He never heard a note, the lights were still on that night when the frat boy took acid, and it was pretty funny to watch them trot off with him on their shoulders, with him screaming 'I'M READY. I'M READY.' He was ready, all right."

In addition to all the other changes that have taken place in Austin over the years, the way we travel here has also changed. The city is blessed with (or damned by) several toll roads, something that would have been considered the work of the devil in 1976. Used to be the only road toll you paid was the change you handed out your car window to the homeless guy on the corner. Which, by the way, is one thing that hasn't changed in Austin. Panhandlers are still part of our landscape. I was talking to one of them just the other day, at Interstate 35 and Riverside Drive. He said his name was Thunderbolt, and he claimed his brother had been up for a Grammy. Some traditions just won't die. We've always had colorful street people, and we still do.

Back in the old days, you'd see flower salesmen on the corners. I recall two of these flower children who were local celebrities: Crazy Carl Hickerson-Bull, who played trombone and spun flowers on his hand on the street, ran for mayor in 1988 and lost; and Max Nofziger, who can sing, ran for City Council and won. Max served on the Council from 1987 to 1996.

In the new Austin, chances are slimmer that a former street person like Max Nofziger can move from the side of the road to City Hall.

The neighborhoods where we live have changed as well. In the 1980s, all sorts of new ones began springing up to accommodate all of the newcomers moving to Austin. In 1984, a brand new subdivision called Wells Branch was just opening up in far North Austin, right next to Interstate 35. My assignment was to pick a street in Wells Branch and talk to everybody on the street about why they were moving in. I selected Gold Fish Pond Avenue, but only because it had a funny name. I went to every house on the street. One lady on the street was new to Texas and didn't understand why the town of Manor is pronounced May-nor. She also didn't understand why the locals were calling her a Yankee, since she came from Iowa. She thought she was, instead, Midwestern. She didn't understand the Texas concept of Yankee — anybody who isn't from Texas.

These new residents had moved in for various reasons: to join the high tech wave, to move into a nicer house than the one they just moved out of in another part of town, or even because they liked the scenery provided by the Hill Country nearby.

In truth, though, the scenery at Wells Branch at the time was a bit bleak. The trees in Wells Branch, being brand new, were tiny. Some of the lawns weren't finished. And the neighbors, all of them being new neighbors, didn't really know each other.

We may have fixed that little problem when we took a group photo of the residents for the article. There were a couple dozen folks in the photo, and it wasn't until the newspaper hit the street that the publisher, Jay Smith, noticed that the little boy toward the right in the photo was grabbing his crotch.

Some things don't change.

Still, even the way we dress has changed. In the Seventies in Austin, it was common to see guys downtown walking around in cowboy hats. Now, if you see a guy in Western attire, he's probably in town from Lubbock, or he's an extra in a Richard Linklater film. Sure, Austin still makes a stab at its Western heritage, sometimes in a lame way. In a subdivision about two miles from my house, you'll see a few street names with a Western theme: Boothill, Whiskey River, Gun Fight, Ammunition, like that.

Several movies have been made in Austin, including the latest Alamo movie, in which I was an extra. I don't think my part made it into the movie, though, because no one has ever come up to me and said, "You know, I saw you in the Alamo."

On the other hand, no one has ever come up to me and said they've even seen the latest Alamo movie — period.

However, some Austin-made movies have made the big-time. Hasn't just about everyone seen Richard Linklater's classic, *Slacker*? If you've seen the movie, which was filmed at various locations around town, you know what sort of off-the-wall folks made up this city in the 1980s and 1990s. You know, the sort of folks who would try to sell Madonna's pap smear on the street. "It's a chance of a lifetime," the gal in the movie said, as she tried to unload Madonna's pap smear on some guy.

With this slacker sort of atmosphere having taken over, you hardly ever see anybody in Western duds anymore, except for Texas Governor Rick Perry, who ran for U.S. President in 2011 in his cowboy boots, and did about as well as Crazy Carl Hickerson-Bull did when he ran for mayor.

Austin was less uptight in 1976 than it is today. You could drink and drive in Texas back then. It was perfectly legal to drive down the street while drinking a Pearl. You'd get busted for driving drunk, sure, if you drank about eighteen Pearl beers, which were kind of watery. (Texas beers in the Seventies were pretty lame; Shiner, which has become quite good, was horrid back in the day.) But the cops weren't as stringent about DWI as they are now.

Right after I moved here, I got pulled over on the access road of I-35 in South Austin by an Austin cop. This was a Sunday afternoon, and I'd been home drinking and watching the Dallas Cowboys play the Washington Redskins.

The cop asked me how much I'd had to drink. I gave him the standard "a couple of beers" answer, and explained that I'd been watching the Cowboys game. "Oh yeah? What was the score?" the cop asked. I got the score right. That was my sobriety test. He told me to go ahead on my way.

As for pot, technically it was illegal in Austin. However, at Spellman's, a beer bar and music club for pickers and songwriters on West Fifth Street, you could often find somebody smokin' a fatty in the back yard. The cops must have known this was going on, but apparently they had bigger fish to fry.

There's the story about Travis County Sheriff Raymond Frank, who was offered a joint while visiting the Soap Creek Saloon one night in the 1970s. The old Soap Creek was the spot where hippies went to drink hard liquor and listen to a comedy band called the Uranium Savages, who had a song that went "I've got blisters on my ears from using pay phones." They also had a guy named Artly Snuff who performed with the band, sometimes in a chicken suit. Artly is still with us. And the Savages, though geriatric, still play occasionally.

Soap Creek, out in the country back then off Bee Caves Road, was known for a bumpy dirt parking lot that looked like the surface of the moon. It was also known for smelling like a bag of weed. So it should come as no surprise that one evening somebody in the crowd asked Sheriff Frank if he wanted a toke.

Sheriff Frank said no thanks, but he didn't bust the guy. If you tried that with Austin Police Chief Art Acevedo today, you'd be in the clink before you could get your Zig-Zags back in your pocket.

We weren't as sophisticated around these parts back in the old days. We weren't as slick. I like a story, told by Roger Bennett, former head of the Southwest Texas State University (now Texas State University) journalism department, about a Reader's Digest editor named Phil Osborne. Osborne had come to Austin for a convention. So he took some of his colleagues down to San Marcos, a small city about half an hour south of Austin, to visit the Cheatham Street Warehouse, a colorful honky-tonk and the sort of place you'd take visitors to show them Central Texas.

After dinner, Osborne asked for a receipt for the beer and food he and his friends had consumed. The college kid tending the cash register fumbled around for a while, trying to find a piece of paper. There was none to be found. So he tore a chunk of curled-up wallpaper off the wall. It took the kid a while to flatten the wallpaper out on the bar so he could write on it. Then it took him a few more minutes to find a pencil under all the junk sitting on the bar. Finally, he wet the pencil in his mouth, looked up at Osborne and asked, "Okay, how do you spell receipt?"

Change has always been in the wind in Austin. Recently we changed the name of Town Lake to Lady Bird Lake. But as early as 1984, Threadgill's restaurant owner Eddie Wilson; Gordon Fowler, then president of 2-Alarm Chili; and Marcia Ball, a legendary Austin singer and piano player, and Gordon's wife, started a movement to make that name change. So it did take a while.

I pointed out that I thought the change was a great idea, since Town Lake was a stupid name, since there was nobody around named Town that I knew about.

Even our grocery stores have changed dramatically. Thirty-five years ago, if you went to the store, you might find frozen snapper — from Korea — in the seafood section. One of the best seafood stops in town in the late Seventies was the blue truck that parked on the east side of South Lamar Boulevard, just south of the bridge over Town Lake. We called it "the shrimp truck." The guy went down to the Gulf Coast most weeks, then drove back to Austin with a load of fresh shrimp and other fresh fish.

The shrimp truck is long gone. But now we've got fancy seafood sections at both Central Market and Whole Foods (which people jokingly call Whole Paycheck, because of the prices). But somebody has to pay for that chocolate "enrobing station," a feature at the big Whole Foods at Sixth and Lamar that opened in 2005. The chocolate enrobing station is really a burbling chocolate fountain. The publicity for the store's grand opening said that you could get anything covered in chocolate if you took it to the fountain.

So naturally, being a wise guy, I stopped at a convenience store on the way to the grand opening and picked up a bag of Baken-Ets Traditional fried pork rinds.

I stuck some of the pork rinds in my sports jacket pocket because I didn't want to carry the bag inside in plain sight. I wasn't sure Whole Foods CEO John Mackey would be cool with it if I brought pork rinds into Six Flags Over Oregano. Then again, he might not have minded, because when he started the first Whole Foods on North Lamar, way back when, his employees called him "Wacky Mackey."

"Can you dip this pork rind in chocolate for me?" I asked politely, pulling one out of my pocket at the chocolate enrobing station.

"You've got to be kidding me," said Dori Beron, who was working at the enrobing station for the grand opening. "We wouldn't want that because if any crumbs got into the chocolate, it would taste like chicharrónes," she explained. They didn't want everything else they dipped in chocolate to taste like pork rinds for the rest of the summer, so they turned me down.

Even our politicians aren't as colorful as they once were. Take City Councilman Mark Spaeth, who married Amanda Blake, *Gunsmoke*'s Miss Kitty, in the 1980s. Then there was Councilman Richard Goodman, who in 1982 had a bit too much fun one evening, mistook his garden hose for a snake in his front yard, and blew it away with a high-powered rifle.

And how about State Senator Drew Nixon, who, in 1997, was arrested after he offered $35 to a chick he thought was a prostitute on South Congress Avenue. Turns out the prostitute was really an undercover Austin cop who, coincidentally, happened to be Crazy Oscar's daughter. A friend of mine named Crazy Oscar used to be my plumber.

And that's another thing. You hardly run into people in Austin anymore who have colorful names, like Crazy Oscar. Oscar got that name because he was born around the time of the Oscars ceremony. So his mother took to calling him "My little Oscar." The crazy part came from him doing things like throwing lit firecrackers out the truck window on the way to the coast for a fishing trip.

Then there was the evening back in the late '70s or early '80s that Crazy Oscar spent chatting with Willie Nelson at the Pedernales Pan, a cozy little beer joint out on Lake Travis. Willie just happened to be hanging out at the bar that evening. So Oscar struck up a conversation with him.

After several hours, Oscar realized he'd be late getting home, which would tick off his wife. Oscar needed an excuse. So he asked Willie to write him a note that would prove he'd spent the evening talking to Willie.

Willie wrote the note and gave it to Oscar, who stuck it in his pocket without looking at it, then showed it to his wife when he got home. The note was addressed to Oscar's wife and it said, "I sure enjoyed spending the evening with your husband."

But, unbeknownst to Oscar, Willie had signed it "Dolly Parton."

Oscar had some explaining to do, if you catch my drift. But he managed not to get thrown out of the house.

Sure, Austin manages to hang onto some of the old ways. For

example, we can brag about some unusual entertainment options you won't find anywhere else. Take Chicken (Bleep) Bingo, which draws hundreds of people to Ginny's Little Longhorn Saloon on Burnet Road every Sunday afternoon. Chicken (Bleep) Bingo works like this. A numbers board is placed on the pool table. You stand in line to buy a $2 ticket on what number you think the chicken is going to bleep on. The chicken is brought from its wire cage in back of the bar into the barroom, and placed on the numbers board. People stand around and root on the chicken. Then, when the chicken goes, somebody wins a little over $100.

So it ain't Vegas. But it *is* Austin.

From Martinis to Yuppies: Big Management Shake-up

In 1984 Ray was replaced by a new editor named Arnold Rosenfeld. Word from a source who worked closely with Ray said the business community went after him for the stories he published. The same source says calls for his tail were made to Cox Enterprises in Atlanta, the *American-Statesman*'s owner. "Free the Press, Fire Mariotti" bumper stickers started popping up on bumpers around town. And Ray probably made some enemies along the way for his less-than-politically correct ways.

For example, there was the evening he walked into the newsroom and noticed that all the copy editors working that night were women. "Well, George," he told the editor, "I see you've got the bitches running the place tonight." Or words along those lines. Ray wasn't what you would call polished.

A guy like Ray wouldn't fit in today's buttoned-down corporate world. If he were still editor, he'd have to send himself to human resources for counseling. He just didn't fit the image management was looking for.

We got a new publisher at the paper when Jay Smith took

the place of Jim Fain. And my guess is that the new management was much more board room-appropriate than Ray.

Ray once explained his demise to me by pointing out that he was usually coming home from carousing about the same time the new bosses were coming to work in the morning.

Austin had been a different place when Ray became the editor. To show new *American-Statesman* employees the town, he'd gather up all the newbies and take them over to Coupland, a small town northeast of Austin, for family-style barbecue. These days an Austin exec would show off new employees by taking them somewhere that had wasabi. Back then nobody in the group could have spelled wasabi.

But by the early 1980s, the city was starting to become one. A real city, that is. So the timing of Ray's demise was fitting. Austin was beginning to become a bit sophisticated, and Ray was a seat-of-the-pants editor, old school, hard drinking and hard playing. You'd be more likely to see him at, say, the Quorum Club interviewing a source than you would to see him talking to the source in his office.

Thirty or so years ago, downtown Austin began getting an actual skyline. Sadly, the old Armadillo World Headquarters rock-and-roll joint closed its doors in the early morning hours of New Year's Day 1981, about the same time downtown started to see some skyscrapers popping up.

For the star of the new skyscraper show, I'd pick the One American Center at Sixth and Congress, a beautiful building that looks sort of like a tiered wedding cake. But you could see how Austin was becoming less free-spirited just by looking at what the designers had put around the building at street level.

On the ledges, they had installed "heinie knobs."

That wasn't the official name, of course. That was the name the public adopted for them. In fact, the first time I ever heard the term, it came from Linda Anthony, a former *American-Statesman* reporter and city editor. So she may have coined the name.

Anyway, the heinie knobs were heavy metal knobs, about half the size of a baseball, put there so that street people couldn't sit down in front of the building's street-level windows.

These unfriendly knobs, it seemed to me, signaled the beginning of a new era — less hippie-dippie, more businesslike— because you certainly couldn't sit on them. If you did, you'd have to call a heinie knob removal specialist to separate you from one of the darned things, and that would be embarrassing. And who knows if health insurance would cover the procedure?

I talked to a spokesman for the building at the time and she told me that yes, the knobs were there to keep away the riff-raff.

After my column about my discussion with her was published, one of her bosses, all hot and bothered, told me that she had said no such thing and that I'd misquoted her. It's one of the few times I've ever been accused of misquoting someone.

But I'm sure that's the reason the heinie knobs were there. They would serve no other purpose than to keep people from parking their butts on those ledges. They certainly weren't attractive, so they weren't there for artistic reasons. Nor were they a tourist attraction. "I know what, ma, let's put the kids in the SUV and go sit on the heinie knobs."

But as they say, what goes around comes around. And about ten years later, an Austin street icon named Leslie, who would eventually become perhaps Austin's best known celebrity, started hanging out in front of the One American Center, dressed only in a thong and high heels and wearing a tiara on most days.

How ironic is that? It was almost as if some higher being had sent Leslie to the One American Center to punish management for its mean-spirited building design.

Austin was turning a bit more staid than it used to be. Take Wally Pryor, for example. For years Wally, the wisecracking brother of Austin comic Cactus Pryor, had been the announcer at Texas Longhorn football games. The University of Texas got rid of Wally in 2000, I suspect, because he just didn't fit the University's buttoned-down image.

During games, it had become a tradition for Wally to announce the score of the Slippery Rock football game going on that day, to lighten things up. The fans loved it and would wait each week for Wally to tell them how Slippery Rock was doing.

Wally was always pulling lighthearted stunts. He was a friend of Hondo Crouch, the self-described "imagineer" who founded the Hill Country town of Luckenbach, the horseshoe-pitchin', guitar-pickin', yarn-swappin' spot introduced to the world in a song sung by Willie Nelson and Waylon Jennings.

In the 1970s, Wally says that Crouch asked him if he could mention his name over the P.A. system at a Longhorn game. During one game Wally made this announcement over the loud speaker: "Hondo Crouch, Scholz Beer Garten called. They want you to pick up your grandmother after the game."

After that, Wally kept up the gag. During subsequent games, fans would wait to hear from which beer joint Hondo was supposed to pick up his grandmother. Granny moved around. One week she'd be at the Rusty Nail, the next week she'd be at the Split Rail.

Another time Wally had some fun with a Texas Longhorn female dance ensemble called the Longhorn Luvs, girls who perform at U.T. basketball games. He started making up names for the dancers over the P.A. system, names such as Luscious Lil, and Sexy Sal.

Naturally, Wally said, somebody complained—so management told him to knock it off. None of Wally's foolishness would starch a Burnt Orange shirt, so Wally was replaced at football games by radio icon Bob Cole, who really wasn't all that starched himself, but at least he sounded like he was. Bob has one of those traditional radio voices. He probably sounds like he's on the radio when he's talking in his sleep.

Anyway, Austin was growing, and with growth, the town was starting to turn just a tad froufrou. For that reason, it wasn't surprising that Ray Mariotti was let go in 1984. He didn't fit the morning meeting mold, and he didn't want to. I'm not sure he was even capable of it.

Ray liked to drink and carouse. It was common for him to hit the local watering holes at happy hour with some big shot, and there he'd get some big scoop.

Then, around 8:00 p.m. he'd come into the newsroom and drop the news on the city editor, and tell him to get a move on and get the story in the paper. The bad news was that the city editor had no choice, because Ray was the boss. The good news was that Ray hung out with the high and mighty so, as often as not, the stories he brought in from happy hour were good news stories. The man had a nose for news. He's the guy who invented the term "the bat cave" to describe City Hall, the image being that the Councilmen didn't know what they were doing, and that they were all down there at city hall hanging around upside down.

Ray was a gambler, and darned good at it, too. He was an expert at betting on the greyhounds, or, if you will, playing the dogs. Austin didn't have any greyhound tracks, but back when Ray had been the editor at the *Palm Beach Post* in the 1970s, he and some of his editors from the paper would hit the local dog track nearly every work night. And after the evening was over, those who put money in Ray's pool would get a cut of the action. It was a team effort. Ray would send his colleagues to the various betting windows with instructions on what bets to place. One time they even won big, a five-figure prize, about $12,000, if I remember right.

Ray was also a pretty darned good pool player. He had a hustler's mentality. He had a way of making you think he was going to beat you, even though, if you hadn't thought that, you might have had a chance of beating him. He'd stick this evil little notion in your head that you were doomed. And pretty soon, you were watching him sink the eight ball.

After Ray left the paper in 1984, he pursued greyhound gambling as a career, along with traveling around the country collecting antiques and selling them. The man was not your average suit.

After he left, I got along fine with Ray's replacement, Arnold Rosenfeld. Ray was kind of scary, while Arnold seemed all soft and fuzzy—heavy emphasis on fuzzy. He used to draw these little stick figures that he'd run with his columns. To tell you the truth, I don't remember what any of his columns were about. Maybe they were about stick figures.

While Ray was the kind of guy who would tell you what he thought, even when it wasn't pleasant, Arnold was the opposite. I could take just about any one of my columns into his office and show it to him and he'd say, "Great story. Really great story."

I think I could have taken a roll of toilet paper in there and handed it to him and he would have said, "Great story. Really great story." I enjoyed the pats on the back, but after a while a guy starts to wonder whether they mean anything.

Arnold wasn't always your best friend, and when you needed a little support from above, he would sometimes come up short on guts. Back in the 1980s, for example, my buddy, Pulitzer Prize-winning cartoonist Ben Sargent, saw a news story that he thought would be worthy of a column. High school kids in the Eanes Independent School District — that being swank West Lake Hills — were holding a food drive for the homeless. Nothing wrong with that, of course. But along with the food drive, the Westlake High kids were having a twenty-four-hour fast. The event was called "Fast In '88."

This daylong fast was the part Sargent figured was worthy of my gooning in my column, and I agreed. Not that I'm trying to shift the blame to Ben here. I didn't have to write this column. It was my choice, and I got after it. Shoot, I wrote, not eating for hours isn't a fast. Sometimes I forget to eat for close to that long. So my column made fun of the fasting part of the project.

"West Lake teens fill weekend by not stuffing their mouths," the headline read. "It must have been awful," I wrote of the daylong deprivation. "Thankfully, nobody passed out behind the wheel of his Beemer." Poor little rich kids miss lunch and think they're doing something special. That was the tone of the column.

You would have thought I'd burned the American flag with my fly unzipped on national television. Westlake High School parents called the newspaper wanting my head. I mean, they wanted my butt on a stick over an open flame. What they really wanted was my job. And I think they darned near got it.

One lesson I learned from this: you don't make fun of people's children—especially if the parents are well-heeled.

Anyway, when the West Lake Hills folks complained, Arnold didn't exactly stick up for me. In fact, he dragged me over to Westlake High to apologize in front of a classroom full of high school kids. During the session, I remember Arnold telling the students that it really didn't matter what John Kelso said. What mattered was that they had performed a service for the community.

@#$%^ *you*, I thought. This was a humor column, folks. Couldn't anybody take a joke? That aspect of the situation was being ignored completely. Rosenfeld could have defused the situation by simply explaining that I write a humor column, but humor wasn't even mentioned.

"No Fritos. No tater chips. No ketchup, and hold those fries," I wrote. "No cruising the aisles at Simon David. It must have been worse than thumbscrews." Well, now it was the parents who wanted to apply the thumbscrews — to my happy hands.

I wasn't the only writer at the *Statesman* whom Arnold hung out to dry in front of the readers. Sometime in the 1980s, our wonderful food writer, Kitty Crider, now a grandmother and retired, had done a story on a small bodega in East Austin. In the story, she mentioned that she had been yelled at by some guys as she was leaving the store. I guess it was the old macho "Hey, Baby" thing. No big deal, but Kitty felt her readers should know that sort of thing could happen at that store. I guess she didn't want some bowhead from West Lake Hills getting embarrassed.

Now this was back before the East Side had become gentrified, so the store was in a relatively poor Hispanic neighborhood. In those days, Interstate 35, which runs north and south through Austin, served as the divider strip between well-off white Austin on the west side of the highway, and the not-so-well-off minorities on the other side of the highway.

So some people from East Austin complained to the paper about the line in the story that mentioned that Kitty was hollered at. Some thought the observation was racist (even though Kitty doesn't have a racist bone in her body). Certainly she had no racist thoughts in mind when she wrote the column, which was fairly straightforward. This was not George Carlin material, in other words.

Rosenfeld handled this situation the same way he'd handled my run-in with the West Lake Hills parents. He organized a meeting. He and Kitty would go over to the bodega and talk with the neighbors.

"Arnold was very big on interacting with the community," was the gracious way that Kitty put it when I talked to her in 2012. "He was trying to build relations with the community."

Anyway, when they got to the store, a contingent of people led by East Side activist Paul Hernandez was there to meet them and excoriate Kitty. "It was not necessarily a happy time," she told me.

I felt sorry for Kitty. She's one of the sweetest people you'd ever want to meet. And it's not like she called the neighborhood a bunch of Commies or something. Somebody yelled at her and she pointed it out for her readers. Big deal. Why embarrass your own troops over something like that?

"Well, it was a learning experience," said Kitty, who is much more forgiving than I am.

I remember Rosenfeld commenting on the surprise greeting from Hernandez and his friends when he and Kitty arrived at the store.

Arnold told me that he didn't mind "getting mau-maued." Of course he didn't. He wasn't the one being "mau-maued." It was his food editor.

One important thing to remember if you're a newspaper writer is this: if you don't have the backing of your editors, you're in trouble. Lucky for me, most of the years I was at the *Statesman*, I had such backing.

The Meanest Man in the Newsroom

You often hear stories about how some newspaper people are hard as nails. For the most part, that's bunk. Deep down inside, most news people are soft and squishy. They do things like collect used books for the school children, and hold Christmas present drives for the poor. Every year at the *Statesman*, the newsroom gathers presents for school kids. And writers and copy editors run around like crazy people, lugging presents and wrapping paper.

Then there was the copy editor name of L.D. Long. This guy made Dirty Harry look clean. L.D. was mean as a snake, and he wanted everybody to know it. He terrorized the copy editors who worked under him. He had the reputation of being the meanest man in the Western Hemisphere.

A friend of mine who was an assistant city editor didn't like L.D. worth a flip. He joked that the L.D. stood for "Loping Dipstick."

Another friend recalls that the picture on L.D.'s computer monitor was of him toting a Tommy gun and grinning. The inscription said something like, "You can get more with a smile and a machine gun than you can with just a smile."

Let's just say this guy wasn't shooting for a job with the Welcome Wagon. As a copy editor is supposed to be, L.D. was a stickler for detail, but he took it beyond the limit. No copy-editing error went by without reprimand. I joked behind L.D.'s back that he was working on a book called, "Slap-Happy: One Word or Two?" That was the kind of critical decision L.D. would twist himself in a knot over.

Actually, L.D. wasn't twisting himself near as much as he was twisting his workers. Legend has it that L.D. freaked out a copy editor who worked for him so badly that she got in a car wreck on her way home from work, broke her arm, and never worked in journalism again.

Personally, I never had any trouble with L.D. As far as I could figure, he couldn't touch me without a bazooka. When you've been in the Army for a couple of years and dealt with drill sergeants, water cooler jockeys don't scare you all that much. So what L.D. did didn't faze me in the least. And since he knew that's how I felt, he didn't mess with me.

That is, except for one time. Sort of.

A fellow columnist at the newspaper had just gotten busted for DWI. Great guy. Anybody can get busted for DWI. All you have to do is open your mouth, swallow, and turn the keys. You don't have to be a serial killer to get popped for DWI, and this columnist who got popped was a real sweetheart. Nicest guy in a three-county area.

Even so, the editors felt compelled to run a news story about it. That's because when Ray Mariotti was editor, he started up a policy of running the names of everybody in town who got busted for DWI. And when he said everybody, that included this particular writer.

So one morning I'm sitting at my desk in the newsroom, minding my own business, reading the morning paper. I see the story in the B section of the paper about my friend who just got popped for DWI. So I'm feeling sorry for him. The paper is open on my desk to that particular page. All of a sudden I look up and there's L.D., leaning on the back of my desk, looking at the story, then glaring at me. And he's got his usual grumpy look on his usual grumpy face.

"You're next," L.D. said, coldly. Then he turned on his heels and walked off. His message was that I was likely to get busted for being drunk behind the wheel, just like my friend. Charming. Maybe L.D. thought he was funny. Actually, I did think it was funny. By the way, I've never been caught for DWI. Although I have mooned people twice — once at a party, and once on the way into a friend's house while people were watching NFL football on TV.

One school of thought in journalism holds that the best way to get results is scare the heck out of the troops. I think that works for some people. But I think L.D. thought it worked for everybody. And I've seen others in the news business who got results the same way.

At the Columbia Missourian at the University of Missouri's journalism school, we had a legendary copy chief who seemed to have taken the same personal warmth class as L.D. Legend has it that one day a student reporter at the Missourian came in late with a story that he thought should get in the paper. Trouble is, it was just past deadline time. The copy chief, apparently, was not impressed with the kid's plea to get the story in the paper.

"PRESSES WILL ROLL," he hollered dramatically, loud enough for everybody in the newsroom to hear. Somebody needed to give that guy an Oscar. And somebody needed to give L.D. a Valium.

Days of Wine and Toot

The 1980s were the years in Austin that I refer to as the Toot Years. This is because it seemed like everybody in town was doing toot. Cocaine was the most annoying drug on the planet. Not only was it really expensive — a night's worth would run you $60-$120, depending on what kind of night you were planning — one where you'd embarrass yourself before a small gathering, or one where you'd make a complete ass of yourself in front of a variety of groups, some of them made up of people you'd never seen before.

Another bad thing about coke was that it wore off in about twenty minutes. So just a few minutes after you were feeling really good, you were feeling really bad. Or as a wise friend of mine put it, "A line of cocaine will make you feel like a new man. Trouble is the new man wants one, too."

In the 1970s, Austin's drug of choice was pot, which encouraged the pleasant attitude of sharing and brotherly love. You could light a joint, and pass it around. In fact, you were *supposed* to pass it around. Hence the expression, "Don't Bogart that joint, my friend." This practice also enhanced the easygoing relationship between hippies and cowboys that occurred during Austin's 1970s music scene.

Coke, on the other hand, led to selfishness and greed. The new man not only wanted one, too, but also the new man didn't want to give any of his to anybody else—unless she was cute and blonde.

But I'm telling you, the stuff was everywhere. One day I walked into Smitty's, a lobster restaurant on the lower end of Guadalupe Street, a few blocks before you crossed Town Lake into South Austin. A friend of mine who cooked there (and I'm talking about food now) came out from the back with a little round dish, one of those dishes you'd use for dipping sauce. Yep, it was filled up with cocaine. Filled up and over the top, and rounded off. Honest. There must have been a couple grand's worth of toot in that dish. And this wasn't midnight. This was around noon on a workday. This gave a new meaning to the expression "Let's do lunch." Actually, it rewrote the expression to "Let's blow off lunch and do some blow."

Eventually, Smitty's got busted and some people involved with the restaurant got sent up the river. And I'm not talking about the Colorado River. I had two friends who did time because they were caught up in the cocaine world. I was one of the lucky many that didn't get caught. I would advise anybody who gets the chance to try the stuff to bang your head against a concrete wall instead. Or smoke a joint.

On the Bar Trail

For about five years in the late 1970s and early 1980s, I went barhopping for a living. Okay, so it wasn't as cushy a deal as it sounds. But in my early days as a columnist for the *American-Statesman*, along with my regular three columns a week, I did a weekly feature called "The Bar Trail."

Over the period that I was writing that feature, I figure I visited literally hundreds of watering holes in and around Austin. I went to bars you may have heard of: the Dry Creek Cafe, the Scoot Inn, Jake's, the Broken Spoke, the Stallion, Hut's, the Austin Outhouse, Maggie Mae's, the Chaparral, the Hole in the Wall, Knebel's Tavern, the Horseshoe Lounge, Snuffy's Place, Mike's Pub, Deep Eddy, Xalapeno Charlie's, the Possum Creek Inn, Katz's Deli & Bar, Ego's, the Dam Saloon, Posse East, the Cheatham Street Warehouse, the Hippopotamus Lounge, and the Poodle Dog Lounge.

And I went to bars I can't even remember existed: Old Jocko's Lounge, the Okey Dokey, the Wild Hare Pub, and Piggy's Bar and Grill.

I went to so many bars that I still use former bar locations to give directions. "Yeah, Matt's El Rancho? It's where the old Hanging Tree used to be."

Finally, I quit doing the Bar Trail because I ran out of interesting bars to write about. I had been to them all. It got so bad that I even wrote about the bar at the airport. Nobody cares about the bar at the airport.

Most of the places I frequented were unpretentious. One, Cox's One-Hole in Cedar Park, was so named because when it opened, it had an outhouse out back. The place was in a trailer that I described as looking "something like a junk pile on LSD."

And I went to another bar, The Rocking V Inn on Ranch Road 620 that had an eight and a half foot live alligator out back in a concrete pen. At one point the pen came with a sign that read, "See the Alligator. Free."

"My daddy gave me that alligator for my seventh birthday," explained Randall Ward, whose daddy, Cotton Ward, originally owned the property. "I throw him a fish or a rabbit about three times a week. You can tell when he's hungry 'cause he eats real fast."

The first bar I went to for this project was the Scoot Inn, on East Fourth Street, which is still with us, but is called Red's Scoot Inn these days. And the decor has changed. In March 1980, the Iranian hostage crisis was still a hot topic, so the bar had a poster on the wall with the following caption: "Let's Play Cowboys and Iranians." Above those words was a photo of several good ol' boys in big hats holding shotguns, fixing to hang a guy with a towel on his head from a tall tree.

That poster wouldn't fly today, but that's because times have changed. When I visited the place half a lifetime ago, Maurine Spiars, one of the owners, told me about how the bar had raised around $1,000 for a customer who was wanted for murder.

"But he was a good customer and he had to pay his lawyer," she explained. "I never did ask him if he was guilty, but I don't think so." To help the guy out, the bar sold donated boiled eggs, chili meat, cases of beer, homemade afghans and German chocolate cake. "We even had the folks guess my daughter's weight for two bits a shot," Maurine said. "You'd be surprised what a group of people who don't have much money can do, if they just chip in."

Then there's the Poodle Dog Lounge, still jumping out on Burnet Road. The Poodle Dog used to have one amusing problem. When it opened, poodle owners would call up and try to make grooming appointments.

You're probably thinking I got loaded now and again during the course of this bar trail assignment, but the truth is, that only happened once. Oh, I'd have a beer or two over the course of a couple hours. But I played it pretty straight, the way you would any reporting assignment. I can only recall becoming snot-slinging on one occasion. It happened at the old Aus-Tex Lounge. I got so drunk that I couldn't interview and chew gum at the same time. In fact, I got so loaded that I had to go back a second time and start all over again.

Looking back on it, I think the reason that happened is that a friend had given me a ride to the bar that evening. If I'd had to drive, I would have minded my manners.

So the Bar Trail worked like this. I'd walk in, grab a barstool and keep an eye out for interesting characters and happenings. I found out quickly that the best way to find out what was what was to sit right in the middle of the action, at the bar or at a table. Only rarely did I run into a troublemaker. Once while I was at a biker bar called Beverly's in South Austin, a menacing guy who, I suspected, might have a knife or gun in his boot, asked me repeatedly, "How do I know you are who you say you are?" He scared the heck out of me. He had ex-con written all over him. Maybe not even _ex_, come to think of it. I kept a close eye on this bozo.

After the article appeared in the paper, a reader wrote in and described Beverly's as "that skull orchard."

But most of the time, the work was just funny stuff. For instance, there was the good old boy drinking beer mid-afternoon on Valentine's Day at the Clachan Inn, a bar out by the old Bergstrom Air Force Base east of town.

Suddenly, this guy's wife showed up in a rage. She threw two white garbage bags and a blue suitcase full of his clothes, and his cowboy hat, in back of his truck. Then she charged inside, tossed his glasses case and glasses on the bar, and hollered about how much she hated his guts.

As she was leaving, some guy with his train engineer's hat on backwards while playing electronic poker at the bar looked up and said, "Goodbye, darlin'." The woman was racing out the door so fast that I'm not sure she even heard the darlin' part. I mean, she was chapped and she was gone.

It was like a scene out of a Willie Nelson movie.

Did I mention they held cockroach races out at the Clachan Inn? No? Well, they did. It was win, place, or squash. No, seriously, the cockroach races were impromptu. First, the bar patrons would wait for a roach to show up. Then they'd put a plastic ashtray over the roach. And it went from there.

I went to some groundbreaking bars, too. In 1984 I went to a new bar on North Lamar called Barwash. It was called that because it was a combination bar and laundromat. You could sit there and have a few drinks while you were doing your clothes. In other words, it had two kinds of suds: the kind you drink and the kind you stick in a washing machine. This, at the time, was a unique concept. "If you get so drunk you can't fold your own clothes, we'll do it for 30 cents a pound," said David Walsh, one of four brothers who, along with their dad, came up with the idea.

One of the more popular parts of the Bar Trails article was a regularly occurring blurb in which I described each bar's "Level of Peace." Under "Level of Peace," I would tell how likely it was that a fistfight would break out in that particular establishment. Under "Level of Peace" for Barwash, I said, "So far, nobody has climbed into the dryers to ride 'round and 'round…"

During the course of hitting all those bars, I saw just one fight. It occurred in January 1985 in the Side Saddle Club, a red-necky little establishment on East Ben White Boulevard.

The funny thing about it was that just before it happened, the manager, Woody Wilson, had told me how the place rarely had any trouble. I had just walked down to the other end of the bar from Woody to read some funny signs on the wall. There was this longhaired kid sitting there.

"Did you notice how we're surrounded by fat people?" he asked the young guy who was with him. The two of them were in their twenties and looked like construction workers. I tried to remain invisible while this kid kept crabbing about being "surrounded by fat people."

Well, sitting on the left side of the mouthy kid was a bearded guy who wasn't fat, but he *was* big and burly. He finally told the kid to shut up. The kid did not. He kept harping on fat people.

The big guy told him to be quiet one more time and asked the kid if he understood the order. "No sir, I don't," the kid said, standing up and turning toward the big guy.

At that point I got up and ran behind the bar so I could be next to the female bartender. I figured that was the safest spot in the joint. And as I explained in my subsequent article about the incident, the Kelso family crest shows a guy running.

So this kid with the mouth took one step off his barstool before the big guy grabbed his long hair. Then he rammed the kid's head, face first, into the coffee maker. The coffee maker won. The young guy was suddenly dazed and confused, and he told his partner that they ought to be going. So they left. It was more of a beating than a fistfight, actually.

I also saw a couple of funny things go down at the Aus-Tex, a popular live music dive on South Congress. One afternoon, I was sitting around minding my own business when a hippie van pulled up to the side of the building. The place had a side wall that doubled as a sliding door, which provided a small loading dock of sorts.

The door slid open, and a couple of guys popped out of the van. One of them chucked a large, dark green garbage bag into the building and onto the barroom floor. Three or four guys rushed up to the bag, and one of the guys from the van started handing out small packets of something. I figure they were ounces of pot.

Then suddenly everybody disappeared. Zip, and everybody involved in the exchange was gone. The whole operation lasted probably two minutes, if that. I never did figure out for sure what was going down, but I don't think they were handing out Gummy Bears.

Another evening when I went to the Aus-Tex, I left a brown paper grocery bag in the back seat of my VW bug. The bag had light bulbs and some toilet paper in it. When I came back out, the bag was gone. I philosophized that it was probably for the best, since it meant some hippie didn't have to poop in the dark.

Most of the places I visited were less than fancy. "Don't wear your ascot into the Hi-Ho Inn," began my article about the old Hi-Ho on far North Lamar. Then I went on to tell the story about a patron named Curly, who took off his shirt at the bar in hopes that the young lady standing beside him would take off her shirt and trade. But as it turned out, this was a case of unrequited laundry.

Some of these bars held special events. Dee's C & W, a small beer joint across from Bergstrom Air Force Base (now the Austin-Bergstrom International Airport), had a Saturday morning gathering known as the Lone Ranger Club. What it was, a group of about a dozen guys showed up every week to watch the Lone Ranger at 10:00 a.m. on the bar TV set. For the occasion, everyone wore black Lone Ranger masks except for Bill Brown, the one black guy in the group. Bill wore a white Lone Ranger mask. He did this because his black mask just didn't show up that well. "He had him a real shiny black one, but the lighting in here ain't too good, so we had to change it," said a club member named Pappa Ray.

Then there was the Rodeo Inn, in Bastrop, a beef jerky, Tums and Tylenol place located up on the hill outside of town. That's how people described it. In conversation, people weren't drinking at the Rodeo Inn. They were drinking "up on the hill." The Rodeo had a three-legged house dog named, you guessed it, Tripod. A photo accompanying the June 12, 1982, *Statesman* article about the Rodeo Inn shows several regulars on barstools, with Tripod getting his ears scratched by some gal. "Tripod likes to go for rides, and delights in jumping into any pickup that has a door open at the time," I wrote about Tripod. Tripod was so well loved that when he passed away, the Rodeo Inn held a wake for him. They packed the place for Tripod.

The things people would say at bars in the old days sound like something a writer wishes he could make up. At the Hanging Tree, a beer joint on South Lamar, a customer described his divorce this way: "She got the gold mine and I got the barbed wire cluster." And, of course, he pronounced it "bob war." A guy named Arthur Schuelke owned the Hanging Tree; for live entertainment, Arthur would play a bass that he made out of a washtub and a push broom.

You may not recall the Hanging Tree, but you'll recognize the location. To this day you'll see a big oak tree out in front of Matt's El Rancho, the esteemed Mexican food restaurant on South Lamar. That tree was the hanging tree the bar is named after. Best I know, nobody was ever actually hanged there — but plenty of folks hung out there.

Some of the bars I wrote about were notable because of their flamboyant proprietors. In 1982, Bill English, owner of English's Restaurant, at 3010 Guadalupe Street, said he used to shoot bottles of champagne off customers' heads, if they requested that service. "It became sort of a cult thing," English said. "It's just astounding how many people wanted to go through that experience." You might ask why English was shooting bottles of champagne and not bottles of Bud off people's heads. Well, English's was an upscale restaurant, with a fancy menu that included roast duckling, Oysters Florentine and Chicken Alfredo.

Then there was the Raw Deal on Sabine Street near the Austin police station, and its newer cousin, Another Raw Deal, over on West Sixth. Both were owned by Fletcher Boone, a cranky artist, and Jim "Lopez" Smitham, who was just plain cranky. These two spent the day sharing pointed bon mots. One time some high-toned woman was looking at the menu board at the Sabine Street joint, trying to decide what to order. Finally, after holding up the line for way too long, she asked Lopez, who was running the counter, "What would you recommend?"

"How about another restaurant?" Lopez said. Lopez was a funny guy, but he would never have done well at the Chamber of Commerce.

One morning right after it had opened for the day, I walked into Another Raw Deal on West Sixth and sat down at the bar next to Lopez.

"F@#$ you, Kelso," he spat.

I looked at Fletcher and asked, "What's his problem?"

"Aw, he's just warmin' up," Fletcher said.

Bubba's Press Agent

A good chunk of my efforts as an Austin writer over the years has gone into pumping up South Austin, a.k.a. Bubbaland. My appreciation of that magic land south of the Colorado River began in 1978, when I moved to the little house in a modest neighborhood near Crockett High School. I lived there for thirty years.

Prior to that, I had been living in an apartment complex in Northeast Austin, and it didn't take me long to notice a big difference in the culture on the other side of Town Lake. I liked it, so I wrote about it. In fact, I wrote about South Austin so much that I gave it a name that stuck — Bubbaland.

You can tell just about anybody in Austin you live in Bubbaland these days, and they'll know what you're talking about. And you can thank — or blame — me for that.

Here's how it started, with my first column on the subject: "When one is connected with North Austin society," I wrote, "one must learn so many different names. North Austin men are called Dick, George, Michael, Fred and Robert, and their dogs are Spot, Rover, Freckles, Sparky, and Pal."

By contrast, I pointed out, in South Austin life was much simpler since all the men and their dogs were called, you got it, Bubba. "Don't take my word for it. Check it out for yourself," I wrote. "Simply stroll into any South Austin neighborhood and scream, 'HEY BUBBA, HOW'S SHE GOIN?' and watch what happens.

"About twelve guys in big hats will holler 'HIDY' back at you, and all the dogs in the area that are not chained up will begin following you down the road."

I have no idea how many readers tried out that experiment to see if it worked. And you may have gotten the same results if you'd hollered Skeeter, Tiny or Hoss.

I pointed out various differences between living in South Austin and living in North Austin. I observed that North Austinites had AAA memberships, while South Austinites didn't need to join AAA, since we all have jumper cables.

In North Austin, I noticed, the waiters ask, "Would you like some wine with your meal?" In South Austin, they ask, "Braid or crackers?"

I noted that North Austin kids spent their time taking piano lessons, while South Austin kids listened to the jukebox. In one column, I explained the concept of South Austin aerobics. Instead of jogging, South Austin aerobics is when you drive to the plant store and buy a fifty-pound bag of sand for the bottom of your barrel-on-wheels barbecuer, so it won't rust out, and you carry the bag to your truck yourself. When you cart all the junk out of your garage for a garage sale in your driveway, that's South

Austin aerobics. When you set up a keg in the back yard, that's South Austin power lifting.

I wrote about South Austin neighborhoods and characters. There was Michael Priest, the Armadillo World Headquarters music club poster artist, who lived on Gibson Street in a rent house people called the Lost Boys Ranch because so many roommates came and went over the years. Another name for the place was even better: Home for Unwed Fathers.

I also had a Bubba advice column. "Dear Bubba," a question began. "'I'm an outdoorsy type who just moved here from up north. What can I catch in the Colorado River between Austin and Bastrop?"

"Son," Bubba answered. "I'm here to tell you that it depends on whether or not you fall out of the boat. If you fall out of the boat there's a lot of things you can catch, but Bubba ain't no doctor so he isn't quite sure what all of them are. Ask your family sawbones."

And when someone asked Bubba why people were starting to use the word "party" as a verb, when historically it had been a noun, Bubba explained it was because folks were unfamiliar with the South Austin expression "Let's blow the doors off."

I praised the South Austin entrepreneurial spirit. Erasmo (Eddie) Rodriguez, and his wife Dolores, whom everyone called Dodie, ran the most eclectic business I've ever seen — Eddie's Optical, Dodie's Beer-to-Go, and Eddie's Used Furniture, at 1801 South First Street. Eddie, an optician, took care of the eyeball part of the operation, as well as the lamps and tables, while Dodie sold beer out the window. So you could improve your eyesight, then fog it over with a few cold ones out of the same building, and also go home with a used couch.

I chided South Austin establishments when they behaved in a snooty North Austin way. In 1985, when a then brand new pool hall called the Warehouse, on Ben White Boulevard, put in a dress code banning shorts and T-shirt, of all things, I wrote, "I'll bet management at Academy Surplus never thought they'd be next-door neighbors to a place with a dress code." And I quoted somebody who said, "Call in an air strike. That's why God invented tactical nuclear weapons."

I even did a column on an imaginary South Austin wedding ceremony. "The bride and the groom were pretty hung over during the ceremony, especially the groom," I pointed out. "The night before, some of his friends held a party for him, after securing a selection of stag movies from the owner of the Dew Drop Inn. Among them were the films *Lewd Grant* and *Thirty-three's Company*, which are takeoffs on popular television shows, sort of."

That entire column was a spoof, of course. But later on, I covered and wrote about a real South Austin wedding—held in front of a pawnshop on Ben White Boulevard.

I kept up the drumbeat well into the '80s. In 1984, when my editors suggested that I go back to high school for a week or two and report back, I chose Travis High, because it's south of the river. I also chose it because Crockett High, the other South Austin high school I tried to get into, turned me down. I guess they were afraid of what I might report.

Travis was glad to have me, though, and I was glad to have Travis. However, I did have one problem. Like an idiot, I was a heavy smoker back in those days. And I had to keep sneaking outside to have a cigarette. I probably spent more time smoking than I did in physics.

Speaking of physics, I didn't understand physics any better in 1984 than I had back in 1961, when I was taking physics at Laconia High School in New Hampshire. I got a C back then, but only because Mr. Davis was being generous.

While physics at Travis baffled me, I did pretty well in English. And I met a lot of cool high school kids. Two of them were gals named Pinky and Punky. Well, their real names were Betsy Garrett, a.k.a. Pinky, and Tracey Paxson, a.k.a. Punky. Pinky was called Pinky because she wore something pink to school every day — pink heels, pink purse, and pink dress. Pinky told me she wore pink all the time because the guys told her she was one of the guys, and she wanted to add something feminine. "If it ain't pink, I don't want it," she told me. Punky was Punky because she always wore punk outfits and had one side of her head shaved.

I've often wondered what happened to Pinky and Punky. They may have grown up to start a successful business called Pinky Punky LLC, who knows?

In 1988, I explained South Austin chic in one of my columns. Dom Perignon was out; Dom DeLuise was in. Ordering the Peking duck was out; cheering for the Taylor High Ducks was in. "He's away from his desk" was out, "He ain't here" was in.

I'll admit I laid it on pretty thick. I managed to tick off some South Austinites who thought they were being culturally downsized, while also stirring up some North Austinites who didn't like being portrayed as snooty. The portrait I painted was an exaggeration, of course, but all of it was based on truth, which is the true trick to getting laughs. The closer to the truth the observation, the funnier it is. That's just the way it works.

So I rode this South Austin horse for at least ten years, maybe fifteen. It became my trademark back in the 1980s, and readers were well aware of it. People assumed I was a good ol' boy, and that I must have a rusty pick-up sitting in the driveway. I did not. I was an advocate of the lifestyle, and I still am, but let's put it this way. I'm a fan, but I'm not a full-blooded practitioner.

Even so, readers would call in to give me a story idea and say, almost apologetically, "I'm not from South Austin but…" It was as if they thought I wouldn't give credence to their story if they weren't from South Austin. I tried to assure them that wasn't the case.

But the guys turning rotors for a living, or banging out dents at the body shop, or putting in a new roof in 100-degree weather, seemed to enjoy my schtick because maybe for the first time ever, somebody was recognizing South Austin as a distinct cultural entity, with its own special lifestyle.

Turns out I had glorified the working man. I wrote about working guys a lot. I remember writing a column about a backhoe operator who won a local backhoe competition. Another time, I did a column on a 6-foot 250-pound bearded electrician named Charlie Hinchman, who could tear the top off a full beer can with his teeth. Not the pop-top, but the whole top of the can. I described Charlie as one of those guys who looks like the bears you see hauling salmon out of the river on television.

One day Charlie gave me a demonstration. He ripped the top off a Bud can with his choppers in four seconds, then chug-a-lugged the beer in another four seconds, after which he commented, "Burp."

I asked Charlie how many times he'd ripped the tops off beer cans and he said "2,422 times — less than a million and more than a thousand."

Charlie had learned how to do this stunt while he and a friend nicknamed Spaghetti, who had just gotten out of the joint, were trying to make progress with two chicks they'd picked up. Charlie was getting edgy. He explained, "You know how you sit there sometimes and bite your thumb? Well, I bit my beer can."

Incidentally, Charlie lived north of the river, but what the heck? His was a South Austin sort of trick.

Another time I did a big story on Joe Bednarski, who grew up in South Austin and wrestled for years as "Ivan Putski, the Polish Strongman." He was also known as "The Polish Hammer" and "Polish Power." In other words, he was Polish, and proud of it.

We had a big color picture of Joe in the newspaper, his biceps bulging like balloons as he held two enormous potted plants as if they were daisies, one in each hand. "I think you gotta have meat," Joe said, explaining his strength. "Yes sir, I believe in it. I'm a meat eater. I eat a lot of meat. You know, back in those caveman days, all they ate was meat."

By the middle of the 1990s, I was backing away from the South Austin riff for a simple reason: South Austin wasn't Bubbaland anymore. When I had moved here in the 1970s, it was a heavily blue collar and garage-band, rent-house area. Rents were cheap, and a college kid who wanted to start up his own band could afford to move into a place with his friends, and they could practice their music in the garage.

A couple of decades later, the garage was being renovated into a high-dollar rental space, and property values in the Bouldin Creek neighborhood — that's the 78704 zip code — were shooting through the roof.

I should have seen this coming. Come to think of it, I did. In 1988, a study conducted at Texas A&M University showed that the greeting "Howdy" was on the way out in the state of Texas. In fact, forty-four percent of the 1,005 Texas adults surveyed said they favored "hi" over "howdy." "Hello" finished second, at thirty-six percent as "howdy" dragged across the finish line in last place, at a meager six percent. If "howdy" had been kicked out, could "fixin' to" be far behind? It was not looking good for the good ol' boy lexicon.

Sure, the independent spirit of South Austin still existed. If you wanted to see yard art, such as Vince Hannemann's Cathedral of Junk, a thirty-three-foot tower made out of tossed objects, South Austin was the place to go. At one point Hannemann estimated his artistic creation included sixty tons of junk. In 2010, the city tried to get rid of it, saying it was a health hazard. Hannemann won the day, though, and the Cathedral still stands, although the City of Austin made Hannemann decrease the size of the thing, and get rid of some of the junk.

By then the area was changing from a blue-collar area into what I called a no-collar area. Instead of jeans and boots, it was jeans and flip-flops. Instead of CBs, it was cell phones. And when people barbecued in the back yard, they were more likely to smoke a portobello mushroom than a side of beef.

I had carried the South Austin flag for so long that when fancy curio shops and antique stores started popping up on South Congress Avenue, I complained about the upgrade. South Congress was a low-rent district with some colorful clubs, such as the Aus-Tex Lounge and the Continental Club (which is still there). It had Central Feed & Seed, a farm supply store, with resident goobers hanging out all the time. And it had prostitutes roaming the street.

When the change came, though, they were running off the hookers to make room for the fancy new shops. And in the middle of this upgrade, they came up with a trendy new name for South Congress — SoCo. I wrote that, since they were running off the hookers to make this upgrade, instead of SoCo they should call it NoMoHo. For some reason, NoMoHo never stuck and I had so looked forward to seeing the bumper stickers.

Back in the day I used my dog, Bubba, to pick the NFL games. Bubba was a pound hound. He wasn't one of those North of the River "purchased" dogs. Bubba was a mutt I got at the pound, and he got started picking the NFL games because of a weekly football pool in which some of the employees at the newspaper took part. It was just for fun. Only the weekly winner made any money, but for a buck or so you could make your game picks. Whoever got the most games right won about a hundred dollars.

One week a gal named Frances, who worked in the newsroom's photo department, won the pool. I figured this lady didn't really know anything about football. She was a poetry type, a hippie chick. A flower child. You could tell just by talking to her that she didn't know a field goal from a geranium, or care about the difference. But she had won the weekly pool, so I went and asked her how she made her NFL picks.

When I found out she'd pick her winners based on cities where she'd had good drug experiences back in the Sixties, I thought to myself, *My dog Bubba can do better than that.*

So my late wife Sally and I designed a system that would allow Bubba to pick the NFL winners each week. We wrote down the names of each NFL team on a sheet of paper. Let's say, San Francisco was playing the New York Giants that week. So I'd put the sheet that said 49ers on the floor next to the sheet that said Giants. Then I'd break a dog biscuit in half and place a half on each sheet. Why half a biscuit? There were twenty-six NFL teams at the time, or thirteen games a week. That's a lot of picks and a lot of dog biscuits. And I didn't want Bubba to get fat.

Meanwhile, Sally would be in the living room holding Bubba by the collar. And when I'd command, "Release the dog," she'd let Bubba loose, at which point he'd come racing down the kitchen hall to grab a treat.

The dog biscuit Bubba ate first was his pick. We'd do the picks during the halftime of Monday Night Football. Bubba would always whine to come inside the house when we'd drag out the sheets of paper and the dog biscuits.

Bubba loved this game. As I pointed out in my obituary about Bubba, who passed away in 1987, some dogs live to chase cars, but Bubba lived to swallow.

Now, the first time we ever did this stunt, in September 1984, Bubba got twelve out of thirteen games right, and won a little over $100 in the office football pool. The only mistake Bubba made was when he picked the L.A. Rams to beat Pittsburgh. I don't know what he was thinking.

We used his winnings to take Bubba to the vet and get him all cleaned up. I've told this story multiple times when speaking to various civic groups, and I've wondered whether many of them thought I was making it up, but I wasn't. It actually happened. Each week our newspaper would run the NFL picks made by our sportswriters Kirk Bohls, Rick Cantu, and so on. After the little doggy experiment I pulled, Bubba's mug shot was soon appearing weekly in the sports section, right next to the sportswriters' photos, and his predictions were published right alongside theirs.

After that first round of remarkable success, Bubba's keen eye for prognostication seemed to fog over. Over the long haul, he got about half of the games right. So the system became little more than an amusing game, just a creative way of flipping a coin. But I was honest about it. Usually. Over the weeks I noticed that Bubba had a tendency to pull to the right — in other words, eat the biscuit on the right side first. So I would go out of my way not to notice which team name I set on the right. Most of the time. Okay, so I fudged a couple of times when the game looked like an impending blowout. I didn't want Bubba picking, say, the Cardinals over the Chicago Bears.

Perhaps the coup de grace of South Austin culture was the Tug of Honor, a massive tug of war featuring teams of five hundred from South Austin and North Austin trying to pull each other into Town Lake. The brain behind the event was a clean-cut young guy named Charlie Gandy, who had been a State Representative from Mesquite. In fact, he was the youngest guy in the Texas House at the time. "I was the only member who ever reached puberty on the House floor," Gandy joked.

Gandy didn't look the part of a Bubbaland advocate. He was much too scrubbed to come across as the promoter of such a raucous event. But he had a keen sense of humor, and he lamented the loss of the old Armadillo World Headquarters rock 'n roll music hall. He wanted a unique way to raise money to build a youth hostel on Town Lake.

So he talked an engineer friend of his into creating a special rig that would accommodate a thousand people tugging against each other. Put that many folks on a single rope, and if the rope snaps, people can get seriously injured as the rope flies apart. It wasn't easy for Gandy to find an engineer to do the work, either. "We couldn't find an engineer who wanted to risk his license on it," he said.

Making matters tougher was that *American-Statesman* editor Arnold Rosenfeld almost pulled the plug on the event. The *Statesman* wasn't sponsoring the event at all, but I was instigating it by writing about it. Rosenfeld had safety concerns, so Gandy and I had to meet with him and explain how this would work without maiming the masses.

Here was the plan: Five hundred-yard ropes on either side of the lake would be attached to iron bars on both the north and south shores of Town Lake. And folks would line up on the ropes, grab on, and have at it.

On Saturday, April 25, 1987, between 1,200-1,500 people showed up on the shores of Town Lake, about a half-mile east of the Congress Avenue Bridge, to try to drag one another into the drink.

"Uncivil war: South pulls off 2-1 tug victory," said the big headline on the front page of the *American-Statesman* the next day. "It was sheer brawn and enthusiasm versus slick strategy Saturday afternoon on the shores of Town Lake, when a contingent of screaming, hooting, beer-drinking South Austinites went up against a more subdued group of North Austinites in a tug of war," I wrote.

That was a colorful affair. "The way I've described it was that it was the city's first city-wide jerk-off," Gandy said when I talked to him in 2012.

On the south shore, a guy walked around with an empty 12-pack box stuck on his head. That was his hat. Another guy had on a T-shirt that said, "I'll have what the gentleman on the floor is having." And when some guys with no shirts on found a crawfish on the bank, one of them said, "All right! Supper."

Meanwhile, on the north shore, a booth served quiche and wine.

The South Austin team easily won the first tug in a best-of-three match. The North Austinites plopped into the drink "somewhat reminiscent of lemmings reaching the ocean. It was just plop, plop, plop," I wrote. The South team took the whole shebang, 2-1.

"I thought they were gonna take 'em to Buda," said Charlie Burton, who drove the shuttle boat that taxied event officials from one side of Town Lake to the other.

The event was a lot of fun, nobody got hurt, South Austin's civic pride was lifted even higher, and Gandy raised enough money to get his youth hostel built.

Ironically, the only damage done was to the Alpha Romeo owned by the engineer who had put together the rope device. He had his car parked nearby, and when the South team managed to jerk the North team into the lake on one of the tugs, they ended up wrapping the rope around the engineer's car.

A master organizer, Gandy even managed to finagle a free trip to the U.S. for an Australian blues band called the Bodgies. These guys hailed from Adelaide, Austin's sister city Down Under. Gandy used that fact to get the group a free ride to Austin on Continental Airlines so they could participate in the festivities. Gandy says he pulled this off by talking to George Christian, LBJ's press secretary, who Gandy says had connections with Continental. At the time, I wasn't aware of how Gandy managed to get those free plane tickets. He kept that little detail from me, probably suspecting it was a conflict of interest issue. And it might have been.

Gandy even got the Bodgies free rooms at the swank Four Seasons Hotel on the shores of Town Lake. Gandy could talk the squirrels out of the trees without using an acorn.

The tug-of-war was so successful that even nationally known syndicated columnist Mollie Ivins weighed in on it. She did a piece for NPR on the differences between North and South Austin, Gandy recalls. Gandy recalls Ivins pointing out that, "If you want to get an education, go to the north side, if you want your furniture reupholstered, go to the south side."

We had the Tug of Honor for three years running. The South Austinites won each time. But after those three runs there was really no reason to keep doing it. The rivalry between North and South Austin was dwindling. As South Austin property values went up, the landscape began to change. Bubba just wasn't Bubba anymore. He was retiring from his roofing job, and would rather stay home and watch a ballgame, or play with the grandkids.

You want to know how much South Austin has gone downhill? Here's a living metaphor that should help explain it. As I write this, I've just bought a high-dollar mattress from a salesman at Factory Mattress in Southpark Meadows, an enormous shopping center next to Interstate 35 in far South Austin where you'll find Wal-Mart, Best Buy, Target, and lots of other big box stores. This place is so huge that I still get lost in it, even though I've been living a few miles away for five or six years now.

So the mattress salesman told me that he's a musician, and that back in the day he played with the late South Austin music legend Rusty Wier, famous for his song "Don't It Make You Wanna Dance?" which became famous from the John Travolta movie *Urban Cowboy*. But this guy working at the store can't make it in music anymore, so he's selling mattresses.

In 1984 and 1985, Willie Nelson held his annual Fourth of July picnics at Southpark Meadows, with Joe Ely, Neil Young and Johnny Cash among the headliners. This was back when Southpark Meadows was an open field full of beer-drinking revelers, instead of a paved–over place where you can max out your Visa card. That's how much South Austin has changed. Oh, I still keep my hand in writing about Bubbaland when the occasion arises. Seven years ago, when the city's health department tried to run off Nik the Goat from his home on West Mary Street in South Austin, I stuck up for the goat, and so did Austin Mayor Will Wynn.

Seems that Nik, the pet of semi-retired washer and dryer repairman Joel Munos, was violating a city ordinance that restricts livestock in the city limits. However, Nik was a popular attraction. Parents would bring their kids to Munos's front yard, where Nik lived, so the kids could pet the goat through the fence. For all these reasons, the mayor gave Nik the Goat an executive pardon.

Then there was Chad Swisher, owner of an Austin ad agency called Big Blue Sky Creative. In 2005, the business was just getting a roll going so they didn't have a lot of money. Swisher and his business partner Tony Lopez worked out of a small travel trailer parked in Swisher's South Austin back yard. Swisher had bought the 14' x 8' Scotty for $650. Sure, it was a little tight on space, but instead of paying a couple grand a month for rent, they'd sit in the trailer with their laptops and create ads. Incidentally, they've since moved their agency into a small rent house in North Austin — for $1,400 a month. That's considered a good deal in Austin these days.

Then there's the Broken Spoke, on South Lamar Boulevard, the last real honky-tonk in Austin proper and a real Austin icon. The Spoke has been around since the 1960s. In the '70s the State Legislature used to drink there. They called their gathering at the Spoke Speaker's Night. The low-slung building is nothing fancy. The ceiling in the dance hall in the back sags and the band members performing on the tiny stage nearly bump their heads on it. Willie Nelson, George Strait, Dolly Parton, Roy Acuff and Ernest Tubb have graced the Spoke, among others.

Trouble is, thanks to development, we're going from Ernest Tubb to hot tub.

As I write this, a couple of posh four-story apartment buildings are shooting up right next to the old country music joint, one on the north side and the other on the south side. The construction work created such havoc that for a time the Spoke began using valet parking, paid for by the developers, so that customers could have a place to park. Valet parking, at a place with a pool table and people dancing backwards in cowboy hats; how out of place is that?

And it's not like the Spoke is the only old-timey business on South Lamar being crowded by ritzy new condos and rental units. High dollar complexes are popping up like gigantic concrete mushrooms up and down South Lamar. There are even apartments going in across Lamar from the Goodwill Store. What a view. Residents will pay good money so they can look out the window and see what stuff Austinites are tossing out.

So there goes the neighborhood. Soon the Broken Spoke will be surrounded by upscale housing for the well-heeled, and the heels won't necessarily be on cowboy boots. James White, the Spoke's owner, is hoping his new neighbors will like his chicken-fried steak and doing the Cotton-Eyed Joe. Maybe the new residents will go next door to listen to country music. The jury's still out on that one, though.

ILLUSTRATED

I look relatively respectable in my high school yearbook picture: Laconia (N.H.) High, early '60s, back when I was taking part in a four-man exercise known as a "group sneeze".

Spec. 4 John Kelso gets the V Corps Professionalism Award from V Corps Commanding General Willard Pearson. Kelso is scowling because he's in the process of losing his buzz. (U.S. Army photo)

Thomas B., my fiercely independent friend who helped make the cream gravy at Hut's hamburger joint on West Sixth Street before it got new linoleum. Thomas claimed he once pawned his teeth.
(Photographer unknown)

The bumper sticker from my 1980 campaign for President of the United States.
(Bumper sticker by Ben Sargent)

A Kelso for President rally at the
University of Texas introduces a creative
style of campaign T-shirt.
(Photo by Ed Malcik)

Texas Governor Rick Perry and
I have one thing in common.
We both ran for U.S. President
and made fools of ourselves
doing it. This political cartoon
by American-Statesman
cartoonist Ben Sargent captures
the magic.

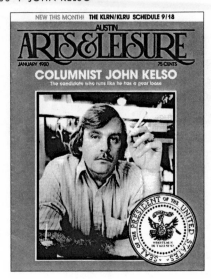

My Presidential campaign didn't lead to a major motion picture, but Texas writer Pete Szilagyi wrote a damn fine article about it for Austin Arts & Leisure magazine. Pete even spelled my name right, while the New York Times did not.

Austin fun from the '70s: Soap Creek Saloon clientele wore festive paper bags over their heads for the George Majewski lookalike contest. The bags, with eyeholes, included a cartoon likeness of Majewski, Soap Creek's beloved owner. It bore a striking resemblance to Alfred E. Neuman.
(Poster by Kerry Awn)

Former Texas State Rep. Charlie Gandy (left) with me at the Tug of Honor, a tug of war across Town Lake between teams of 500 from North and South Austin. For three years running the South Austin Bubbas dragged the North Austin yuppies into the drink. (Photo by Austin American-Statesman)

*Wavy Gravy, who ran No-
body for President and has a
Ben & Jerry's ice cream flavor
named after him, stopped at
my house back in the '80s
with a busload of about 40
hippies who came inside to
take showers.
(Photographer unknown)*

*For three years I held a contest
to find the ugliest pickup truck
in Texas. Nobody ever out-ug-
lied the scary-looking number
owned by Clyde Puckett, who
used to write his to-do list in
chalk on the hood and hauled
trash for a living.*

*My buddy Edd O'Donnell and me, posing as retired players from the old UFO, the
United Football Organization, at the Dallas Cowboys training camp at St. Edwards
University. (Photo by Austin American-Statesman)*

I was the only contestant who filled out the disclaimer form while wearing reading glasses when I tried out unsuccessfully for the TV show American Gladiators. (Photographer unknown)

Big Bird Kelso at the polls to vote for President. The big guy in the dark suit is Big Bird's Not So Secret Service agent Edd O'Donnell. (Photo by Ralph Barrera)

If the lead article of this series of Texas "perfects" had run, I probably would have gotten fired. Turns out the East Texas sheriff I was touting was being investigated by the Department of Public Safety. Hey, nobody's perfect, right? (Poster by Austin American-Statesman)

I was proud of my expense accounts, particularly this one that paid for a large box of cow pies mail-ordered from Beaver, Okla. The pasture pods were used to make an Oklahoma Sooner likeness called Okie Pokie.

A couple of Texas Longhorn cheerleaders visit with Okie Pokie in Dallas before the annual Oklahoma-Texas football game. We wheeled this cow dung art piece into the Texas State Fairgrounds for a photo shoot with Big Tex. (Photo by John Kelso)

What an Austin trifecta: street icon Leslie Cochran, a nearly naked woman protesting furs for the People for the Ethical Treatment of Animals, and somebody in a cow suit—all on the same corner. (Photo by Bob Wade)

My good friend Gary Rice, who climbs mountains for fun and teaches journalism at Fresno State in California. Gary used to manage rock bands in Austin and go to stock car races all over the country. (Photo by Gary Rice)

Big Shots I Have Met

During my career at the *American-Statesman*, I didn't rub elbows with the famous as often as I rubbed elbows with regular Joes. That's because seeking out the stars wasn't my job or my intention. Even so, every once in a while, I'd run across somebody you might have heard of — or they'd run across me.

Take the evening in the Eighties when Joe Ely, the rock and roll star from Lubbock and Amarillo, dropped by my South Austin home. I had no idea he was on the way. To this day I still don't know how he found my address. This was way before the Internet, back when things were harder to look up. If I had known he was coming over, I wouldn't have baked a cake, but I might have put out some chips and hot sauce. Why hot sauce? I'll tell you.

It was around 10:30 at night when the doorbell rang. My doorbell rarely rang at 10:30 at night. Oh, there was that time in 1980 when the doorbell rang at 4:30 in the morning, and it was the police. Seems three goofy friends of mine — Dick Terry, who went on to sell cars and called himself "The Walking

Man's Friend;" the late Pat Knight, who was a good writer and a talented cook around Austin; and somebody else (I forget who) — had toilet-papered my yard. They were hammered, and they were standing there behind the cop at the door, looking sheepish. They had assured the cops they knew me, and the cops wanted to know if that was true.

I told the cops that yes, I knew these clowns, and so the cops let them go. Even though they appeared somewhat loaded to me. I got a quick laugh out of it and went back to bed.

But when the doorbell rang on the occasion I'm remembering, it was Joe Ely standing there. At that time I was working on a story about what famous people around Austin keep in their refrigerators. At first glance, this sounds like a stupid idea, but I'd interviewed Ely for the story, and he'd rattled off some foods.

However, he'd forgotten to mention one item: the hot sauce. I don't remember what brand he liked, but he had a favorite salsa, and he wanted to make sure it was mentioned in the article that he kept this type of hot sauce in his fridge at home.

Ely hung around in my living room for about half an hour. We chatted. Then he got up and wandered off into the night. I asked him if he wanted a drink because back in those days I would make that sort of offer at 10:30 at night. Ely said no thanks, and he was gone.

So the hot sauce made it into the article.

I interviewed Ely later about the presidential candidates, particularly Ronald Reagan, and he gave me a quote I still remember, because it sounds like vintage Joe Ely. I asked him what he thought about Ronald Reagan, and he said he'd be more likely to vote for somebody "who might could roller skate." Not sure exactly what that meant, but it's stuck in my brain all these years.

The only other famous person who stayed at my house was Wavy Gravy, who once showed up at my door with a bus full of hippies. Wavy Gravy was the clown-lookin' guy you might have seen from Woodstock. He worked security there, if you could call that security. He even has a Ben and Jerry's ice cream flavor named after him called, you got it, Wavy Gravy.

Gravy, or should I say Wavy, came to Austin to run Nobody for President. You know, "Nobody in Washington cares about your interests." "If Nobody wins, Nobody loses." That sort of thing. As it turned out, Nobody was a set of plastic chatter teeth set on a plush pillow. An entourage of a few hippies marched the pillow and chatter teeth onto the West Mall at the University of Texas.

I guess you could say Wavy and friends didn't stay at my house, technically, because they slept in their bus. But they did come into the house and use the shower. They also hooked up to electricity in my garage. It was a South Austin commune sort of situation. There were about forty of them.

Another famous person I met was Lieutenant Governor Bob Bullock, the man who ran Texas state government for decades. It was one election night thirty or so years ago. There was a Democratic celebration going on at the Driskill Hotel, and Bullock was walking around sort of pigeon-toed on the second floor of the hotel, just outside the ballroom. I assume he was at least slightly loaded. This was back before he had sworn off booze.

So Bullock pigeon-toed up to me and asked me a few questions. I was the new columnist in town and he wanted to find out some stuff about me. He asked me what I thought about my boss, *Statesman* editor Ray Mariotti. I waffled on the answer, because I didn't know what Bullock thought of Mariotti, and I was being chicken-bleep at the time. Bullock lit into me and said I should back up the man who hired me. (He was right about that.) Then he poked me on the chest a couple of times, and said something like, "I know a lot of people think highly of you, but I don't think you're worth a (bleep)." Then he turned on his heels and pigeon-toed off.

A few years later I started getting Christmas cards from Bullock, family cards with photos of him and his wife on them. Go figure. I always admired Bob Bullock.

Then there was Doug English, the great Texas Longhorns defensive player who went on to be an NFL star with the Detroit Lions. This happened in the late '70s when I was down at the Raw Deal steak place, a literati hangout downtown by the police station, on Sabine Street. I turned a corner in the little restaurant and suddenly in front of me was this enormous presence, this man who blocked out the light coming off the light bulbs.

He was looking right at me. *What the heck did I do?* I wondered, and then I thought, *Uh-oh.*

"You John Kelso?" he asked. I admitted it, and he stuck out this massive paw. "I really like your columns," he said with a grin.

Thank God, I said to myself. Doug English is one of the good guys. For one thing, he never took his star status that seriously, and he does a lot of stuff for charity. Plus, he was a fan of the chicken-fried steak at Jake's on West Fifth Street, where he was always kind to the owners, Pee-Wee and Marie. And anybody who hung out at Jake's was a friend of mine. Jake's had the best fried oysters in town.

I ran into Willie Nelson one night out in Bee Cave but it wasn't much of a story. There's a famous old building out there on Texas 71 at 620 that's been a barbecue place, a wine bar and grill, and all sorts of other things over the years. Today it's a Planet K novelty store. But this story took place back when the venue was a downhome place to eat. I walked in around 9:00 one night, and Willie was there, sitting alone at a table. We were the only two people in the restaurant. Willie seemed like he wanted to be left alone, so I went over and introduced myself. We shook hands. And that was all she wrote.

I didn't really want to bother the guy.

I talked to U.S. Rep. J.J. (Jake) Pickle on numerous occasions, but who didn't? Pickle was one of the representatives who got around and met his constituents. I don't think there was a building in Travis County he hadn't been in. He was one of those guys who could remember a face, too. If he'd ever met you, five years later he'd recall your name.

I remember one time when he came into the newsroom after I had shaved off my beard. I could see him peering at me with a befuddled look on his face. I think it was bugging him that he couldn't place me. I finally went over and told him who I was. He never let on that he hadn't known all along.

Jake Pickle got out there with the people and shook hands and talked to everybody. Years ago at the Watermelon Thump down in Luling, parade officials told Jake that, for safety reasons, he couldn't throw his plastic pickles from the parade car to the people along the parade route. Pickle distributed these little toys when he was campaigning. But the people running the parade asked him not to toss them to the crowd. Some kid might get his eye put out by a flying pickle, they explained.

But that didn't stop Jake Pickle, who solved the problem by walking the entire parade route and personally handing out his campaign pickles.

Imagine a Tea Party candidate doing that. He'd probably charge for the pickles.

Then there's Kinky Friedman, writer, singer, humorist, Texas gubernatorial candidate, animal lover and general bull@#% artist. Some people are always on stage and Kinky is one of them. To illustrate: Kinky and I walked into Conchita's Mexican Cafe in Kerrville one day in 2005. The 17-year-old gal waiting tables had the hiccups. Loud hiccups. You could hear her going off all the way from the kitchen. Kinky told her to come on over to our table. Then he laid out six $20 bills — $120 in all — on the table. "Go ahead and try to hiccup, and if you can, you get the $120," Kinky told the waitress. She stood there, blinking. She couldn't. She didn't get the money. But her hiccups were gone.

Kinky told me he learned that trick from an old cowboy named Grady Tuck. He says it works every time. He says how much money you have to put up depends on the hiccupper. If the person with the hiccups is loaded, you have to put up more money, because the amount has to be enough dough to startle the hiccup victim.

I stayed at Kinky's house out in the Hill Country a few nights, and you never knew what would pop out of his head. One day he wondered aloud how many journalists he could off and bury their skulls on his property out there in the boonies before anybody noticed.

Maybe he was trying to get me to leave. Kinky's goal in life is to never be boring. Or bored. At least that's my best guess. I guess everybody knows by now that Kinky puts out steaks on the floor of his house for his dogs.

Another famous guy I've met is Texas artist Bob "Daddy-O" Wade, the man who put the big iguana on top of the Lone Star Café in New York City. Wade is a close friend of mine, and we do stuff together. He's good company because he's always in good spirits, and up for a laugh.

In 1999, while I was working on my funny travel book, *Texas Curiosities*, Wade and I drove from Austin to Irving together, to observe the Dallas Cowboys' cheerleading tryouts. No, we weren't trying to make the team. I was doing a little research for a blurb to go in my book, and Wade was along for the chuckles.

On that particular day, Oliver Stone was filming a movie called *Any Given Sunday* on the field at Cowboys Stadium. The film starred Al Pacino and Cameron Diaz, so it was a big deal.

Meanwhile, hundreds of good-looking gals were dancing and strutting their stuff on a disco floor set up in one of team owner Jerry Jones's offices. Wade started talking with some of them. He explained that yes, famous director Oliver Stone was filming a movie on the field below, but the only way they could see the action was to get down on the floor on their hands and knees and peer through the bottom of the blinds, which were closed. Next thing you knew, you had four or five attractive gals all lined up on their hands and knees, peeking through the bottom of the curtain to try to see Oliver Stone.

With that, Wade got out his camera, took a couple steps back, and quickly snapped a photo of the ladies' fannies. As far as I know they never knew they'd been photographed.

Wade, whom I suppose you could call a dirty old man, since he was sixty-nine years old in 2012, does stuff like that. Somehow he manages to get away with it, though, by smiling a lot and maintaining an entertaining demeanor. It's as if Wade is the world's oldest fraternity boy. In fact, he still spends a lot of time with his fraternity brothers from Kappa Sigma, the frat he belonged to at the University of Texas. Wade likes pretty much everybody, and pretty much everybody likes Wade. I've never seen him grumpy or out of sorts. He's always upbeat.

But what can you expect from a guy who put together the world's largest cowboy boots? At forty feet tall, they loom over Saks Fifth Avenue in San Antonio.

I met Merle Haggard in October 1977, a few months after I'd started working for the *American-Statesman*. I like Haggard's music, and I'm almost always glad to hear it in my car on the outlaw music radio station. However, I don't always agree with Haggard's politics. In other words, I appreciate my Social Security checks.

When I interviewed him, Haggard had just released a song called "I'm a White Boy" that struck my boss, the city editor, as being a bit racist. And since Merle was playing at the Silver

Dollar, a honky-tonk in North Austin, the city editor asked me to go out there and ask him about the song. Sure, I was nervous. Here I was, about to interview an American country-western music legend, an Okie from Muskogee, and ask him some tough questions about racism.

Here are some of the lyrics of "I'm a White Boy":

"Some folks call me ramblin' man, I do a lot of thumbin' and kickin' cans.

And it wouldn't do an ounce of good to call my name,

'Cause daddy's name wasn't Willie Woodrow.

And I wasn't born and raised in no ghetto,

Just a white boy lookin' for a place to do my thing."

The song also tells us that "I ain't black and I ain't yeller" and "I don't want no hand-out livin', and part of anything they're givin'. I'm proud and white."

I sat down with Haggard in his travel trailer parked outside the Silver Dollar and asked him how he felt about welfare. Nobody else was present when we talked. Haggard said welfare was okay if it was "used right." But he said he thought some people who applied for it "aren't really eligible." He also pointed out that he'd worked hard all his life, hauling potatoes, baling hay, picking strawberries—and that he'd never had to resort to welfare.

So who's this guy Willie Woodrow, I asked. At first, Haggard didn't seem to know what I was talking about, but then he remembered the lyrics of his song and he said, "Willie Woodrow is a fictional character, but if you think you got the message there, I think you got the right idea."

Got it.

Some day maybe we'll get over this white vs. black thing, but I don't know when.

Now That's an Ugly Truck

Perhaps no other story I covered shows how much Austin has changed as my ugly truck contest. For three years in a row, hundreds of good ol' boys and their significant mamas gathered in a vacant lot next to the Hog-eye Bait Shop on Lake Long in East Austin to compete for the title of biggest eyesore truck in the state of Texas, or perhaps the world.

Today you couldn't draw a crowd in Austin with an event like that. Nowadays, to draw a crowd in upscale Austin you'd have to hold an ugly iPhone contest, or an ugly mini-van contest, or a worst mocha latte contest.

But Austin in 1984 was a whole 'nother world.

The seed for the contest was planted in June of 1984, when an Austin lawyer named Stuart Kinard called me from a gas station in Elgin to tell me he'd just seen the ugliest pickup truck in Texas. That Kinard called from a pay phone should tell you something about how the world has changed. Today you'd have an easier time finding uranium in Manor than you would finding a pay phone at a gas station.

Anyway, Kinard was calling about a mostly black Chevy pickup truck owned by Clyde Puckett, who used the truck to haul trash for a living. "This truck is so pristine perfect in its ugliness that you can't suggest anything to put on it to make it uglier, and I'll bet you the next longneck on that," Kinard told me.

When Kinard told me the owner's name was Clyde Puckett, I assumed he was making it up. It was too perfect a name for the owner of an ugly truck. But it turned out that Clyde Puckett was a real guy and that he lived on Hog-eye Road near Manor. Hog-eye Road plus Clyde Puckett: double pay dirt.

I drove over to Elgin to look at Puckett's truck and it really was Stephen King-scary. The truck had started out as a 1970 Chevy, but it was registered as a '63 because of various body changes caused by various adventures. Turns out Clyde had run into a steer with the truck about four months earlier on Hog-eye Road.

"That's where that old bull ricocheted," Clyde said, pointing to the smashed-in right rear fender. He added that the reason the truck had a 1978 engine, a 1970 frame and front end, a '63 bed and cab, and a Buick speedometer, is that a former owner of the truck who had gone out West looking for a job as a movie stunt man "rolled it off an Oregon mountain."

Then, about three weeks before I met Clyde, a Kenworth 18-wheeler had hit the rear end of the truck while Clyde was headed down Interstate 35. "It kind of stirred all my entrails," Clyde explained. "It was like a baseball bat hitting a gnat. I heard this uurrrrrr, ka-boom! And when I looked in my rear view mirror, all I could see was chrome."

Clyde's truck was so ugly that Clyde used to write his daily to-do list in chalk on the fender.

Finding a truck this ugly was the inspiration for me to create the Ugliest Pickup Truck in Texas Contest.

The first of three annual contests, held in July 1984, was a slam-dunk for Clyde. I pretty much knew going into it that nobody could come up with anything uglier than Clyde's truck. I also knew that it would be difficult for anybody to top Clyde's line of bull. Rule of thumb: A colorful quote or three will go a long way toward getting you first place in an ugly contest held by a humor columnist.

By the way, Clyde's truck was so ugly that he said his sister's dog, PeeWee, who is half Border Collie, would chew on the tires whenever he saw it. In fact, Clyde added, the mere appearance of the truck coming down the road would set the dog into a frenzy, and get him "so excited that he suspends himself in mid-air."

None of the forty or so other truck owners entered in that first contest could top that line, or compete with the horrifying appearance of Clyde's truck. I mean, the grill on the front glared at you like it was fixing to run over pedestrians for sport. It would have made a great prop in the movie *Deliverance*.

First prize, presented to Clyde, was a can of an abrasive cleaner called Ugly Off.

There was plenty of local color at that first contest. The trucks broke down into two informal categories: natural, and messed-with. "Messed-with" was a category handed to me by my friend from Kyle, Owen Dorman, who pointed out that a naturally ugly truck deserves higher status than one that is ugly because of add-ons.

And speaking of add-ons, one of the messed-with trucks was decorated with Lite beer cans stuck on the windshield wipers.

Another truck had two stainless steel mixing bowls on top of its cab, painted to look like eyeballs. And when it was announced the judging would start in five minutes, one bozo jumped up and down on the hood of his truck to cave it in some.

The contest wasn't completely unsophisticated, though. One year I talked the late Liz Carpenter, Lady Bird Johnson's press secretary, into being a judge. Liz had a great sense of humor, but it only went so far. I remember her crabbing about the company car I picked her up in to take her out to the contest. I told her she was lucky she didn't have to ride out there in my old beat-up VW. She did have a good time at the contest, though I remember her wearing gloves.

We had the contest three years running, and during that time no other truck entered was ever as ugly as Clyde's. But we declared other winners anyway. It would have ticked off the other ugly truck owners who entered if Clyde had kept winning every year.

During the second annual, in 1985, we had a scandal. We judges initially named a '64 Ford with a bullet hole in the windshield and owned by Leon McMahan, a furniture upholsterer from Austin, as the ugliest. But the problem was the judges, me included, hadn't noticed that McMahan's truck was absent a current inspection sticker. The rules said trucks had to have an inspection sticker because that way we wouldn't be stuck with a pile of junked trucks left in the vacant lot next to the Hog-eye Bait Shop after the contest.

Some people in the crowd noticed the out-of-date inspection sticker, though, and they complained. Several said quite boisterously that the second-place finisher, Doug Celovsky of Bastrop County, should be named winner. So to settle the row, some good ol' boys hooked up Celovsky's '66 model International Harvester to McMahan's truck, and a pull-off ensued. As the crowd hollered, "Take him to town, take him to town," Celovsky's truck dragged McMahon's Ford all over the lot.

Later the judges switched gears and made Celovsky the champion.

Celovsky had won a pair of fuzzy dice for his initial second-place finish. But he never did exchange prizes with McMahon, who had won Mexican food for two at Don Juan's & Only Taco Palace, because Celovsky really wanted to keep those fuzzy dice.

Come to think of it, that's another thing you don't see around Austin much anymore—a guy who would prefer fuzzy dice over free Mexican food.

Austin mechanic L.D. Kemp won the third and final ugly truck contest in July 1986 with a '61 Chevy that featured more rust than Cleveland. The truck sported a hole in the windshield (covered with duct tape) that was caused, Kemp said, by "a mailbox and an old boy's face." After the victory, Kemp told me that his wife Diana would like to get rid of the truck.

"She hates that truck with a passion," said Kemp, who had dressed for the contest in a leather vest with no shirt, a red bandana around his neck, sunglasses and a straw cowboy hat. "The first time we went out, we rode in that thing. But she hates it. She doesn't think she looks good in it. Even so, the truck will be here when I die."

"I think that will be shortly," Diana added.

Big Edd and the Old UFO

A lot of the columns I did were interactive.

What this means is that I'd put on a funny costume and go out and make a fool of myself.

Take the time in 1997 when my friend Edd O'Donnell and I went to the Dallas Cowboys training camp at St. Edward's University in South Austin, pretending to be former pro football players from the UFO.

You know, the old United Football Organization.

For this occasion, Edd, a great big guy (probably 350 pounds and 6-foot-4) who sported a sizable white beard, posed as Edd "Late Train" O'Donnell. I was John "Crusher" Kelso. We wore leather football helmets, and set up a card table to sign autographs. Our table sported a sign that read simply, "Autographs."

"Are you one of the original Cowboys?" asked a guy in his twenties who walked up to our table.

``No, not exactly,'' I told him. ``I was with the old United Football Organization, the old UFO.''

"Oh, yeah. The old UFO," the guy said. Then he wandered

off without asking for my autograph. I guess he didn't think much of the old UFO.

Another guy who came by asked us to autograph his football. "I don't know if we can sign anything made in Taiwan," Edd said.

This wasn't a complete ruse, though. As I explained in my column, Edd and I both have football backgrounds. Edd, an Austin writer, played ball in the Navy — under John Paul Jones. And I watch a lot of it on TV.

I suppose I ought to pay Edd about half of my retirement benefits, since he gave me so many column ideas. He was always thinking up stunts we could pull off together. I don't know how many similar capers we went on as a team. I'd say probably ten. Okay, maybe six.

You might wonder how I paid Edd for supplying these concepts and tagging along. Lunch. I'd take him to lunch. Edd liked to go to lunch. Or as he put it, "putting on the old feed bag."

The big problem with these engagements is that, at some point during the stunt, I'd have to hide my face from laughing out loud at something Edd said or did. Like the time I did the column on Oslo, a pretentious watering hole with a phony Scandinavian decor in Austin's semi-pretentious Warehouse District. This bar had been touted as a hot spot in *Conde Naste Traveler* magazine. The place served a metrosexual martini, which, if you drank three, made you want to put on a black turtleneck and use skin care products.

Oslo is the capital of Norway, so Edd pointed out that the bar's name was way off base, since it didn't match up with the decor.

"What? No smelts?" he asked. "If it doesn't smell like bad cheese and fish, it's not really Norwegian."

While Edd and I were ordering drinks from the bar in the back room, this really cute blonde Barbie Doll bartender asked us, "So how did you hear about this place?"

"We got married in Massachusetts last week, so everyone was telling us about it," Edd said.

That was one of those occasions where I had to hide my face, since I about spit up laughing.

Another of my favorite capers was our participation in the Capitol 10,000, Austin's revered 10-kilometer jogging race. Every year since the 1970s, the race has attracted thousands of people who run through downtown Austin.

Edd suggested that we strap lawn chairs to our backs with bungee cords, so that when we got winded, we could sit down for a spell. Not that there was a reason for us to be winded. We only finished about the last hundred yards of the race. And I'm not sure either of us ever broke into a trot.

For sure, Edd and I did a lot of stupid stuff together. In 2007 we attended a cocktail reception at the froufrou Louis Vuitton handbag store at the Domain.

The Domain is a high-dollar mall in Northwest Austin whose design is stunning. The mall looks like someone lowered Beverly Hills into a field full off chiggers next to the MoPac expressway.

I asked Edd who the heck Louis Vuitton is. "I thought he was the guy who makes the really good tuck and roll upholstery in Tijuana," Edd said.

Neither of us was in the market for a handbag, which was

just as well because neither of us could have afforded a Louis Vuitton model. For example, they had a $1,620 handbag suitable for carrying your dog. It had a little cage side so your dog could breathe while inside the handbag. Trouble was at that price if your dog crapped in the bag you'd have to kill him.

Edd and I, with the help of my friend Clyde Puckett, even closed down the Coyote Cafe, a chichi restaurant on West Sixth Street.

Actually, we didn't exactly close it down. We had lunch on the restaurant's last day of business. Rocky Packard, the executive chef, had written a letter to the editor of the *American-Statesman* saying that one reason the restaurant had been having trouble was that the locals didn't appreciate sophisticated cuisine.

So Edd, Clyde, and I decided to visit the place, to prove to Packard that Austin certainly has its share of sophisticated diners. Edd and I selected Clyde as our lunch mate because he has a really great beard for straining soup. Also, we figured that a man who lived out on Hog-eye Road in the Manor School District could put a realistic perspective on Austin's dining scene.

Clyde admitted that usually he favors the 290 Café, a greasy spoon out on U.S. 290 in Manor. "A hog just can't pass by a good mud hole, and I just can't hardly pass by the 290 buffet," said Clyde, who hauls junk for a living. "The food is home-cooked, all seasoned up, and it's laid out there with those little plates underneath the glass where you can look at it. That gets your taste buds bumping together."

You're not going to find that kind of review in *Gourmet* magazine.

At the Coyote Cafe, our waiter told us that they served nine-grain wheat bread.

"Do you know which nine?" Edd asked. "No, I do not," the waiter said. I felt sorry for the poor guy, being so clueless, so I left him a good tip.

One warm late summer evening, Edd and I went to a biker rally in downtown Austin to observe all the dentists and doctors who had invaded the city on Harleys. We didn't have a Harley at our disposal, so to get to the rally, we rode across the Congress Avenue Bridge in a pedicab, one of those wienie little carts propelled by a guy on a bicycle. It had something of a rickshaw feel about it.

"Does anybody but me feel like he's on the way to a Hong Kong whorehouse?" Edd asked from his seat behind the pedicab driver.

Then there was the time we posed as psychic insurance salesmen at a psychic fair held in a motel on Interstate 35, south of Town Lake. The fair was a marketing opportunity for tarot card readers, palm readers, and people selling essences and herbs and mystical stones. It was a great opportunity to get your aura fluffed, as Edd put it.

As we went from table to table checking out all this woo-woo stuff, we approached several people and told them we were selling insurance that would cover any damages they might incur from, say, an inaccurate tarot card reading, or an errant fortune cookie. For example, I once got a fortune cookie that said, "You like Chinese food." Well, you know what, Sherlock?

At one point big Edd, wearing a doo-rag on his head, as

usual for these occasions, told a woman at the event that he would read her elbows if she wanted. She agreed and held her elbows up, while Edd inspected them. I was having trouble breathing when Edd did that because I was laughing so hard with my face hidden. Sometimes you just wanted to blurt out, "I don't know this guy."

The elbow reading came out well. "You need to learn to relax," Edd told the woman as he looked at her elbows. She seemed happy with the advice. He should have charged her $35 — or at least gotten her phone number.

Although I had some fine partners in crime, sometimes I pulled stunts on my own, like the time the news story came out that lawyers for Barney the Dinosaur were ordering people to stop renting Barney the Dinosaur outfits. Renting the Barney suit was a trademark infringement, Barney's lawyers contended.

So of course I had to go to the Lucy in Disguise costume shop on South Congress and rent a Barney the Dinosaur outfit. I wore the suit around town for a few hours, stopping at various spots, including the Chaparral Lounge, a redneck beer joint way down South Congress Avenue. My old redneck friend, Thomas B, was sitting at the bar. "John G. Kelso," he said when I walked in. He knew who I was, even though I was hidden inside the Barney suit.

I also visited a South Congress Avenue drugstore where Barney the Dinosaur bought some condoms. The drugstore was busy, so Barney had to stand in line to buy his rubbers. While I stood there holding onto the package of condoms, I noticed the clerk at the cash register fighting a losing battle to keep a straight face. He was probably thinking I was about to get lucky with a lizard or something.

In 1992, I tried out for American Gladiators, that TV show where body builders with names like Blaze and Thunder club each other with pugil sticks. As I pointed out in my column, at the time, at age forty-seven I may have been the only person among the 552 competitors who had to put on his reading glasses to fill out the registration form.

For the occasion I was assisted by my attorney friend, Scott Wilson, who brought along my uniform, or at least what he thought should be my uniform. It consisted of a red bathrobe, a floppy-eared World War II aviator's cap, flexible silver Godfather's Pizza sunglasses and an enormous red and white polka-dot bow tie.

"I ain't wearing that bow tie," I told him.

"I wouldn't either," Wilson said. "I just threw it in there to see what your limit was, 'cause I know it's way beyond mine."

As it turned out, I didn't wear the uniform at all. I didn't need to, because I had no trouble making a fool of myself without dressing for the occasion. To make the cut, would-be contestants had to do fifty push-ups on their fingertips. I couldn't do a fingertip push-up when I was five, okay? I tried, but without success. About a thousand people in the arena got to watch this show, by the way.

"You've got to get up on your fingers, Sir," the official who was checking my form kept saying. "Sir, you've got to get up on your fingers. Sir…" I did complete twenty exercises of some sort, but they weren't push-ups in the traditional sense. So I said that I completed twenty Kelsos. A Kelso, you see, is when you push on the floor, your fingers bend, and your breathing becomes erratic.

"I was laughing like crazy because you had your butt sticking way up in the air, and everybody else was flat, ha ha ha ha ha," Wilson observed. But hey, Wilson couldn't do a fingertip push-up, either, unless you hooked his belt to a crane and started cranking.

Another adventure I enjoyed was called The Remote, the performance art piece I organized in 1999 that would have featured a hundred guys lounging in recliners while watching football on television on the Congress Avenue Bridge.

It was the kind of thing pop artist Christo would have done if he watched Monday Night Football. I envisioned The Remote as a dance performance of sorts. Men would display a variety of intricate recliner moves. You know, like getting up out of the chair and grabbing a beer, or changing channels from, say, Oprah to the Longhorns game. I even had a choreographer helping us out. Andrew Long of the Johnson-Long Dance Company rehearsed with a core group of ten guys about once a week. These rehearsals were held in an abandoned bar space in downtown Austin. Men marched about, popping in and out of recliners, practicing.

(And by the way, you can understand why the Johnson-Long Dance Company wasn't named with Long getting top billing, just by saying the name out loud the other way around.)

Perhaps the funniest part of this performance art deal was that Andrew Long expected to get paid for his work by the newspaper. As they say, "When pigs fly."

Anyway, we really were doing this piece. What gave me the idea was a woman's dance and spoken word project called *The*

Bridge, held on the Congress Avenue Bridge. The City of Austin shut down the bridge for a few hours right before sunset one evening so that traffic would not disturb this spectacle. A hundred women dressed in white sat in folding chairs, popping up now and then to take part in the spoken word, while a jazz ensemble backed them up with atonal music. Even for Austin, it was a bit screwy.

I wrote a review of *The Bridge* for the newspaper. Afterward, Ken Herman, currently a talented columnist at the *American-Statesman*, said that if women could shut down the Congress Avenue Bridge for this escapade, what about the guys? Didn't men deserve their own arts event based on guys watching football on TV? I thought that was a great idea, so I went after it hammer and tongs. To put *The Remote* together, I took a week off from work to drive around town, gathering up used recliners from people who donated their old worn out furniture for the arts.

Sadly, though, *The Remote* never happened. We were all set up to break a leg on the day after Thanksgiving, in conjunction with the kickoff of the Texas-Texas A&M football game. While that game was on the tube, we would be doing our stuff on the Congress Avenue Bridge. We had urged guys to show up with their chairs and join in. We were hoping for a hundred participants. We had gotten permission to use the bridge, and we even had our guy movement statement: "We're here. We're changing channels. We're watching ESPN. Get used to it."

Then tragedy struck. I mean, serious tragedy.

Each fall the Aggies would stack thousands of logs and set them on fire to celebrate the coming Texas-Texas A&M football game. But in the early hours of November 18, 1999, about a week before *The Remote* was scheduled to happen, the Aggies' bonfire stack of about 5,000 logs collapsed while under construction. Twelve people were killed while working on the stack, and fifty-seven were injured. It would have been thoughtless and wrong to continue with a joke under those unhappy circumstances. So *The Remote* was called off and never happened.

There was one climate-oriented column that involved my making a fool of myself on purpose. Back in May 1998, Austin was engulfed in smelly smoke that was blowing up from brush fires in Mexico, Honduras, and Guatemala. It was the season in Latin America for the locals to slash and burn the local flora for agricultural purposes. So with the spring winds blowing in from the south, here came the smoke. Weathermen here gave daily particulate reports.

Wondering just how thick the smoke was, I went to Wal-Mart and spent $12 on a small smoke detector. The strap I bought to attach the smoke detector to my head was too short to get the job done. So my neighbor, Rich Mann (and yes, that's his real name) got out his glue gun and stuck it to a red ball cap.

I went to various places around Austin wearing this hat to check for Mexican smoke density. I even stopped at Jazz (A Louisiana Kitchen) on East Sixth Street, since they were cooking blackened shrimp.

"What's that on your head?" asked Tracee Hoffman, the manager.

The blackened smoke did not set off the smoke detector.

On the other hand, when I walked around my South Austin neighborhood wearing the hat, the smoke detector made a few tiny "Zzzt zzzt zzzt" sounds.

What did these findings show? They showed I would do just about anything for a column. But there was nothing here for *Scientific American*.

No one was safe from these pranks. In 2008 I picked up my daughter Rachel from school in the Oscar Mayer Wienermobile. The Wienermobile was in Austin at the time for the Wiener Dog Races in Buda, an event in which dachshund owners race their dogs against each other. I should mention that Rachel is a serious vegetarian. I figured what better way to tweak her than to show up at Austin High in the afternoon in a gigantic motorized dog-lookin' thing.

Let's face it. Parents live to embarrass their teenagers, right? Besides, Rachel already thought I was goofy. She used to call me Kelsoid. So I figured I might as well get some points with the meat car.

My wife Kay, Rachel's mother, set this up by telling Rachel I'd been having car problems, so we'd be picking her up at school that day "in a big ol' orange car."

Rachel looked stunned when she came out of school and saw the Wienermobile about twenty feet in front of her at the curb. She had no idea what was up. So she got on her cell phone and called her mom to ask where she was.

"I'm in the Wienermobile," her mom told her.

We were later told by one of Rachel's friends that at that point Rachel kept saying, "No, no, no, no, no."

But she was a good sport about it. "You came and picked up a vegetarian in a large meat mobile," she said. "That's the best part of the whole thing."

But, she added, "Y'all are weird."

The Wienermobile did draw a small crowd. My favorite response was the high school kid who came up and asked the driver, "What's your business here?" Guess he was looking for a free hot dog.

Talking about stunts, though, I have to report a recent one: wearing a full, extremely yellow Big Bird outfit to the polls here in South Austin to vote for president of the United States. The hardest part of that deal was putting on the suit, which I rented from the Lucy in Disguise costume shop. The suit came in three pieces, and if you didn't put them on in the right order, you'd get trapped inside the suit.

To begin donning the Big Bird outfit, you're supposed to stick your legs into a couple of holes. But I screwed up and ended up putting that part of my suit over my head. After I'd done this, I realized I'd dived in backwards. But when I went to start over, I discovered that the hole through which I'd jammed my head was so small that I couldn't get the damn thing off, since it was stuck around my stomach.

I had to get my wife Kay to help me escape from the suit by yanking on it for two or three minutes. "When I married you, I didn't see this in my future," she said.

Big Edd went with me to the polls as my Secret Service agent. Mostly, though, his job was to keep me from walking into walls, because with the Big Bird head on it was hard to see much. For the occasion, Edd wore a conservative dark suit, and red tie, and he kept cupping his ear as if he were listening to an earpiece for instructions on would-be terrorist threats on Big Bird or whatever.

"I'm from the Acme Security Company," Edd kept repeating as we stood in line. Throughout the caper Big Edd kept calling me "Sir." He wanted to appear official. "I shaved my legs for this?" Edd joked.

By the way, I called ahead to the Travis Clerk's office to make sure I wasn't breaking any laws. I don't know about you, but I don't want to go to jail in a Big Bird outfit. It would make the what-are-you-in-for questions hard to explain.

The line at the polls was fairly long, since it was the last day of early voting. Most people just ignored me, but several voters, almost all of them women, jumped out of line to take my picture. Everybody's got a camera these days because everybody's got an iPhone, right? And the picture takers were all getting a smile out of it.

There were a couple of grumps, though. "Vote right, Bird," some woman (who I assume was a Republican) said in an unfriendly tone as she walked past Big Bird.

Another woman asked one of the poll workers about funding. She wanted to know who was picking up the tab on Big Bird's security. This woman was completely duped. She apparently was concerned that Big Edd really was Secret Service, and that her tax money was paying for this extravagance.

Actually, Big Bird paid for his own security. I took Big Edd to lunch at Lucy's Fried Chicken in South Austin. He had the chicken basket.

Want to know why I pulled this caper? You can thank Mitt Romney. The unsuccessful Presidential candidate had said during one of his debates with President Obama that, even though he loved Big Bird, he was considering stopping federal funds to public broadcasting. Since federal funding of PBS is such a drop in the federal bucket, I thought somebody ought to come out swinging for Sesame Street.

I'll take credit for Obama's victory on election day. I'm certain that my voting in the Big Bird suit swayed many undecided voters to support the President. After all, the caper made national news. The Huffington Post wrote about it, as did ABC. One reporter, I think she was from ABC, asked me why I'd done it. "Two simple reasons," I told her. "I did it for laughs, and I like public broadcasting."

But there was a third reason. I wanted something funny to write about, and that's always a big motivator.

Not all of my stunts were successful. Sometimes I went overboard, if you can imagine that. In retrospect, for example, I shouldn't have gotten dressed up in my Arab outfit a couple years after 9/11 and gone into the Yellow Rose topless bar posing as Sheik Yer Booty. For one thing, the name was a rip-off. Frank Zappa had used the name, or one close to it, for one of his albums. If you're going to invent silly names, at least be original. That's the lesson I learned from that experience.

Besides, getting a lap dance while dressed as an Arab was offensive to just about anybody you could think of: Arabs, women, the troops, and most people in the United States of America, probably.

So when I wrote the column about it, editor Fred Zipp quickly killed it. He called me into his office and told me some of the stuff in the column was funny, but most of it wasn't. Zipp was a good editor. Put another way, he saved my butt on that occasion.

Hey, they can't all be home runs, right?

Trouble At The Top

When you work for a newspaper you are at the mercy of the editor. It's a pretty simple arrangement. You write the story, it goes to the boss, and the boss decides what to do with it. You put your trust in these people. And usually, if you take good notes and the story is accurate, and you've got a story worth telling, bang. The booger gets in the paper and everybody's happy.

But it doesn't always work that way.

In the late 1980s it seemed to me that the American-Statesman went into an investigative funk. I remember one time when it got so goofy that we did a readership survey that consisted of a dummy front page with a centerpiece story about, of all things, chimney sweeps.

I know about this because I wrote the story about the chimney sweeps.

Should such a story take up such prime space in a daily newspaper? That was the question.

Since the readership survey was done in mid-summer, when only the certifiably insane in Austin crank up their fireplaces, the answer from the readers taking the survey was a resounding no. You wouldn't think the paper would have had to ask. But that's the way it was in those days around the old newsroom.

Meanwhile, more serious issues — such as Austin growth — were caught up in a battle and hard nose coverage was going by the wayside. It seemed to me that the developers in town were the beneficiaries of a hands-off policy. Not that you could slap up a high rise and dump, say, 98,000 barrels of crude oil in Town Lake and the paper would look the other way.

It was a little more subtle than that. But this was a time in Austin history when you had a war going on. You had the new developments going in on the one hand, and the old Austin hippies who wanted to save Barton Creek, and thought the developers should be consigned to hell.

Then, in steps Maggie Balough, a really good person who I suspect was in over her head.

Maggie Balough was the *Statesman's* editor from 1987 to 1994, and she had been assistant managing editor before that. She was easily the most careful editor we had during the thirty-five years I worked at the *American-Statesman*. That's the nice way of putting it.

The good thing about working for Maggie Balough? You didn't have to worry so much about making mistakes in your stories, especially if they were hard-hitting, because she might not let them get in the paper in the first place.

The nasty way to put this tendency would be to say Maggie kowtowed to the city's big shot developers. This is not to say that she wasn't a nice person. Some people even consider her a top-flight journalist. I saw on-line that she was nominated for the Indiana Journalism Hall of Fame. She was also great to her dogs, and I really think she meant well. And actually, this business was not all her fault.

A source who should know tells me that Ray Mariotti, the newspaper's editor from the mid-1970s until 1984, was fired from the *Statesman* because of pressure from the business community. Ray went after the high and mighty while he was boss, and the high and mighty didn't appreciate it. Ray wouldn't back away from a story, even if it was about some Chamber of Commerce type he admired.

And Maggie, this same source tells me, didn't want to suffer the same fate as Ray when she followed him. So she just didn't always show the backbone it takes to be a newspaper editor. And yes, it does take a leather hide. You can't please everybody when you're the editor, and I think Maggie tried to please everybody — except for her reporters.

I first noticed her tendency to coddle local developers back in the early 1980s, when I wrote a column about some new developments built by big-time homebuilder Bill Milburn. New Milburn homes were appearing all along Manchaca Road. Prior to that, a drive from Austin to the town of Manchaca on Manchaca Road was a drive in the boondocks.

And now, all of a sudden, new homes with fancy amenities were jumping up like weeds—or bluebonnets, depending on your view of Austin growth.

An ad in our newspaper in the spring of 1984 touted the new Milburn homes by talking about their fancy-schmancy European design touches. The headline on a newspaper ad for a couple of these developments mentioned that the homes would come with "English bay windows" and "Swedish corner fireplaces." The ad even mentioned a number to call if you wanted "to find your corner of the Old World in Austin."

"Great," I wrote, tongue planted firmly in cheek. "Now Austin's got toney European design on Manchaca Road — about halfway between the A&M Drive-In Grocery in downtown Manchaca, and Andy Granatelli's Tune-Up Masters at Stassney Lane and Manchaca Road."

I pointed out that the new Milburn homes were built so close together that if you hit a tennis ball off one house, it would bounce off the house next door and keep bouncing back and forth two or three times before it hit the ground.

Apparently Bill Milburn didn't find those observations amusing, because soon after the column ran in the paper, Maggie Balough was calling me over to the city desk for a little talk. "Next time you're fixing to write about one of our advertisers," she said, "please run up a 'red flag'." That way, I suppose, she'd know what advertiser I was about to infuriate.

I thought about going out and buying a little red flag on a short stick to wear around the newsroom in my Hawaiian shirt pocket. Back in the day I was known for my Hawaiian shirts.

But I controlled myself and never got around to flying my flag. See, I needed the work.

For years I wondered why, every time I wrote something funny about infamous Austin developer Gary Bradley, the column never saw the light of day. Years later, I heard from an excellent source at the newspaper that it was common for Gary Bradley to have Balough's ear, because he was tired of the newspaper picking on him.

'Scuse me while I get out the world's tiniest violin.

Bradley developed Circle C Ranch, a large master-planned community in Southwest Austin that was involved in a long and tortuous environmental legal fight over Barton Springs and the Edwards Aquifer. Barton Springs Pool is the center diamond of Austin's environmental tiara, a spring-fed pool cherished by the community.

Circle C, which comes with an 18-hole golf course, a tennis club, an Olympic-size swimming pool, and a bunch of Californians who just moved in from San Jose, went bankrupt during the savings and loan scandal of the 1980s. Every time you turned around, Bradley's name would be in the news, and rarely (if ever) in a complimentary account. He was about as popular with Austin's tree huggers as Rick Santorum would be at Eeyore's Birthday Party. On KVET radio, a pissing contest between Bradley and environmentally rabid City Council member Brigid Shea was a magic moment in Austin's environmental wars. The two stood there toe to toe (perhaps I should say lip to lip) and vilified each other, much to the delight of the listening audience.

So I took advantage of Bradley's fame and wrote a few columns making fun of him. We're talking maybe three columns over a period of five years. After none of them ran, I finally gave up.

After Balough left, I finally managed to get a few columns about Bradley in the paper. Before that, though, no such luck. One that she blocked was a tongue-in-cheek piece about the secret romance between Bradley and Shea. Of course, the romance never existed, since they hated each other. (They have since made peace.) But I wrote the column in such a way that people would realize I was kidding.

That column never saw the light of day, and neither did the few others I wrote about Bradley while Balough was in power. I always wondered why she kept killing these columns, but eventually I decided I must just be paranoid about Maggie. After all, in person she can be as sweet as pie. But after talking to several old-time *Statesman* reporters, I've found out I wasn't alone. Several of them think Maggie was kissing the developers' butts. And protecting them.

"The *Statesman* has had a lot of good people as reporters and editors, and it's also had Maggie Balough," said Robert Cullick, a former reporter for the paper who covered Austin development in the 1980s. Cullick, who went on to become the spokesman for the Lower Colorado River Authority, left the *American-Statesman* in the late 1980s for a job with the *Houston Chronicle*. He split, he said, because Balough sat on a story he'd written about some alleged funny business going on in a Municipal Utility District (MUD) established by Bill Milburn.

You see, Milburn created a MUD in Austin called Maple Run. Municipal Utility Districts set their own tax rates for their homeowners. When Maple Run was born, Cullick recalls, the tax rate on homes there was pretty doggone low. But after only a few years, he adds, Maple Run's tax rate jumped 100 percent. Milburn claimed this was because growth had slowed, and Maple Run needed the money, but Cullick looked into it and found out

Milburn had been planning to raise Maple Run's tax rate from the get-go.

"I have the documents to prove he had always intended to raise taxes," Cullick told me. "After he kept taxes low to get people to buy the houses, he sprang the tax raise on them." So, like a responsible journalist, Cullick put the story together. But there was a problem. As usual, it was Maggie "Stonewall" Balough. She wouldn't run the story. According to Cullick, she sat on it like it was a show-room sofa.

"Maggie wasn't at all happy with it," Cullick recalled. "She sent it back four or five times to be rewritten." Meanwhile, a *Houston Chronicle* reporting job opened up, and Cullick grabbed it. You know things are bad when somebody willingly moves from Austin to Houston. "Clearly I wasn't getting anywhere writing these kinds of stories at the *Statesman*, so I just got another job and quit," he said.

Cullick said the situation with Balough left him feeling helpless. That's the same way I felt whenever she killed one of my Bradley columns. "When it was happening to me, it felt like there was nothing I could do ever to get that story in the paper," Cullick told me.

Actually, the Milburn MUD story did run — under a double byline after Cullick left. Reporter Laylan Copelin worked on Cullick's story, and eventually it got in the paper under both reporters' names. Cullick says Milburn sued both him and the newspaper over the story but ultimately Milburn dropped his suit.

These days, Balough lives in Indiana and runs the United Methodist News Service, the official news service of the

Methodist Church. She says she doesn't remember the Maple Run story at all. After all, it has been about 196 years in dog years. You may remember that Balough loves dogs.

"You might want to call Jeff Bruce," she said, referring to another former *Statesman* news executive. "He might have some recall of the story, but I don't remember."

There were others who went through the same Balough development news story meat grinder. A friend who was an editor under Balough said he just never could get the water tap story in the newspaper.

Again, we're talking about a 1980s Austin development story. *American-Statesman* reporters had found out that one of the big developers (thirty years later, my friend can't recall which one) was selling water taps, or water hook-ups, to other homebuilders, which was a no-no. To build a house, a developer had to have a water hook-up first, but builders were skirting the rules by purchasing water taps from one of the developers. When the reporter got wind of this and wrote a story about it, Balough wouldn't run the story.

"The reporters had already called the developers to get their side of it and it was ready to go," my friend the editor said. "And it was one of those things that Maggie, day after day, [said], 'It's not ready, you've got to talk to one more person.' She was famous for tying you up with so much tangential detail that you didn't know which way was up."

After the story had been held for weeks, word broke at City Hall about the shenanigans that were going on with the developer and the water taps. At that point, the matter was settled, which meant there was no more story to run. At least not a hard-hitting story.

"Basically the story came out before we got it in print," my friend said. "It just took the wind out of the sails of the story."

Looking back, my friend said that Balough's, uh, thorough ways had a major impact on the newspaper's reputation. The *Austin Chronicle* was on us like a cheap suit on a used car salesman for being in bed with the developers. My friend says you can thank Balough for that, and he's right on target. During her reign, the paper became known around town as the *Austin Real Estatesman*.

"I think that sort of bias is why we didn't get the respect we should have," Cullick said. "The environmentalists thought we were in the developers' back pockets."

Little makes a reporter madder than to work his butt off investigating a story, coming up with the facts, putting a meaningful piece together that might do the public some good, and then see it die on the cutting room floor because of favoritism.

Bill McCann was another *Statesman* reporter who left the paper because of Maggie Balough. Management didn't like Bill McCann. I know that because of a brief conversation I had one day with one of our editors back then. The editor said something about how McCann wasn't one of the paper's best reporters. I think this had to do with McCann's flap with management over his wife.

"The crowning glory, the last straw," as McCann put it to me, came along when his wife at the time, activist Susan Toomey Frost, decided to run for City Council. After Frost did well enough to make it into a run-off, McCann says that Balough told him his reporting could cause a conflict of interest with the City Council.

McCann says there was no conflict of interest. "I was (writing) in the business section at the time, and I very rarely had anything to do with City Council," he said. Besides, he went on, the business editor back then, the late and much loved Michelle Kay, assured Balough that she would not give McCann any writing assignments that had anything to do with City Hall.

McCann figures Maggie was catching heat from local politicos about one of her reporters being married to a Council candidate. So she was covering her keister by messing with him. "Maggie couldn't stand up to any kind of heat, so she told me I was going to go to work in the Lifestyle section," McCann said.

But McCann didn't want to work in the Lifestyle section. So after taking a couple of weeks off, he came back to the paper and pulled a Johnny Paycheck. "As soon as I came back, I told Maggie I didn't want to work there anymore," McCann said, pointing out that he's just one of several experienced reporters who fled the newspaper because of Balough.

"She ran off a lot of good people. She ran off a bunch of 'em. She ran me off, she ran Cullick off. She ran (reporter) Tony Tucci off. Heck, she ran off lots of folks who were really good journalists. It's unfortunate because this city deserved better." McCann said.

McCann still fumes over Balough's handling of an investigative piece he wrote in the mid-Eighties about City Attorney Albert de la Rosa. Bill found out that de la Rosa was using city funds to take his wife to New York City when he was there on city business. McCann said it was kosher for de la Rosa to use city money to pay for himself to go to New York on city business. But using city funds to pay for his wife to travel to New York was illegal. So McCann called up de la Rosa and asked him about it.

"He was very apologetic," McCann recalled. McCann says that when he turned in his story, Balough held it up. "She kept coming back to me, and this was what she was would do. She would just hold up a story," he said. "She wouldn't say 'I'm not going to run this story.' She would just keep asking questions about it until you gave it up."

By the time Maggie allowed the story into print, McCann said, de la Rosa had settled the matter with the city and paid back the New York trip money he owed on his wife's expenses. Therefore, there was no real story left. Here, though, is the real coup de grace: "Maggie said, 'Your lede's wrong. You need to rewrite the lede and say this guy's paid it back,'" McCann recalled. The "lede" is journalism jargon for the opening paragraph of a story.

McCann said, "So I rewrote the lede, and the story barely got to the outside of the B section."

McCann said the next day several reporters came up to him and said they were upset and embarrassed by what was done with his story. "The sports editor, Paul Schnitt, stopped at the elevator and apologized on behalf of the newsroom. I thought that was pretty classy on his part."

Balough says she remembers the de la Rosa story, since her ex-husband, attorney Richard Balough, worked under de la Rosa in the City Attorney's office. But she claims she didn't get involved with the story, since Ray Mariotti, the *Statesman*'s editor at the time, told her to stay away from it because of a possible conflict of interest. "I wasn't involved in that whole process playing out," she said. "Ray said you need to stay away from all of this, so I did."

Statesman reporter Tony Tucci got so fed up with Balough's chicken-hearted ways that he left the newspaper in the late 1980s to start up his own little publication, called *The Austin Agenda*. "I felt like I had stories that the paper didn't want or couldn't find or whatever, so I decided to go out and start my own newsletter," said Tucci, who's in his seventies these days, and retired. "And I would beat the *Statesman* every week with my little newsletter. The *Statesman* had to read my newsletter to find out what was going on in town. It was silly. It was just silly. They were totally unaggressive."

Tucci arrived at the *Statesman* in 1982, fixing to break some serious news. He'd been a reporter and the city editor at the *Cleveland* (Ohio) *Press*. He said he'd been a "muckraker" up north and was darned proud of the term. "I came from Cleveland where we had two newspapers, and the rule was 'Get it first, but first get it right,' so here in Austin I was disappointed, because they didn't care if you got it first or not," he said.

Tucci described Maggie Balough's attitude this way: "Don't make an accusation or a charge that might cause waves." Tucci ran into Balough's stonewall while working with fellow reporter Bob Banta on a story about Brackenridge Hospital, the city-owned hospital then.

"Whoever it was in charge of the hospital had a private company that was doing business and getting favors from the hospital," he explained. "We had this all documented. There was no question about it at all. We'd write the story, hand it in and Maggie would give us that rubbing her forehead thing that she did and say, 'You need to check this and you need to ask this,' and every day it was a different obstacle."

Tucci said that, for another example of the lede getting in the way of a good story, Balough had a problem with the hospital story's opening paragraph. "One day she said, 'I just don't like the lede,'" Tucci recalled. "I said, 'I'll tell you what, Maggie, you write the lede.' And you should have seen the lede she wrote. I think it was fifty-seven words or something like that. It was so unintelligible that I just shook my head."

At that point, Tucci had had enough, and he gave up on the hospital story. He handed it to Banta, who confirms this. Shortly after the city manager called a press conference and fired the hospital director, Tucci recalled. And the *Statesman*'s story still hadn't run. The big trouble was that "everybody else" in town had run it, so the *Statesman* had been beaten to the punch because of Balough, according to Tucci. "We could have broken the story a week or two weeks ahead of time, but she was afraid of it," he said. "It just made me so mad; I'm not used to that kind of reporting. I want to be in the lead and have the city manager react to my story. I was furious. That's one of the reasons I left the paper, to tell you the truth."

When asked about Tucci's Brackenridge story, Balough said, "I don't remember the specific story, but the question I would ask you is whether it ultimately got published." It did get published, but according to Tucci, it was published so late in the game that it wasn't much of a story anymore.

Tucci did some hard-hitting stories while at the *Statesman*, including some about Austin Mayor Ron Mullen, a former cop who also had an insurance business. "I did story after story about his ethics violations," Tucci said. "He was an insurance executive and he was having his agents call people who had cases in front of the planning commission, rezonings and that sort of thing. And his agents would say, 'Well, Ron Mullen suggested that I call you and that you might need some insurance.' My, how nice."

Tucci said he also did a story about local housing developers Bradley and his partner John Wooley buying a $4 million life insurance policy from Mullen. Those stories made it into the newspaper, but they didn't get a nod of approval from management, Tucci said. "It was like I was a pariah almost. What got me the most was that not one of those stories was ever entered for an award. Not one of 'em. Not one story. And no one ever complimented me on the stories."

But what goes around comes around. In 1994, Balough was fired by publisher Roger Kintzel. What got her? It was probably a lot of things, and probably it wasn't her fault. While publisher, Kintzel was the head of the Greater Austin Chamber of Commerce, which a lot of people in the newsroom thought was a blatant conflict of interest. And my source tells me that on some days, after visiting with Kintzel in his office, Maggie would come downstairs, downtrodden, and say, "I just don't know what he wants. I just don't know what he wants."

But the old heave-ho did come for Balough right after a story about the Coyote Cafe's hot sauce ran on the front page. Seems that the restaurant's salsa was going to be toned to please the tastes of newcomers to town. A well-known restaurant taking the bite out of the salsa is a big story in Texas, but not front page big, apparently.

I should add one other little detail here that still frosts my petunias. While Maggie was wielding power, the newspaper moved my column (and Mike Kelley's column, as well) to the back page of the B section, underneath the weather map. I suspect it was really publisher Kintzel's call. But I don't know.

Either way, the explanation I got from above was that the new spot was a great location for my column. Yeah, right. I had been on the front page of the B section since 1977, and now I'm underneath Key West on the back page. If that's a step up, I'm a Bulgarian tap dancer. Just call me a sorehead.

After Maggie got fired she asked me to visit with her so she could tell me her woes. My wife and I met with her at a chain place in Brodie Oaks. Chili's? Not sure. It's been almost 20 years.

But we sat there and listened for a couple hours. Maybe more. She just didn't understand why she'd been fired. It was kinda sad. I don't think she realized the problems she had caused so many reporters. There was a blind spot there somewhere.

Ironically, she didn't get fired for the stories she killed. She got fired because the newspaper sucked and the publisher knew it. Of course, part of the reason the newspaper sucked was she had killed some really hard-hitting stories.

When I started writing this chapter I had my doubts about

doing it. I thought maybe it was just me.

But after talking to about a half dozen folks who went through it too, I realized it wasn't just me.

But she did love a good feature story about Christmas cookies. Really.

By the way, Balough was replaced by Rich Oppel. And under our new editor, the paper started winning a lot more awards than it had before. And the investigative pieces starting to show up in print.

Rick Perry

If there's a guy I should thank for providing me with so much material, it's Texas Governor Rick Perry. Toward the end of my career, I started messing with him a lot. At first, I think I homed in on the guy because the stupid stuff he was doing was simply amusing.

But as time went on, it appeared to me that he just didn't care about people. What's the saying? Absolute power corrupts absolutely? I think that's the case with the Texas governor. What kind of guy moves into a $10,000 rent house at the taxpayers' expense while so many Texans don't have health insurance? What kind of guy turns down federal money for Medicaid when a quarter of the people in Texas don't have health coverage? What kind of guy runs a state where, if you make more than $5,000, you're not eligible for Medicaid?

A guy who doesn't care about the poor having health care coverage, apparently.

I never would have thought, years ago, that I would spend so much time and space gooning one particular politician. Earlier in my career, I had stayed way from politics, for the most part, thinking it was out of my league. I just didn't hang out in those circles, so I figured I didn't know enough about them.

Oh, every once in a while I'd take a stab at Republicans. I've always thought the Grand Old Party wasn't as concerned about the regular folk as the Democrats are. Take the expression "trickle down theory," for example. The idea here is that if the rich have a lot of money, some of it will "trickle down" to the masses.

Who wants to live on a trickle?

So when a chance arose, I would pop the Republicans' balloon. Take Ronald Reagan's 1984 rally at Auditorium Shores, for example. I was there. The refreshments weren't worth the trouble. You had to stand in line for an hour to get a hot dog and a tiny Coca-Cola. And they charged a quarter for the hot dog.

"I like quarter hot dogs, but I thought they would be cooked," said my friend Ed Born-Long, who attended the event. Ed, who used to haul dirt for a living (his business card said "Call Ed for Dirt") bought two dogs and he said they were raw. Of course, at a Democratic rally they'd give you a hummus burger, but at least they'd put some heat to it, right?

But years ago I was more likely to write about an elected official's barber than the elected official. In fact, I wrote a column about Governor Ann Richards' hair stylist in Austin, and another one about presidential candidate Ross Perot's barber up in Dallas.

Then here came Rick Perry, repeatedly stepping in it and begging to be gonged. He made so many ridiculous moves while running for president in 2011 that, after his campaign was over, one in three Texans said their view of the man had dimmed. Why? People thought Perry's run had made Texas look stupid to the rest of the country.

No wonder. Here's a guy who, in a Presidential debate, can't remember all three of the Federal departments he wants to eliminate. Let's see, there were Commerce, Education, and Oops, remember? Many people probably didn't realize there was a Department of Oops until Perry brought it up in the debate.

It occurred to me that if people had been paying attention before Perry's presidential run, they would have already had a bad taste in their mouths about this state. Either way, I couldn't leave it alone. It was like someone had handed me a box of chocolates, and I couldn't stop eating.

I first met Perry when he was Texas's Agriculture Commissioner at the annual Cowboy Breakfast, on the shores of Town Lake (these days called Lady Bird Lake). Perry seemed like a regular good old boy, and Austin radio personality Bob Cole introduced us. I was happy to meet the man.

We shook hands, he told me he enjoyed my columns, he smiled, I smiled. Like that. He didn't seem like the type who would ever get jiggy widdit, so to speak, but he was okay, I thought.

But later on, I started picking up on his disingenuous nature. So I began gooning him. I'm not sure the columns ever did any good, except to entertain. I doubt if I changed the guy's nature a bit. Not that I thought I had that kind of power anyway. But I had a good time writing about Perry, and a lot of people seemed to enjoy my making fun of the guy. I first monkeyed with Perry in print when he got pulled over for speeding by a Department of Public Safety officer in June of 2000. Actually, Perry wasn't doing the speeding. His driver was.

But when the officer started writing Perry's driver a warning ticket, Perry, who was Lieutenant Governor at the time, began to protest as if he expected special treatment. He jumped out of his Suburban, and uttered this now famous line: "Why don't you just let us get on down the road?"

It wasn't a big deal like Watergate or anything, but to me it was another way of saying, "Don't you know who I am?" Or, "Don't you realize I'm a special person and above the law?"

Another line Perry tried out on the DPS officer was, "So, if you'll just let us go on, that would be better."

For the column, I even came up with a new syndrome. I wrote that Perry was obviously suffering from "big shot rage."

I wrote, "Big shot rage is kind of like road rage, but with a narrower victim base. Big shot rage occurs when somebody who thinks he's pretty darned important gets in a snit because he's being treated like a guy who has season football tickets on the 2-yard line." I went on to explain that big shot rage was a mental condition that affected the powerful, but that it was treatable by explaining to the sufferer that "the bass didn't start biting just because he went fishing."

I never did hear from Perry after that column. Come to think of it, I didn't hear from Perry after any of the other columns I wrote about him, either. I didn't even hear from him after I left a signed copy of my book, *Texas Curiosities*, at his office in the Capitol. I thought that was rude. Don't governors have a staff person who sends out thank you notes? I mean, even if he didn't like the book, and even if he didn't like me, shouldn't he acknowledge that he got it?

I never heard a word from him, though. And I don't expect I ever will.

On the other hand, when I met First Lady Barbara Bush at a Kinky Friedman fundraiser for dogs at the Four Seasons Hotel in Austin, she said she enjoyed the "big shot rage" column I had written, and that she could relate.

She told me that sometimes she mentions the expression "big shot rage" to her husband the former President. I'm thinking she should have mentioned it to George W. right before he decided to invade Iraq.

With the speeding Suburban column, I was just getting started with Rick Perry, because as it turned out he was just getting started at screwing up, and doing and saying asinine things.

There was the time in 2008 that Governor Perry told the Chamber of Commerce in San Antonio that Texans will continue to drive their gas-hog pickups regardless of the price of gas. "You can't put a bale of hay in the back of a Prius," he explained. "It don't work."

Well, that sounded like a double-dog dare to me, so I borrowed Omar Gallaga's Prius. Omar is one of the *American-Statesman*'s tech writers. I drove Omar's Prius out to Callahan's General Store in southeast Austin, and had three of the guys working out back stuff as much hay in the car as they could jam in there. Naturally, I expense-accounted the hay.

The Callahan's guys seemed somewhat nonplussed at first

when I asked them to stuff the Prius with hay. But I explained to them why I was doing this, and they got the joke.

"I'm glad (Perry) didn't say how many chickens can you fit in a hybrid," said Wayne Slayton, one of the three guys who loaded the Prius with hay. "That would be a lot of mess right there."

The Callahan's crew managed to squeeze five bales of hay into the Prius, with only the driver's seat remaining hay-free. As I noted, "It looked like a farm had exploded inside the car." I had to take it to Genie Car Wash afterward just to get the car to the point where you could stand sitting inside it again. I think I even expense-accounted the car wash.

The hits just kept on coming. In 2006, the Governor invited the press to come up to his office in the Capitol to see his slide show of the Iraq war. Perry had used taxpayer money to go to Iraq, Kuwait, Afghanistan, and Belgium for about a week. While a student at Texas A&M University, Perry was a yell leader, the Aggie version of a cheerleader. And his slide show was little more than a bunch of pictures showing Perry schmoozing with Aggie troops stationed in Iraq, with Perry telling us how great a job our troops were doing.

You might wonder what the purpose of the trip was. "Sometimes the picture that's painted is different from what you find yourself," Perry said. There were about fifteen of us sitting around a long table in the Governor's office, with Perry up front by a screen, commenting on each slide. It was kind of like when you go to somebody's house and they show you their photos from their vacation to Hawaii, but without the drinks with the flags in them.

One slide showed a group of young Pakistani boys who, Perry explained, came outside and "and showed me their goat."

I pointed out he was lucky they didn't kidnap him and ransom his hair for $100,000. I've probably written enough Rick Perry hair jokes to fill up a Letterman monologue, or a Prius, come to think of it. During his Iraq trip, Perry wore a helmet part of the time, so his hair was flatter than usual in some of the slides.

In 2010, Perry's gubernatorial campaign coughed up $225,000 to put his name on a NASCAR car at the Texas Motor Speedway in Fort Worth. Earlier in his career, Perry, thinking the mike was off, had once said to a television reporter who had annoyed him, "Adios, mo-fo" at the end of an interview. So I put two and two together and said Perry's NASCAR should be named the Adios Mo-fo Mobile. I'll tell you, writing about Perry was all just too easy.

Did I mention that while Perry moved into that $10,000-a-month rent house west of Austin that the State of Texas was suffering from a $9.1 billion budget shortfall? I understand he had to live somewhere, since the Governor's Mansion had been torched by an arsonist and he was waiting for the remodel to get finished. But did he really need to live in a gated community, in a house with a pool, when many of his constituents were having a hard time making ends meet? Arkansas Governor Mike Huckabee had lived in a trailer on that state's capitol grounds. Why couldn't Perry slide into a wobbly box during these troubled financial times and save the taxpayers a few bucks? Wouldn't that have made him look better to his people? Wouldn't that have been the classy move to make?

Regardless, Texans apparently didn't care all that much about Perry's choice of real estate, because they kept voting him in as governor no matter how he was spending their money. So I can't really blame him. Under the same circumstances I'd probably stay at the Ritz instead of the Super 8, but then again, I'm not the governor. I'm just the local smart-ass.

Perry was a great outdoorsman, sort of. He bagged a coyote, or at least he said he did. I never saw the coyote and as far as I know nobody else did, either. Anyway, Perry allegedly bagged the coyote while jogging out by his fancy rent house. He bagged the coyote with a Ruger .380 that he carries when he jogs. Who carries a Ruger .380 while jogging near a gated community? And how come he never produced the coyote? Do we know he didn't really bag a jackalope by mistake?

But hey, it could have been worse. At least he didn't bag the coyote while driving a tank through a gated community.

Perry had a habit of saying things that I figured he really didn't believe just to curry favor with this group or that. When the Tea Party hit the scene, he hinted that Texas should secede from the Union. It sounded good to the yee-haw crowd, but I doubt he really meant it.

If At First You Don't Secede...

After Obama was re-elected president in November 2012, Texans started up a petition on the White House Web site, demanding that Texas secede from the Union. By November 26, 117,355 Texans had signed it, which isn't a major movement when you consider that as of 2011 about 25 and a half million people live in the Lone Star State.

Why such a small figure, since Republican presidential candidate Mitt Romney beat Obama by a whoppin' 1.3 million votes?

Here's my theory. Perhaps most Texans don't want to quit driving on interstate highways, lose the protection of the U.S. Army when the Chinese invade, have to get a passport to go to New Orleans for Mardi Gras, or get not an ounce of Federal help the next time a hurricane blows Galveston Island away.

Also, there's the currency thing. Whose photo would we put on the Texas $1 bill? Jerry Jones? Kinky Friedman? Willie Nelson? Red McCombs? Rick Perry? And would Perry's hairdo fit on a $1 bill?

After the Texas secede petition was born, a counter-petition asking that Austin secede from Texas and remain in the Union showed up on the White House Web site. By November 28th, that petition had received more than 5,000 signatures. A blue city surrounded by a sea of red, Austin would rather be linked to, say, Portland, Oregon, than deal with a bunch of cotton pickers from Lubbock. On the other hand, there were parts of Texas that the Austin signers wanted to keep. Their petition included this request: "We would also like to annex Dublin, Texas, Lockhart, Texas, & Shiner Texas." In other words, Austinites wanted their Dr Pepper, barbecue and Shiner Bock.

My opinion on all this foolishness? I figure the White House should dismantle the petition option from the Web site. Heck, I may start a petition demanding just that.

I'm not saying Perry is dumb, but let's have a look at his grades from Texas A&M University. The liberal online news Web site, the Huffington Post, somehow got hold of Perry's college transcripts. During the pursuit of his higher education, our governor got two A's (in "Improv of Learning" and World Military Systems), twenty B's, twenty-seven C's, nine D's, and an F in Organic Chemistry II. Twenty-seven C's, nine D's and an F: not exactly Rhodes Scholar material, especially when you consider that Perry got a D in Meats, one of his required animal science classes.

How come an Aggie got a D in Cheeseburger 101? It seemed implausible. And imagine going in for a job interview and having the interviewer ask, "Uh, Mister Perry, I see by your college transcript that you nearly flunked Meats." How does a guy who nearly flunks Meats get to be governor? That's what I want to know.

Perhaps I screwed up and stepped over the line when I wrote about how Perry's wife, Anita, didn't exactly look happy in her photographs.

In 2011 we ran a photo on the front page of the paper that showed Perry and Anita at Perry's gubernatorial inauguration. The picture showed the Perrys marching under some swords held aloft by Texas A&M's Ross Volunteers. Perry was smiling and giving a queen's wave.

Anita, meanwhile, had this look on her face that said to me that she would rather be just about anywhere else. "It's not quite as bad a look as the guy in *A Clockwork Orange* when they jam his eyes open to interrogate him," I wrote. "But it's close."

Here's how I got the idea for the column: In the editorial meeting at the newspaper, some of the editors got to jawing about the Perry inauguration photo and suggested among themselves that maybe I should write a column about it. This happened fairly frequently. The editors would see something in the paper they thought was funny. Then someone would say, "Maybe Kelso should write about it."

So I did a little research, looking through a bunch of file photos of Texas's First Lady.

In almost all of the news photos, Anita Perry looked like she had stepped on a skunk or something. In retrospect, the Perrys never cottoned to the press, to put it mildly. So every time a news photographer took her picture, maybe Anita was thinking, "Oh, my Gawd, here comes another one of those liberal pinko commie nosy news photographers again."

Regardless, I said in my column that Anita Perry didn't look like she was having a good time. There was a photo of her at a pre-election night gathering at El Arroyo in Austin, showing off her red shoe with the elephant on it to the crowd. She was holding up the shoe, with this look that said, "How come I have to stand up here in front of everybody with one bare foot holding up this stupid shoe?"

When the column came out, some politicos at the Capitol were chapped. See, there had been rumors about Perry's supposedly strained family life that I never believed or paid much attention to.

To me it was just a bunch of gossip. But I think a lot of politicos who read the column thought I was hinting that there was trouble in the Perry household. Who knows? And who cares? Most every household has troubles now and again.

My friend Gardner Selby, one of the *Statesman*'s political reporters, and a damned good one, said the part in the column that bothered him was this: "There are a few pictures here showing the governor trying to kiss her, and her turning her face. I don't want to get into that, so let's be gentle here."

By saying I didn't want to get into "that," Gardner said, I was alluding to the rumors of Perry being gay. And I guess I was. But like I said, I never believed them anyway. As much scrutiny as the guy was getting over that rumor, if it'd been true, it would have come out.

Politics in Austin is a cottage industry, although a great big, tight-knit, everybody-knows-everybody-else cottage industry. And some press members and elected officials closed ranks and bitched to each other about how I should apologize. Gardner said somebody at the Capitol even hollered across a room at him that I should apologize.

But nobody called me about it. Like I said, I don't travel in those circles.

A writer for the *Texas Tribune* even wrote a column about my scowling Anita Perry column, questioning whether it was over the line, and this person added that the column probably would have been better if it had been funny. That's the truth. It's always better when a humor column is funny. In the column, I did offer to take Anita out for a beer, but she never called.

I seriously considered the idea that I had gone too far, so I talked to our editor, Fred Zipp, who was the kind of guy you'd want to be with in an alley fight. I suggested maybe I should apologize to Anita Perry. "You have nothing to apologize for," he said. And when he was questioned about the column by others in the press, he stood by it and said it was accurate.

I stopped messing with Perry quite so frequently once he jumped into the Presidential race. But I was still on his case. And why not? While Perry was Governor, millions of dollars were cut from public schools, and teachers were digging into their wallets to pay for classroom necessities, such as chalk for the blackboard.

Meanwhile the state was paying hundreds of thousands of dollars for his security on his presidential campaign trips to New Hampshire, Iowa, and South Carolina, and to what end? The guy got one percent of the vote in the New Hampshire Republican primary. Heck, that was only one percent better than what I got when I ran for President, and tried to get my name on the New Hampshire Presidential primary ballot. And I only spent $3,600 for my entire Presidential campaign, including the cost of a keg for my going- away party.

I began easing off on Perry for a couple of reasons. (a) It's not good form to kick a dead horse. (b) My boss told me to stop picking on him. The thinking was that, by keying on Perry so often, it looked like the newspaper was biased.

Maybe so, but the man had it coming. Here's a guy who hinted that it might be a good idea for Texas to leave the U.S. Was he fixing to run for the Presidency of the U.S. or the Confederacy? And by the end of his presidential campaign, it seemed like he was saying just about anything to try to save his campaign from total oblivion.

Explain to me how a Republican Presidential candidate can come out against the free market system. Perry essentially did that when he called his main competitor in the Presidential race, Mitt Romney, a vulture capitalist. It would be one thing if he really meant what he said. But I think at that point he was so far behind in the race that he would spit up just about anything to keep his head above water.

Or, as I put it in a blog, the man seemed to have one advantage over everybody else — an extra head: one for talking out of one side of his mouth and the other for talking out the other side.

Do I think what I wrote about him changed the world? Nope. But do I think it made a point? Yup, and I would add that it brought a few laughs. Definitely. And that was the name of the game most of the time when I sat down at a keyboard.

Did I Actually Write That?

I've written some columns I wish I'd never written.

Perhaps the stupidest one I ever did was the time I tried to fry an egg on the sidewalk. Actually, this stunt occurred on the pavement in front of the *American-Statesman* building.

When you have to come up with three columns a week for thirty-five years, you can get a little desperate sometimes. This must have been one of those times.

As we all know, summer gets extremely hot in Austin, even "hot enough to fry an egg on the sidewalk," as the expression goes. So I came up with this gem of an idea to fry an egg on the sidewalk.

The wife of one of my bosses was not impressed when she read the column. She said something like, "I'm sure glad I don't have his job."

Anyway, at high noon one July day in 1986, I set a cookie sheet in front of the newspaper building and let it heat up in the sun for a couple of hours. By 2:00 p.m., it was about 101 degrees out there. At five after 2:00, I cracked an egg directly onto the pavement. I also put some butter on the cookie sheet, and then poured two raw scrambled eggs with cream cheese onto it. Then I dropped yet another egg on the cookie sheet.

"Why don't you eat out of the vending machines like everybody else?" a friend asked. Yet another observer suggested it would work better if I dropped an egg on the hood of somebody's car.

When you try to cook an egg in the sun, everybody's an expert.

Here's the outcome: None of the eggs sizzled. None of the egg whites turned white. The cream cheese broke up a little bit but it never melted completely. After about half an hour the yolk on the egg sitting directly on the pavement began to undergo some sort of disgusting metamorphosis, though you couldn't describe it as cooked.

The scrambled eggs eventually turned a little goopy, and the lone egg on the cookie sheet got a tan.

You're wondering why, if I lament writing this stupid column in the first place, I'm doing it again in this book. Friend, that's a darned good question.

In any case, I never got a call from any of the local TV stations offering me a job as a weatherman, or a spot doing my own cooking show.

For another column I wish I'd never done, I nominate my Polish Pope jokes column. I can blame this one partly on my rookie status. I wrote it in 1978, when I'd been doing columns for just a year and a half. I can also blame a lack of good taste, and a shortage of sensitivity. The occasion was that Cardinal Karol

Wojtyla had been named Pope John Paul II. So we had a Polish Pope, who replaced an Italian pope, Pope John Paul I. (George and Ringo never made the cut).

John Paul I had died in office after a very brief stint of Poping, which lead to my headline suggestion on that story, a headline that never saw print: "Too Pooped to Pope." I'm not sure which is more embarrassing to recall: that completely tasteless headline idea, or the pope jokes that actually made it into the paper.

I wrote the column as if other people were coming up and telling me these jokes. But I don't think that was the case. I think I was coming up with them in my own sick little head. Or maybe I was hearing them from equally tasteless people at bars around town. Like this:

A guy comes up and asks me if I know what town crier Cardinal Pericle Felici chanted after Cardinal Karol Wojtyla was chosen to be Pope John Paul II.

"What?" I ask.

"Annuntio vobis gaudium magnum: habemus Papam," he says.

"What's that mean?" I query.

"It means," he says, the silly leer taking over his face, "how many popes does it take to screw in a light bulb?"

I also wrote that "a man who should be dressed in a red rubber nose and large polka dot shoes" had asked me if I'd heard about the Shoes of the Fisherman.

"What, pray tell, about the Shoes of the Fisherman?" I ask in the column.

"They're bowling shoes," the guy says.

Like that. It was awful. I got a few complaints from Catholics. One was so heartfelt that I felt very small. What I mostly got, though, was the overwhelming silence that accompanies a complete flop.

You remember these bad ones years later, maybe even more than you remember the good ones.

Another disastrous story I did took place in 1987, when I drove with a news photographer all the way from Austin to the Texas-Louisiana border to interview N.L. Tindall, the sheriff of San Augustine County. Tindall had been the county sheriff in this small East Texas county since the 1940s. I was working on a ten-part series on "perfect" things and people in Texas: the perfect barbecued ribs (at the Country Tavern in Kilgore) the perfect job (ice cream taster at the Blue Bell plant in Brenham), the perfect truck stop (the Circle Bar Truck Corral in Ozona), and the perfect county sheriff.

I'd picked N.L. Tindall for this statewide honor because he was colorful, and because he had managed to stay in office since before David was a Las Vegas hotel statue. Tindall was known for letting the inmates in the jail in the county seat of San Augustine go home for Christmas Day, with the understanding they'd check themselves back into the lockup the next morning.

These sorts of "perfect" stories are subjective, of course. It's not like I interviewed every sheriff in the state to find the top lawman. I should have known from the get-go that there might be a problem. When we walked into Sheriff Tindall's office, he gave us a suspicious look and asked what kind of story I intended to do. (That should have been a clue. On the other hand, I get that question a lot. And that look.) I told Tindall the nature of the story, and he smiled.

All that day and the next morning, Sheriff Tindall put on a good ol' boy show for us. He loved, loved, *loved* the spotlight. He brought around some of the minority folks in town who were eager to give out quotes about what a great guy the sheriff was. The photographer, Lynne Dobson, who is now retired from the news biz (her family started the Whataburger chain, by the way), figures she shot five or six rolls of film, or around two hundred pictures, of the man. The sheriff had some ham in him, and he had no problem posing.

Over and over.

"He seemed like a good ol' boy sheriff, typical Texas sheriff," said Lynne. These days she's shooting photos for non-profits in Africa. She said, "I remember him being kinda heavyset and, you know, just kind of a regular guy. I remember him as not too country — he wasn't too extreme, like you'd expect for a small town county sheriff. He was a little more normal than I thought he would be."

When I got back to the newspaper from my East Texas trip, I mentioned to one of my fellow reporters, John Harris, the story I was doing on Sheriff Tindall, naming him the perfect Texas county sheriff. The story, I explained, would lead off a ten-part series on bests in Texas: the best ribs, the best cab driver, the best sheriff, and so on.

"You do know," John told me, "that Sheriff Tindall is being investigated for drugs by the Department of Public Safety."

Um, no, I hadn't known that. I made a phone call to DPS

and found out that indeed the sheriff was under investigation for some sort of drug violation. And I doubt if it was for smokin' pot. I freaked out on the spot and made a beeline for the editor's office to tell editor Arnold Rosenfeld the problem. As it turned out, the sheriff never got busted. But we didn't know at the time that that's how it would turn out. San Augustine is a close-lipped community, and finding out information about the sheriff wasn't easy. In 2012, I called the local newspaper in San Augustine, and the editor told me that his paper had no biographical information on the sheriff. Not a stitch. That despite the fact that the town's justice building is named the N.L. Tindall Building. That's East Texas for you.

"I remember being really bummed that the pictures were never going to run," Lynne recalled. "He was a photogenic type of guy and it was a beautiful historical city. Also, we had driven all that way (more than 300 miles). I was kinda disappointed after we had done all that work."

So the story went to waste, along with all those wonderful photos. The best sheriff in Texas story obviously never made it into the newspaper. Can you imagine the fool I would have looked like if it had? I would easily have made it into *Texas Monthly*'s Bum Steer Awards, maybe even the *Columbia Journalism Review* in a recap of idiot journalistic moves. Also, I probably would have gotten run out the front door of the *Austin-American Statesman*.

Because of the hole in my series that Sheriff Tindall's sudden absence had created, I had to rush over to Houston and do a filler piece on the best cabbie in Texas. Fortunately, the cab driver wasn't being investigated for drugs. Unfortunately, along with being Texas's perfect cab driver, he ~~may~~ also may have been Texas's most boring cab driver. But I slapped the story together as best I could.

Not nearly so bad, but perhaps even more spectacular, was a colorful headline I wrote back in Florida, to top a college football story when I was working on the sports desk at the *Palm Beach Post*. This occurred in the early '70s. Just about anyone who's ever been assigned to write headlines for a newspaper can tell you a yarn about the worst headline they ever wrote. Headlines are written on deadline, in a hurry, and they have to fit the space. Not only that, they also have to tell what the story is about in a few words. It's not an easy job.

So people come up with all sorts of embarrassing goofs. Goofs you wish you could grab and put back in the box.

The headline I wrote for the story on a USC-Oregon State football game was the most spectacular one I've ever come up with, and it was done completely unintentionally. USC had won the game. So the headline read, "Trojans Plunge Through Beavers."

I wonder how I'd look in a security guard uniform, I thought to myself when I picked up the paper the next morning and read the headline. Fortunately, I'm the only person who noticed it, as far as I know. At least nobody ever mentioned it.

All I can say is, "Whew."

Another column I wish I'd never done is the one I wrote in 2006 about Robert Gates, former president of Texas A&M, when he was named Secretary of the Defense replacing Donald Rumsfeld. I've written plenty of columns making fun of A&M,

and this is the only one I regret. It's not that the column was totally without merit. It had some pretty good lines in it. For example, I pointed out that Texas A&M and defense go hand and hand. And that before Dennis Francione was named football coach, the Aggies actually had one.

I also wrote that Gates was in for it, because if he thought the Aggies' game against Army was tough, wait 'til he had to deal with the Mahdi army. Where I screwed up was the line that followed that remark: "On the other hand, Corps of Cadets, Abu Ghraib: what's the difference?"

I never should have included that observation. Aggies around the state were incensed that I was comparing their beloved Corps of Cadets with the prison abuse in Iraq. I kind of knew it was coming. The day before the column ran, I went to my boss Fred Zipp and asked him about it. Fred said maybe we should substitute the Abu Ghraib line with a better one. But we couldn't think of a better one, so we went with what we had.

Big mistake. If I had it to do over again, I wouldn't. Sorry, Ags.

Some Little Stuff I Liked

For a series of articles about the oddest jobs in Texas, I spent a couple of days hanging out at Frank Funai's Poultry Sexing Service in the East Texas town of Nacogdoches.

The chicken-sexing gig entailed workers sitting up all night looking at chicken butts. Yes, literally all night. The crew would show up for work around 11:00 p.m. and work until daylight. And there was no time for goofing off. A good chicken sexer could inspect about a thousand chicken butts an hour. No kidding. I'm not sure I'd want to look at that many chicken butts in my entire life, let alone an hour.

The boy chicks went in one box for shipping, and the girl chicks went in another box for shipping. This job required several steps, the first of which was "squirting the chicken."

Squirting the chicken works like this, although you kids shouldn't try this in the living room. You pick up the little yellow chick, aim its hind end at a coffee can, and squeeze the tailbone lightly.

This sends a stream of digested egg yoke into the can. The

chicken sexers did this out of self-defense, "So you don't get it in the face," Funai explained.

Covering this story was so memorable that I still keep my Frank Funai's Chicken Sexing Service souvenir pen in my desk drawer at work. I take it out every once in a while to impress people.

Most people, however, don't seem all that bowled over by it.

Another part of that eight-part series on odd jobs around Texas was a story about the tourism director of Killeen. Killeen, home of Fort Hood, a gigantic Army base about an hour north of Austin, isn't the sort of town where you'd expect to see a lot of tourists. There were twenty-four pawnbrokers in town when I wrote the story in 1988. Pawnshops, fast food joints, and used car lots: that's Killeen.

Still, Killeen Tourism Director Joanie Duncan came up with the most clever tourism campaign slogan I've ever seen. "Tanks for the Memories," read the side of the souvenir olive drab first aid kits the town gave out to visitors. For years, I kept that first aid kit in the glove box of my car. I wish I still had it. I'm not sure how many people based their vacation plans around that campaign slogan, however.

On the other hand, Killeen could also boast of having a $7,700 wax dummy of a hollow-eyed Saddam Hussein, looking as disheveled as he did when he was found hiding in a hole near Tikrit, Iraq, by U.S. Forces in December 2003. The statue could be found at the 4th Infantry Division's Museum at Fort Hood. And if that doesn't get you in the car headed to Killeen, I don't know what will. That wax dummy sure inspired me to drive to

Killeen to take its picture, as soon as I heard about it being on display.

Another story that caught my fancy? The tale of Russell Slaton, of Malakoff, another little town in East Texas. Russell is a University of Texas football fan who can play the Aggie War Hymn under his armpit. He used to wear a completely orange outfit to Longhorn football games. He looked like a tangerine with ears. He learned armpit music in grade school, and he could also do the Star Spangled Banner, and Boomer Sooner, the University of Oklahoma fight song. However, he refused to armpit the Eyes of Texas, because he thought that would be demeaning to the University of Texas.

Russell's talents were so remarkable that I managed to get him an appearance on the Jay Leno show. (I used to get calls a couple times a year from one of Leno's staff members, who was in charge of finding eccentric guests for the show.) Russell fit the bill. He also got a mention in *Texas Monthly*'s Bum Steer Awards, which are reserved for people who do stupid yet colorful things.

Russell performed his music by cupping his hand under his armpit, and flapping his arm like a chicken trying to take flight. "Either you get someone rolling on the floor or you get a blank stare. There's no in-between," Russell said. I was in the rolling-on-the-floor category, but then I'm easily amused.

Also worthy of mention is D. Alan Calhoun, the El Paso furniture maker who could hammer a nail up his nose. Calhoun made it into my funny travel book, *Texas Curiosities*, which I researched by driving about 13,000 miles all over the State of Texas in 1999.

Calhoun had learned his nail-up-nose stunt while working at a carnival. The carnies showed him how he didn't need a hammer to get the job done. If you placed the nail just so, you could push it right on up there. The hammer was just for effect. So Calhoun took me into the office of his furniture business in El Paso and performed the trick for me. But he closed the door first because he said it freaked out his employees.

Before he put the nail up his nose, he asked me if I minded a little blood. He just said that for effect. There was no blood. But he did use the hammer for tapping purposes. Tink, tink tink, and the nail went right up his nose.

Then there was Joe Doyle, who said he had known a guy in Army basic training back in 1969 who could perform the tune of Yankee Doodle by breaking wind.

Joe was working in Austin as locations manager for Heartbreak Films when I interviewed him. He said that the kid's name was Byndum, and that he had one show business flaw: he only knew one song. But he could get far enough into Yankee Doodle so that people knew he wasn't performing the 1812 Overture.

I found that impressive.

In 1987, Dino Lee, an Austin musician who had a band called Dino Lee & His Luv Johnson, said the reason he was stopped on South Congress Avenue in a rented purple '86 Caddy was that the cops thought he was a pimp.

This occurred back in the day when prostitutes were marching up and down South Congress, looking for business. As it turned out, Dino, who wore a purple pompadour wig on stage, spent the night in the City Jail for an unpaid traffic ticket.

When he was pulled over, Dino's rented Caddy was packed with his stuff, which included a blue-streaked wig, and a rhinestone decorated fur coat with a pink lining.

The cops nabbed Dino while he was checking out room rates at the State Motel. "The first cop questioning me said, 'You're a pimp, aren't you?'" Dino recalled. "'Nobody but a pimp could afford a car like this.'" I hope Dino remembered to tell the cop it was a rental.

In the spring of 2010, Patty Everett was driving on South Congress Avenue, near Hill's Café, when she noticed a snake coming out of the AC vent of her SUV. Patty, from Spicewood, had her grandbaby in the back seat at the time.

I asked Patty if she was scared when she saw the snake, and she replied, "Well, somebody crapped in my pants." Turns out the snake was probably a harmless bull snake and nobody got hurt. But it did cause a stir. "I'm thinking about three and a half to four inches of his body was hanging out of my vent," Patty said. "I started screaming, 'There's a snake in the car.'"

So she pulled over, grabbed the grandbaby and scampered out. "I didn't realize I had lost a shoe," she said. You know you're making a dash for it when you outrun your shoe.

You hear about college kids who have a hard time nailing that degree? Bill Scarborough, who was 39 when I talked to him in 1988, may have set the record. At the time he had been going to college off and on for twenty years, and he had piled up 241 semester hours from three different schools: Austin Community College, Southwestern University in Georgetown, and the University of Texas.

And he still didn't have a bachelor's degree.

Funny thing is, you only need 120 credit hours for a bachelor's degree, but as Bill pointed out, "You need the proper courses, in the proper places, and in the proper sequence."

Part of Bill's problem may have been that for fourteen years he lived in the Loud Hall at the Ark, a long-gone student co-op on Pearl Street, near the University of Texas campus. The Loud Hall was for students who didn't mind loud distractions, such as a guy in the room next door playing "Smoke on the Water" on electric guitar at 3:00 in the morning.

On the other hand, maybe Bill just took the wrong courses — such as one called "The Vampire in Eastern Europe," which studied vampire lore. It's pretty hard to get your degree in vampire, I guess.

There isn't a lot of colorful gambling in Austin, but you take what you can get. Back in 1987, when I visited a chili cook-off at VFW Post 8925 in Pilot Knob, southeast of downtown Austin, some of the cook-off spectators were gambling on rats. If you ask me, this was gaming at its finest. The rats were honest, and there were no lines.

Let me set the scene for you. The Post had put together this circular wooden contraption with colorful holes on the top — yellow, red, blue, white, and grey. Meanwhile, a retired Army sergeant named Robert Walden, a.k.a. Bob, was serving as rat handler. Bob was holding a live rat underneath a plastic motel ice bucket.

People were betting quarters on their favorite hole. If the rat ran into your hole after its release from the ice bucket, you'd win some money. Bob explained the game was called "the rat race." He added that extra rats were kept on the premises in a box or a garbage can, in case the rat under the ice bucket got "tired" or "lazy" and needed another rat to take over.

All of the money the rats brought in that day went to charity. On the day of my visit, they raised $170.55.

Oh, almost forgot. Most of the rat holes paid 2-1, but the yellow hole was the biggie, paying off at 8-1, since there was only one yellow hole.

Furthermore, the rats put on an exciting display. "And all the people who are playing, they usually holler at 'em to go in a certain hole," Bob said.

People in the Austin area have long been concerned with preserving the environment. Charlie Loving, of Round Rock, did his part to save the planet by not mowing his yard.

In 1986, Charlie discovered the reason he'd never have to mow again when he looked out the window and saw a bunch of people walking around in his yard, some of them wearing pith helmets. They had pulled up out front in a small bus. They hadn't called ahead.

Some were taking pictures. Others were taking notes. All of them were checking out the plants in Charlie's unmowed yard. Some of them "looked like the guys who go out chasing butterflies," Charlie said.

Turns out the unexpected visitors were a tour group brought to Charlie's yard by the Austin Parks and Recreation Department's Nature Preserves System. Seems that Charlie's yard was an acre of undisturbed prairie, and it had all sorts of rare grasses and plants flourishing in it — such as blue grama and sideoats grama.

And Charlie had thought they were a bunch of weeds. But what made Charlie happy was that now he had an excuse not to do yard work. Not that he really needed one. He said he had gone out with a Weed Eater once during the two years he'd been living there, "but it was hot and I lost interest pretty quick."

It was funny little stories such as these that made my day.

Expense Accounts

I didn't do a lot of it, but I was always proud when I managed to expense-account stuff that looked particularly goofy on the form you fill out to get your money back. Like, say, "dog massage."

On these occasions, the point wasn't to screw the company out of money. Far from it. The point was to create an expense account for something so unusual that the expense-account form would be suitable for framing. So just for the thrill of it, I took my little dog Harry to Paulette Glorya Gutchess, a certified animal therapist who lives in South Austin, to get him massaged doggy-style, so to speak.

I left Harry off at Paulette's second-floor apartment for a few hours of canine rubbing. Frankly, the whole thing freaked him out. Harry had been shipped around during his life, having lived with different owners. So I suspect that Harry thought I was leaving him there. You would have thought Paulette's Enya tape playing in the background would have helped sooth the dog's nerves, but it didn't. Harry was a nervous wreck.

By the way, if a dog starts getting hyper during the massage, Paulette sprays it with an essential oil called Calm and Peace. "The spray just calms them down," she said. "It releases endorphins." I wrote about this in my column, holding that the spray also makes the dog want to go to a Grateful Dead concert.

Paulette has a way with critters. She told me that she actually communicated with animals, and once talked to a cow out at Krause Springs, a beautiful spring-fed pool and swimming hole about thirty-five miles northwest of Austin in Spicewood Springs. Paulette said that during the conversation the cow was "nonchalant."

"I just happened to be camping one time, and I saw this cow, and I said, 'How you doing?' and he goes, 'Okay,' " Paulette said of her meeting with the cow at Krause Springs. "I said, 'How do you feel about people eating you?' He said, 'I don't care.' He was just happy to be a cow."

So you vegetarians who are worried about the feelings of the animals you are eating: don't. They're cool with it, if you can trust this conversation Paulette had with a cow. On the other hand, this might have been one particularly laid-back cow, and not representative of cows in general.

I thought Paulette's prices for her services were fairly reasonable. She charged me $30 for Harry's massage. Seems like she could have charged a lot more. Hey, if somebody is silly enough to spend money on a dog massage, you could probably soak 'em with a big bill and get away with it.

Anyway, I was so tickled with the dog massage that I had the expense account framed. I think today it's sitting somewhere in my closet. I'm pretty sure I also framed the expense account for the $3 ticket I bought in 1992 to get into the pig races at the Texas International Livestock Exposition, held at the Texas Exposition & Heritage Center northeast of downtown Austin.

The racing pigs, under the direction of Colonel Mel Silverlake, swine master for Robinson's Racing Pigs of Tampa, Florida, ran on a 150-foot sawdust oval decorated with red and white pennants. These hogs, Silverlake said, could hit speeds of about fourteen miles an hour. I asked what gets them to pick 'em up and lay 'em down at that incredible speed, and Colonel Silverlake said, "It's the Oreo cookie we place at the finish line."

I should mention that among the eight running pigs competing at Pork Chop Downs were Hammy Faye Bacon and Arnold Snortzenhogger.

I'll bet nationally respected columnist George Will never saw Arnold Snortzenhogger run. And if he did, I'll bet he didn't bother to expense-account the ticket — or have it framed.

So the race starts when Silverlake plays "Old McDonald Had a Farm" on a small tape machine ("Here an oink, there an oink...")

Sometimes management would get stingy over an expense account. In 1990 the newspaper sent me to Earth, Texas, population 1,512, a town in the south plains, to write about the Earth Day Celebration, which was held a day before the real Earth Day. It was done that way so that Earth, the only Earth on planet Earth, could go first and get the publicity.

So this was the biggest Earth Day ever in the U.S., on planet Earth, or in the town of Earth, Texas. For the occasion, nine trees had been planted in Earth, which is a lot of trees for a farming community in the south plains. That's not a part of the country that is exactly ate up with trees. I remember that morning as I drove toward Earth that the early-morning fog was the thickest I'd ever seen in my life. Not that the fog blocking the view mattered. Aren't a lot of scenic visits in that part of the state.

VISTAS

Anyway, this Earth Day celebration was a big deal, because up 'til then, Earth had enjoyed its biggest moment when allegedly the entire town had gathered at the Dairy Queen for a group photo that was used in a Dairy Queen TV ad. You may remember it. (Or not.) But this Earth Day celebration was almost as big as that DQ moment. They had a dunking booth. Agriculture Commissioner Jim Hightower spoke, among others. Speakers spoke about planting and other green subjects from a flatbed truck usually used to haul hay. You could get a "Hello From Earth" T-shirt (I got one; I wish I knew where it is), and music was provided by the Springlake-Earth Junior and Senior High School band.

The previous day I had been in Turkey, Texas, home of country-western music legend Bob Wills. I was working on a story about the problems at the local landfill, or, if you prefer, the dump. I've always disliked pretense, so I'm a proponent of the word dump, over landfill. Anyway, I was busy during this two-day trip, so I didn't have much time to dine. Besides, this being the remote part of Texas, where would I dine anyway? Would I stop at an Allsup's convenience store for the burritos? No thanks, I just shined my shoes.

So I bought a bag of jalapeno peanuts from a designer peanut shop in downtown Turkey to tide me over. The peanuts cost about

$6, if I remember right. This was the fanciest peanut store I've ever set foot in. It had several flavors of peanuts available, and these jalapeno peanuts I purchased were really tasty.

That's about all I ate during my two days of roaming the Panhandle — jalapeno peanuts. I munched on them out of the bag in the front seat of my rental car as I tooled on down the road. When I got back to the paper in Austin, I expense-accounted the peanuts. "Peanuts — $6," I wrote down on the form, or something close to it. And that was about all I expense-accounted under food, because that's about all I ate on that trip.

A couple days later one of the high-ranking editors at the *Statesman* came out of his glass office. "I've got one word for you," he said.

"What's that?"

"Peanuts," he said.

Apparently the managing editor had crabbed to this guy about my expense-accounting those jalapeno peanuts. At the time, the newspaper's managing editor was kind of a tightwad. And no, I never had the peanuts expense account framed. Maybe I should have.

The Wilson Years

"I don't need no gas or oil,
Long as I got Darrell Royal,
Ridin' on the dashboard of my car..."

To be a proper University of Texas football fan, it helps to have the juvenile behavior gene. One illustration of this is the special way U.T. fans tell time. Texas fans have their own special time zone. Not to be confused with Eastern, Pacific or Mountain Time, O.U. Time provides a way for Longhorn fans to hurl yet another insult at the University of Oklahoma Sooners, Texas's bitter football rival from north of the Red River.

Here's how O.U. Time works:

Somebody in a group of Texas fans, perhaps gathered in a state parking garage in Austin before the game, will holler to the rest of the bunch, "Hey, (Leroy, Buster, Lloyd, whatever), what time is it?" Then the person addressed will holler back, "7:09, and O.U. still sucks."

That's when all of the assembled Longhorn fans, many of them grown men clutching cans of beer, and sporting large bellies under burnt orange T-shirts, will guffaw as if they'd never heard that joke before, even though they may already have repeated it half a dozen times before kickoff.

I didn't know about this tradition until I began hanging out with my friend Scott Wilson in the 1990s. That's when I started going to U.T. football games with Wilson, an Austin attorney who has been to every Texas Longhorn football game since the Arkansas game in 1977. He would have made that one, too, probably. But it occurred the weekend Wilson was moving into his Northeast Austin house, the same one he lives in today. The one that has a game room with the walls and ceilings completely covered in ball caps from various brake job repair shops, barbecue places and the like.

Do I need to tell you Wilson is single?

As of the summer of 2012, Wilson had been to 422 U.T. football games in a row. This includes home games, away games, and bowl games, games in Hawaii, games in California, games in Kansas, games in Wyoming. If Texas scheduled a game with the University of Mars, Wilson would call NASA. This guy has been to so many Holiday Bowl games in San Diego ("Five, I believe.") that he's sick of the place.

How could anybody get sick of a beautiful city like San Diego? "Sometimes if you go to the same place often enough, it starts looking like Waco," Wilson explained.

I asked Wilson what would make him miss a game, and he said, "Death."

It's not that Wilson doesn't have a life. For years he took

care of his bed-ridden mother pretty much all by himself. But what makes him tick is being there for the game.

Wilson has become something of a celebrity in U.T. fandom circles. Like Madonna, he is known by one name: Wilson. He has dedicated his life to attending U.T. sporting events. He scoffs at people who go to games only when U.T. is winning, calling them "front-runners." Wilson is not a front-runner. Winning or clobbered, Wilson is at the game.

Sometimes he flies; sometimes he drives or is chauffeured by a friend to games in his vintage 1975 burnt orange Cadillac with the steer horns mounted on the hood. Right this minute in my iPhone is a photo of Wilson, wearing a smile as big as Texas and standing next to his beloved Caddy with four other guys — guys he might know by first name only.

"Hey, Wilson."

"Hi Bob, you know Jim? Jim, you know Bob?" And on and on. Each of the four other guys is smiling big, too. It's as if they are the best of friends and they haven't seen each other in years.

And for this moment, they are best friends, because they have a common denominator. They're about to go to a Texas football game, and there's nothing you can put in a Christmas card photo they'd rather be doing.

I wonder how many such pictures Wilson has been in, standing and beaming around his Caddy with fellow buddies in orange attire. Heck, it may have reached a thousand snapshots by now. You could paper an entire den with these photos, I'd wager.

This is the second such Caddy Wilson has owned. He paid about $50 for the first one. "Chote's Wrecker Service found it by the side of the road," Wilson said. The engine on the first Caddy blew up on the highway in Tonkawa, Oklahoma, while Wilson was returning home from the College World Series in 2002. Along with baseball and football, he also goes to Texas men's and women's basketball games, softball, soccer, and volleyball games. "And swimming and tennis some, too," Wilson said.

It would take a natural disaster to keep Wilson from making it to a game. One evening on the drive over to College Station from Austin, for a U.T.-Texas A&M basketball game, the engine in Wilson's old Honda burst into flames. So he pulled over to the side of the road, and he and his three ticket-scalper friends who were along for the ride put the fire out by pouring the contents of their cooler — melted ice and canned beer — onto the burning motor.

"What ultimately put it out was the beer," Wilson said later. The four of them left the car by the road and hitchhiked the rest of the way to College Station. They made it to the game in time to see the second half.

Which reminds me: what time is it? Well, whatever it is, O.U. still sucks.

If you go to every single University of Texas football game for thirty-five years, you've got to assume that sometimes it will be hard to get a ticket, particularly to road games. That might be true, but somehow Wilson always finds a way. For example, in 2012, there weren't many tickets available for Longhorn fans who wanted to go to the game at Mississippi. So Wilson solved the problem by buying a season's ticket to all of Mississippi's football games for the year. Sure, it cost him a little over $200 to get into one game. But he figured he could sell the tickets to games he wouldn't be attending to Mississippi fans, who would use them. That way, he'd make his money back and get into the stadium for the U.T./Mississippi game, too.

Another time Wilson and several other friends and I needed to get into a particular football game in Austin. Trouble was, we were one ticket short. As is often the case, Wilson knew the ticket taker working the gate. So we just kinda conga-lined our way into the stadium. And coincidentally the old boy taking the tickets seemed not to notice. If there's a way into the place, Wilson figures it out.

Wilson is a graduate of the University of Texas, but he got his law degree from Baylor University, although Wilson wouldn't go across the street to watch a Baylor game unless Baylor was playing Texas. Yet he would drive all the way from Austin to Ames, Iowa, to watch Texas play Iowa State in a baseball series. In fact, he's done just that. He figures he's been to about twice as many U.T. baseball games in a row as he has football games. As of March 2012, the baseball figure was 784 games in a row, with approximately 2,500 baseball games in all.

Some people go to Paris on vacation. Wilson goes to Omaha for the College World Series every June, whether Texas makes it into the tournament or not. He's been to thirty-three College World Series. There's a special place in his heart for college baseball.

Wilson is a member of a loose-knit group of U.T. baseball fans called the Wild Bunch. They are of an age now that someone jokingly referred to them as the Mild Bunch. The Wild Bunch sits behind third base at Disch-Falk Field, the Longhorns' ballpark, and raises hell with the umpires, the opposing team's players, and even one another. They also cut up on the road. During a U.T. baseball game at Arlington Stadium in 1976, something that Wilson refers to as "the tennis ball incident" took place. The Wild Bunch had brought a hundred tennis balls to the game, which they passed out in the stands. The announcer on the loudspeaker kept reminding the fans to "please return all balls to the playing field."

So after one such announcement, one person stood up and tossed a tennis ball on the field, which was apparently a signal for everybody else to hurl their tennis balls onto the field as well.

Soon the playing field was covered with tennis balls.

Wilson's home in North Austin is a good old boy's living museum. He has a game room with a tiny pool table, and as I mentioned, the walls and ceiling are completely covered in ball caps. Wilson figures there are 2,500-3,000 ball caps in the room.

"I had to box up some of them a few months ago just to clear a path," he said. "There may be a body in there someplace, for all we know." One of Wilson's hats said, simply, "Arkansas State Bird." Another, from a petroleum outfit called Saunco Pump Rentals, says, "Our Pumps Suck." Yet another hat says "I (Heart) Intercourse," a town in Pennsylvania. Then there's the "TCU Crowd Control" hat. "This was from a time when a TCU sports crowd was about three people," Wilson explained.

The living room is plastered with U.T. sports memorabilia, much of it about Wilson, and one small part of it about me. Included on the walls is a letter some old lady wrote to me excoriating me for writing a column about how drunk I got at my first Oklahoma-Texas football game at the Texas State Fair up in Dallas. She laid into me pretty good, and told me I should be ashamed of myself.

Speaking of that, Wilson's garage serves as home to a beer can collection. Wilson being somewhat, uh, overly organized, the cans are lined up by brand, alphabetically.

Traveling with Wilson on road trips can be an adventure, and not only because he loves both his beer *AND* White Russians. Since the man has invested nearly all of his money on attending U.T. sports, he travels on the cheap. Wilson isn't a big donor to the U.T. sports programs. He's not a rich man. But he's undoubtedly given a bigger percentage of his income to U.T. sports than the millionaire contributors.

Be that as it may, if you're staying with Wilson on a football road trip, you're staying at Motel 6, unless he decides to splurge and ends up at the Super 8. During baseball trips, Wilson will stay at higher priced digs. On those trips he likes to stay where the baseball team stays. But during football season, Wilson's idea of hotel amenities are (a) cable TV and (b) a working ice machine. And his concept of fine dining is a double-meat cheeseburger eaten in the back seat while somebody else is driving.

I've seen heated arguments between Wilson and a traveling companion about whether they should (a) eat the double meat cheeseburgers in the restaurant or (b) eat in the car and keep going. Wilson is always a proponent of eating in the car.

On special occasions, like say, sunup, Wilson likes to drink. So over the years he's had hundreds of designated drivers, all of them friends who have volunteered for that duty. Designated drivers get a T-shirt from Wilson for performing that task. Each one says, "I drove the Caddy home" on it, with quotes from the likes of Michael Martin Murphy, John Carlos, and the band Mike and the Mechanics on the back. Over the years I think I've earned at least three of these shirts.

Wilson has had piles of those orange and white T-shirts made up. In recent years, however, he has needed fewer designated drivers. So he gives out the shirts to friends as souvenirs, whether they drive the Caddy or not. Some people like to collect them.

Now don't get the idea that Wilson is some dumb sports jock. His observations on the world condition are pithy, sometimes bordering on redneck brilliant. In 2008 an Austin strip club was sued by *American Idol* for trademark infringement for holding an event called Stripper Idol.

"With the economy the way it is, I would think we'd have a lot more idle strippers than we would have Stripper Idols," Wilson observed.

In 2003, for the first time ever, the Texas House decorated its chambers with a synthetic Christmas tree. Wilson attributed this to the fact that then-House Speaker Tom Craddick was from Midland, where trees of any sort are in short supply.

"I wouldn't be surprised in West Texas if they just dressed up a telephone pole," Wilson said.

It's sometimes a challenge to go on the road with Wilson. There was the football game in Pittsburgh in 1994. We were in a sports bar in downtown Pittsburgh on a Friday night. The place was packed with guys drinking beer. Wilson was leading cheers for, of all things, the Dallas Cowboys. Here he was, in Steeler country, and he was leading Cowboys cheers. Turns out the

Cowboys were playing the Steelers that weekend in Pittsburgh. So to lead the cheers properly, Wilson decided he needed to climb up on a chair.

The bartender, a large guy, told Wilson to get down from the chair before he broke his neck. Wilson dutifully climbed down. But he says he misunderstood the bartender's intention. He thought the bartender was telling him not to hold onto a glass partition near the chair. So he left the partition alone, and climbed back onto the chair.

Wilson thought the bartender was out of line for throwing him out of the bar. He thought he'd done what the bartender had told him to do. But the bartender was in no mood to quibble. So he walked over to Wilson, put his hand around the back of Wilson's neck, pointed toward the door, and said, "You. Outta here," as he led Wilson out of the place and left him on the street.

The bartender's pointing toward the door reminded me of the way Babe Ruth pointed toward centerfield in a World Series game against the Cubs back in the Thirties, right before he knocked that famous home run out of the park. The difference was that this time, Wilson was the ball.

I can still envision Wilson out on the sidewalk in Pittsburgh, looking at us through the sports bar's plate glass window as we finished his beer. Hey, somebody had to do it.

That whole weekend was full of colorful behavior. After watching Texas whip the University of Pittsburgh (just barely) on Saturday, we tried unsuccessfully to get tickets to the Cowboys-Steelers game the next day. The scalpers wanted $200 and up, however. So we blew off the ticket search and settled into a bar to watch the game.

Lance Beversdorff, our traveling companion and another Longhorn fan, decided after a few beers that it was high time to show the people of Pittsburgh a dance he called "The Alligator." This involved Lance, a middle-aged family man, lying on the floor of the bar, stomach down, and flopping like a gaffed fish. The bar wasn't all that full, and those in attendance didn't seem overly interested. This did not concern Lance, however, who put on a real floorshow. Road trips with Wilson are sort of like being in a fraternity house with really old members. For the Pittsburgh trip, Wilson and I shared a room in a motel with some other old guy/friend of Wilson's. I got a bed, the other guy got a bed, and Wilson got the sleeping bag on the floor.

In the middle of the night, I felt this lumpy presence lying on top of me. It was Wilson, who had plopped down on me (back first fortunately), while still asleep. He was walking in his sleep, or perhaps I should say staggering in his sleep.

I swore loudly at Wilson, hollered and pushed him off. He stumbled on back to the sleeping bag on the floor. After that, I started getting my own room.

I recall that even the plane ride home from the Pittsburgh game was, uh, entertaining. In the airport, I saw an old codger wearing one of those annoying envelope-shaped VFW hats that retired military geezers seem to favor. I could tell by the glaze of his eyes that the old boy, who was in his eighties, was in his cups. As it turned out, he had been hitting the wine. He'd spent the weekend at a VFW convention, and now he was heading home to Houston via airplane.

The old man was wandering around stoned in an airport restaurant when I saw him. My mistake was making eye contact with him. Soon he was sitting at our table, uninvited.

I told Wilson on the sly that I hoped this guy wouldn't be on our airplane — but of course he was. He was sitting about five rows behind us on the plane, in the middle of a bunch of U.T. students, who were egging him on to sing *The Eyes of Texas* at full throat. The old man did some other numbers, too, including the French favorite, *Alouette*. He was loud, and he was hammered.

A male flight attendant tried to get the old fellow to calm down and shut up, with no luck. He just kept singing. When the plane reached the runway in Houston for the landing, the old man decided it was time to stand up in the aisle. The flight attendant asked him to sit down. He didn't. "You can't tell me what to do; I outrank you," the old man said from under his VFW cap.

Since the guy wouldn't sit down, the pilot stopped the plane on the tarmac to wait until the old man did sit down. I spoke with the old buzzard on our way out of the plane, and he said, "What do I care? I'll never see these people again."

The airplane crew thought about having the old pest arrested at the gate in Houston, but when they learned his son was going to meet him, they decided to blow it off. I imagine these days he's singing *Alouette* in a nursing home.

Wilson and I also took a trip to the Syracuse game in 1992. In and around the football game we visited both a replica of President Millard Fillmore's boyhood home and the actual location of his boyhood home. We also visited Niagara Falls, as well as a metal kazoo factory and museum.

When you hang out with Wilson, you meet a lot of characters. One was a guy named Gabe Trinidad, the only man who's ever been able to get me to climb inside a police car just as a lark.

About fifteen years ago at the O.U.-Texas football game in Dallas, Gabe and I were walking out of the Texas Fairgrounds after O.U. had stomped Texas yet again. Gabe was nipping on a col'beer when a Dallas cop car rolled slowly past us with two cops in the front. As it did, Gabe hollered, "How about a ride?" He was joking, but the cops stopped anyway and one of them invited us to get in their squad car.

I thought this an extremely bad idea. I mean, Gabe had an open beer, and we'd both been drinking. But he climbed in the back seat and after about two seconds of deep thought, I lumbered in behind him. I was pretty sure we were going to jail.

Instead, the cops started chitchatting with us about the game. They talked about how that evening happy Okie fans around Dallas would be partying big-time, raising hell. These cops were so friendly it was as if they had been sent by the Dallas Chamber of Commerce.

After a couple of minutes of this camaraderie, Gabe asked, from his spot in the back seat, if the cops could give us a ride to our tailgate party a few blocks away. They said sure. Then Gabe asked one more favor.

He asked if they could turn on the bubblegum machine lights on top of the cop car as they pulled into our tailgate area. That way they could scare the snot out of all of our friends who were partying.

They did it. The cops actually turned on their cop lights. Then they jumped out of the car and posed for pictures. They didn't ask us to send them the photos for their Christmas cards, however.

My relationship with Wilson, strangely enough, has also led me to dabble in the arts. If I hadn't become a Longhorn season ticket holder, I never would have instigated the creation of the artwork known as Okie Pokie. Okie Pokie is a likeness of an Okie made out of plywood and cow chips.

In case you're not from Texas, let me explain that a cow chip is a dried-up cow patty.

This escapade started when I found out that the town of Beaver, Oklahoma, collected and sold cow chips by mail order. Nearly every year I write a column dissing O.U., and I'm always looking for new angles to make Oklahoma look trashy. So one year, Beaver was it.

Beaver, you see, billed itself as "the cow chip capital of the world." Seems it's customary in some southwestern states, including Texas, for fairs to have cow chip-throwing contests. And if there's one thing Beaver has, it's cow poop. Thus it was Beaver's contention that if you wanted your contest to be official, you had to use cow chips from Beaver. Only in Oklahoma would cow poop be a marketing tool.

The Beaver County Sheltered Workshop actually sent developmentally disabled people out into the fields around the Greater Beaverplex to gather up the cow pies. Then they'd box them up and send them to customers for a price.

In 2002, I bought a box of Beaver cow chips for $28.34,

after being told a box contains 40-70 cow chips. I don't remember if I counted them. But I did expense-account the cow chips. I even blew up the expense account form, suitable for framing. "Cowchip Sculpture," it says on the form.

Then I got my artist buddy Bob "Daddy-O" Wade to design a sculpture made of cow chips. I named this work of art "Okie Pokie." My idea was to take this Sooner likeness made of cow dung to the annual O.U.-Texas football game at the Cotton Bowl. And that's just what we did. We put Okie Pokie on wheels. The Friday night before the game, Okie Pokie went to a party in Dallas and posed with a couple of University of Texas cheerleaders. Then the next morning we rolled Okie Pokie into the Cotton Bowl right up to Big Tex, the huge talking cowboy statue that greets visitors to the Texas State Fair. We took photos of Okie Pokie standing in front of Big Tex. Talk about your Kodak moment.

We got a bunch of dirty looks from Oklahoma fans, but no fistfights broke out, probably because they had no clue as to what was going on. Okie Pokie, however, didn't get to go to the game inside the Cotton Bowl, and it never made it to an art museum. Okie Pokie is still leaning up against a wall in Wilson's garage.

For years I've thought that the University of Texas should honor Wilson for his loyalty to the school's athletic programs. No, he hasn't given millions of dollars to the school, because he doesn't have that kind of dough. But if he had it, he would sure give it.

So why not put a statue of him over in the corner of Royal-

Memorial Stadium next to Earl Campbell's statue? And, of course, Wilson's statue would be holding a col'beer and wearing a T-shirt that says, "I Drove the Caddy Home." Even if he didn't actually do the driving.

A Rolling Ball of Go

I want to talk about the best editor I ever worked for. I'm not talking big-office, meet-the-Chamber-of-Commerce, run-the-show executive-type editor. I'm talking editor who can read stuff and improve it.

As far as treating his reporters right, and being an interesting character, for my money nobody did it better than assistant city editor Gary Rice.

Gary, who worked at the *American-Statesman* from 1980 to 1989, was the kind of guy who could spot the weakness in your story and tell you in easy-to-understand terms how to fix this mess. Maybe you needed to make one more phone call. Maybe you needed to get in the car and see the subject face to face to get some color. Maybe you needed to move this paragraph down here up to the top.

Gary knew how to do that, and he knew how to do it in a pleasant, confidence-building way. He didn't belittle his reporters. You didn't feel like you were being scolded when Gary helped you with your copy. You figured you were talking to a friend, and your friend knew what he was doing.

Whenever we'd get young reporters in the newsroom, usually Gary would be called on to give them a hand. These days he's teaching journalism at Fresno State University in California.

But even more fascinating than Gary's work were his hobbies. He's one busy mo-fo. Gary is a rollin' ball of go. This guy managed bands around Austin; went on a binge of climbing mountains around the country (in 2011 he climbed 150 mountains, some as high as 14,000 feet); flew around the country to so many NASCAR races one year that he piled up enough frequent flyer miles to take his spring break in Shanghai; enjoyed professional wrestling; and amassed a collection of more than six thousand records and CDs.

Stuff always seems to happen to Gary.

In 1983 Gary, Joe Vargo, the *American-Statesman*'s cop reporter at the time, and I had gone to lunch at the Maverick Steak House, a chicken-fried steak kind of place at 922 Congress Avenue, within spittin' distance of the Texas Capitol. I was there to work on a story about the life-sized brown and white papier-mâché and chicken wire steer that twirled clockwise on a platform over the front door.

The story was that, years ago, the steer hadn't been a steer at all, but an anatomically accurate bull. Bob Mosley, Jr., who opened the place in 1963 and who had fed LBJ, said that the steer had gotten him a late-night phone call years ago from City Council member Emma Lou Long, who was displeased by the precise anatomy of the steer. Mosley said she told him if he wanted to keep his sign permit, he'd better make a few strategic cuts on that bull.

So Mosley and Vince Davis, his then business partner, went outside on Congress Avenue at 2:00 in the morning and performed surgery with a "hacksaw and a damned ax," as Mosley recounted the story.

So I was hanging around gathering information for that story, with Gary and Joe along for lunch, when a fly landed on Gary's strawberry shortcake. Gary tried to backhand the bug, but he missed it and hit the shortcake's whipped cream, which flew across the room and landed on the pants of Mosley's son, Bob Mosley III, at the next table.

Bob III didn't seem to mind, but a gal sitting across the table from him got huffy, glared at Gary, and said, "Well. Excuse me." She had on black business attire, now snow-flaked by the whipped cream. This incident had "trip to the dry cleaners" written all over it. Meanwhile, Gary attempted to become invisible.

It was always something with Gary. He just seemed to attract eccentric people. One time when we were in a convenience store parking lot up in Dallas, for example, some guy with a bunch of stolen musical equipment tried to sell it to Gary, even though Gary had never seen the guy before.

Or maybe it was because Gary went to where the nuts were hanging out. He used to love to go up to the Devil's Bowl car race track in Mesquite, Texas, and on those trips he'd always stay at a trashy motel called the Big Town Inn, which had an equally trashy bar in the basement called Uncle Herman's Lounge.

One night Gary, an Australian friend of mine named Reg Ricketts, and I decided to hit Uncle Herman's Lounge. Uncle Herman wasn't there, but some fat girls were, and one of them came up to our table looking for a dance partner. "Y'all just gonna sit there?" she said.

To avoid the woman, Reg got up from the table and rushed off to the men's room. Meanwhile, Gary pretended to be too "pie-eyed" to get up and dance. That left me, and where I come from it's impolite to turn down a lady. Besides, with everybody else at the table chickening out, I was left with no escape. So I volunteered, and ended up dancing with a woman about the size of a one-car garage. Fortunately, the band played a fast number, which meant I could keep some distance from her and not get my toes crushed.

On another trip to Devil's Bowl, the rain came down in sheets so hard that the mud parking lot turned into a quagmire. The mud was so deep that the wheels on my recently purchased used Honda were packed with mud so thick that they wouldn't turn properly. Trucks were stuck and rednecks were pushing on them, the way people up north push on vehicles stuck in a snowstorm. Mud was flying up from wheels, and people in the parking lot looked like they had been throwing gravy on each other.

My late wife Sally, who had climbed out of the Honda to help push, was so covered with mud that she looked like she had some horrible skin affliction. To get the mud out of the car's wheel wells, we figured we needed to find a truck wash to clean the thing up.

Finally, we made it to a truck stop diner, at which point Sally, who looked like a victim in a Hitchcock movie, bravely marched in and asked a good old boy at the counter if he could direct her to a truck wash. The old boy at the counter looked up from his coffee, saw Sally's legs covered with mud blotches that looked like scabs, and told her, "Lady, your lotion just ain't workin'."

Things like that always seemed to happen when I spent time on the road with Gary. Not a man of pretense, on his racecar jaunts Gary picked his accommodations based on price. On one stay at the Big Town Inn, I found an unopened can of Budweiser in one of the drawers in my room, along with a folder. A previous guest had cut some photos of nekkid women out of a skin magazine and stuck them in the folder. Who needs cable TV when you've got that sort of entertainment option?

Gary is a music expert. The guy could have won a bunch of money on the old TV show *Name That Tune*. In 2012 we were sitting in a barbecue joint in East Austin when an obscure novelty song came on the jukebox.

"'Let It All Hang Out.' The Hombres," Gary said. "It was recorded in the Sixties." Then he recited the lyrics.

Who knew? Gary did. I always figured Gary had a photographic memory. He would hold these oddball film festivals in his back yard and other places in South Austin. One night it might be 1950s teen rebel movies. Another night might be cheesy horror flicks, featuring monsters with huge webbed feet stomping through Tokyo. Sometimes he would fly in celebrities to go with the movies.

On Halloween weekend one year, he flew in Al Lewis, the actor who played Grandpa Munster on the comedy TV classic *The Munsters*. Lewis came all the way from California. Another time there was a visit from bad boy Eddie Haskell, from *Leave It to Beaver*. For yet another film festival, he brought in Russ Tamblyn, a hoofer of note who performed in the movie *West Side Story*. I recall that Tamblyn spent the better part of his Austin visit somewhat loopy. Part of that was my fault. Russ Tamblyn snorted a line of toot in the back seat of my VW bug. He appreciated it, but I didn't tell Gary about it until twenty years later.

"I didn't know there were any narcotics at my party," Gary said, matter-of-factly. Gary, for his part, never touched that kind of stuff. He stuck to beer.

It was 1982 when Gary and Vargo picked up Al Lewis, aka Grandpa Munster, at the old Robert Mueller Airport. Al had flown in for the Halloween film festival in Gary's back yard, and he was wearing an expensive suit when he arrived. Gary and Joe picked him up in a hearse with the top cut out. They'd gotten the hearse from Doug Breeding's car repair shop, Red River Motors, on Rainey Street in Austin. The repair shop was a favorite with Austin hippies who drove pieces of junk and were looking for reasonable prices, and they found a kindred spirit in Doug Breeding.

Grandpa Munster was not a hippie kind of guy, though. At one point during the trip to Gary's house, Lewis bitched about the ride. He told Joe and Gary they should take the messed-with hearse to Memorial Stadium and leave it on the 50-yard line.

Lewis's opinion of the vehicle might have been swayed by the hearse's weak battery. During the trip, the engine repeatedly quit running. So Gary and Joe had to make several stops to jumpstart the thing.

Their first stop was at a recording studio at about 12th Street on North Lamar Boulevard. One of Gary's bands, the Commandos, was recording a song there called "My Baby Loves Monster Movies." (You can't make this stuff up.) So Gary asked Lewis if he would help out by adding some sound effects to the recording.

Lewis complied by giving out some blood-curdling screams toward the end of the number, which can still be heard when you play the song. After his performance, Lewis looked at the band and said, "Get lucky, kids." Then they left.

Next, it was on to Robert Burns' creepy home in South Austin. Gary figured Al Lewis needed to meet Burns, who lived in a dusty old house decorated with props from the horror classic, "The Texas Chainsaw Massacre." Burns worked as the art director on the movie, designing all sorts of macabre accessories, such as "The Arm Chair," a gory chair with prosthetic human arms, that he kept in one of his living rooms. His was not your normal abode.

So here came Gary and Joe up to Burns' door, dragging along a famous TV actor dressed in a slick $2,000 suit. Burns was not similarly attired. Gary recalls that Burns was wearing a grubby white T-shirt that looked like he had just changed oil in it. And his white belly was sticking out from beneath the shirt.

By this time, Al Lewis was thinking, "What the heck have I gotten myself into?"

Meanwhile, Burns was eating a peanut butter and jelly sandwich, with the jelly dripping off the sandwich and onto his gut. So he wipes the jelly on his grubby T-shirt, leaving purple skid marks on his belly. Then he switches the sandwich from his right hand to his left, and he reaches out to shake hands with Al Lewis, who said in an aside to Gary and Joe, "That guy might be normal, but not on this planet."

When Gary wasn't showing old movies in his yard, he was traveling around the world. In 1992 he hiked in the lower Himalayas, outside Kathmandu. His guide was a friendly and energetic guy named Llaman. Llaman was overly concerned about customer service, apparently, because he wanted Gary to be happy. He kept asking Gary if he was happy in his hiking. He even carried Gary's backpack.

"Almost constantly, he asked me, 'Are you happy, Sir?'" Gary recalled, and he adds that he was happy the whole time. So after about three days of being asked if he was happy, he said, "Llaman, have you ever had a tourist who was not happy with the trek?" Llaman replied, "Just one time, Sir. We high in mountains. Tourist fall off mountain. Tourist die. Other tourists unhappy. Trek end. I unhappy, too."

Earlier in the trek, the two stayed at a rugged roadhouse with no electricity. The place did provide a couple cots and a hot meal, however. And while they were sitting around the dining room, they were impressed with four extremely beautiful Swiss nurses who were on their own trek. "They were tall, shapely, drop-dead gorgeous in every regard," Gary remembers. "Later that night, when we were in our room on our cots, Llaman was still thinking about the babes. He asked me: 'Tell me, Sir. Is it true that American boy have different girl every night?'"

Gary thought about it, and then said, "Yes, Llaman, that's true."

To that, Llaman replied, "Some day, Sir, I come to your country."

Now that's what I call being a great American ambassador.

Look! Up in the Sky . . .

Over the years I've done a lot of stories that weren't humor columns. I worked my butt off doing extra stuff. Why? Simple. I didn't think I was all that good, for one thing. So I figured I could get around that by working extra hard. I'd always thought that Mike Kelley, the guy who was writing humor columns on the days I wasn't, was a much more gifted writer than I was. So I was constantly worried about that. When it wasn't at the back of my mind, it was right up front. Partly because I'd already been threatened with being fired by Ray Mariotti, my first editor at the *Statesman.*

So if there was an assignment or story I'd dug up myself of any kind, I'd jump on it. And when I say any kind, I'm not kidding. The weirdest story I ever worked on was the one about the two women and the little boy in Dayton, Texas, who were suing the Federal government for $20 million because they claimed they'd been nuked by a UFO. In September 1985 I traveled to Dayton, a little redneck town about forty miles northeast of Houston, to check in with Vickie Landrum, who used to wait tables at the

Truck Stop Café north of town, and her friend, Betty Cash, who used to own the café and had since moved to Birmingham, Alabama.

Landrum, Cash and Landrum's 11-year-old grandson Colby all had medical problems. Cash and Landrum suffered from a sensitivity to sunlight so severe that they stayed inside most of the time. Cash said sunlight made her break out in big water blisters. All three had skin and eye problems. Cash had breast cancer and had had a double mastectomy. Colby had nightmares. And all three said they vomited and had diarrhea the night the mysterious flying object came out of the sky.

Their story began around 9:00 p.m. on December 29, 1980, when the three were riding in Cash's car down a country road about twenty miles from Landrum's house. They had gone to nearby New Caney to play bingo, but the game was closed for the Christmas holiday. So after eating supper in a café in New Caney, they headed down FM 1485 toward home.

That's when they say they saw the diamond-shaped flying object. It was the size of a small water tower, and the flames shooting out of the bottom reached almost down to the road. The three were claiming the object must have been some sort of military experiment. Hence the lawsuit against the Feds.

The trio got out of the car to look at this machine from beyond. Cash said that when she got back in the car, the door handle on the driver's side was so hot that she had to use her coat like a potholder to open it. It was about forty degrees outside, but the interior of the car was so hot that they turned on the air conditioner, Landrum said.

The flying object later rose into the sky and took off with what young Colby called a "roaring noise." And of course there followed a Jesus quote.

Landrum explained, "I said, 'Colby, you look at that light, and if you see a man step out of that light, it will be Jesus Christ, and he will take us to a better place.'"

If I'd been there, I would have brought up Sammy Davis, Jr., and a trip to Vegas, but that's just me.

Landrum reports that they counted twenty-three helicopters hovering around the flying object. "It was a sight of helicopters no one has ever seen," she said. "They just kept coming to it."

Dr. Bryan McClelland, the Birmingham, Alabama doctor who treated Cash, said he thought her skin problems were the result of radiation. However, he couldn't say where the radiation came from. And L.L. Walker, a Dayton police officer, told me he saw six to nine military helicopters bearing Army insignias in the area that night, flying in a V formation.

The suit was eventually thrown out of court, but I didn't know what to make of this story. I joked to my friends and figured that maybe Cash and Landrum had stuck their heads in the microwave over at the truck stop.

Meanwhile, I'm not sure which was weirder — the story, or the town of Dayton. I am a friend of the chewin' tobacco set, really. But this place gave me the Willies. It was a minor case of the Willies, but the Willies just the same.

For example, I walked into a local beer joint to get a few quotes and talked to the owner, whose name I don't remember. The guy started out being friendly enough, but when I started taking notes he came unglued. He said he'd gone to journalism school at the University of Texas, and he knew that the rules of journalism said that you were supposed to get permission before you took notes. That was a new one on me.

The guy was being a jerk and trying to intimidate me. I'd already introduced myself to this bozo, and told him what I was doing, and that I was a writer for the *American-Statesman*. So there was no reason for him to be surprised when I started scribbling on my legal pad.

While I was in Dayton, I stayed in the Sands Motel, perhaps the worst fleabag I've ever stayed in. You know the motel is a special place if you remember the name twenty-seven years later. I had asked a relative of Landrum's to tell me the best place to stay in Dayton, and he recommended this dump.

Prominently displayed on the front check-in cage (notice I didn't say desk) was an illustration of a telephone with the international "no" sign drawn over it. "No phones in rooms," the sign said. The door to the room didn't even lock, which left me with a somewhat unsettled feeling, especially after talking to that clown in the bar.

But I got out of there alive. And the story ran on the front page, so what the heck? I'm surely not the only newspaper guy who has ever run across weirdness with a tabloid story. I had a columnist friend in Florida named Jim Quinlan, who worked briefly for the *National Enquirer*. The *Enquirer* had its office in Lantana back in the 1970s, and Quinlan had worked with me at the nearby *Palm Beach Post* before he moved on to the *Enquirer*.

Quinlan had been sent up to Connecticut by the *Enquirer*

to interview a woman who said she had spaceships in her house. When Jim got to the woman's address, she wouldn't let him in the house to talk to her. So Jim called his boss about the problem. There were no bleeding hearts at the *Enquirer*. If you were looking for sympathy and a warm heart, *Enquirer* management was not the place to go. Jim's boss told him he'd better get in that house and talk to that woman, or he was fired.

Jim gave it some thought and came up with a plan to save his neck. The woman still wouldn't let him in for an interview, so he called his boss back and made up a story. Seems the woman had told Jim she was going to kill herself if he didn't quit bothering her. And she was going to leave a note blaming the *National Enquirer*.

At that, Jim's boss told him to send her a dozen roses, and come home. Pretty smart, huh? I hope Jim remembered to expense-account the flowers, and I'll just bet he did.

The Wild Goodbye

Nobody could make an exit quite like my friend Robert Burns, the eccentric guy who did the gruesome artwork for the horror movie classic *The Texas Chainsaw Massacre*. I've know a lot of creative characters in my time, but Burns was the only one who has been able to contact me from the dead.

Really.

It was June 2004. Robert Burns had been found dead in his old house in Seguin, a small town about an hour southeast of Austin. His house was near the town square, which, by the way, is decorated with the World's Largest Pecan. It's concrete. Burns had killed himself by setting fire to charcoal briquettes and breathing the fumes. He had terminal cancer and he just didn't want to deal with going through the cure.

Having suffered through radiation my own self, now I can relate.

But before Burns checked out, he posted a picture of himself on his Web site. The photo showed him stretched out in front of a mock tombstone with the name "Burns" on it. This shot was accompanied by the following message, which Burns left for his friends:

> I've never understood why people would stay in the theater after it became obvious that the rest of the movie would not be enjoyable. Due to physical and psychological reasons too tedious to bore anyone with, it became obvious that the rest of my movie would not be enjoyable, so I left the theater (me and Elvis, you know.)

And that's not even the exit I'm talking about.

A few days after Burns was found dead in his home, I got a postcard in the mail from him. He'd put the postcard together, obviously, before he checked out. Talk about planning ahead.

"THANKS FOR BEING A FRIEND," it said in large black letters on the front of the card. On the back, Burns had printed the same message he had left for his friends on his Web site. Beyond that, Burns personalized the message to me. "Kelso," he wrote, "Next time you get a column tip from me, you'll know it's time to sober up!"

The card was signed, "Adios, Burns."

On the front of the envelope, postmarked the same day Burns was found dead, was a post office cancellation stamp that read, "Greetings From Far, Far Away."

There's an understatement. I'm surprised he could get it sent that distance with just one 37-cent stamp.

Most people would probably be startled to get something like that in the mail. But if you knew Robert Burns, you might not have been surprised.

The guy had a maniacal sense of humor. After his mother died, Burns kept a collection of her hats, strung up on wires in a room. One was a large floppy red number. I had heard from a mutual friend that Burns didn't get along with his mother.

I remember Burns taking down the hat, putting it on his head, and saying dramatically, "Mom, as Super Fly."

I visited Burns at his eerie old South Austin house years ago. I'd never seen *The Texas Chainsaw Massacre*, so he was going to show it to me on his television.

Meanwhile, a bloody wind-up rubber hand with a knife sticking out of it was crawling across the wood floor upstairs. Burns had designed the hand for another horror movie he was working on.

I recall Burns' frightening yet funny Halloween get-ups, which he designed himself and usually involved some character or other messing with him. A favorite of his was the outfit that made him appear to be a baby being carried around by a French maid. And there was another costume that, when Burns put it on, made it appear that he was being carried down the street against his will by some deranged person. The arms of the costume appeared to wrap around Burns' body.

He would wear these nutty costumes to Austin's annual Halloween celebration on Sixth Street, which attracted throngs of folks in various outfits. I think his creations won him some first place awards in Sixth Street Halloween costume judging, and if they didn't, they should have.

I suspect Robert Burns was one of those MENSA-level

geniuses who bored easily, because he was always working on something daffy. He wrote a song called "Colonel Sanders' Thighs," a takeoff on the 1980s hit "Bette Davis Eyes." Sing along if you will:

> *Her eyes are Big Mac brown.*
> *Her hair is like French fries.*
> *She's blown up like the clown.*
> *She's got Colonel Sanders thighs.*

After Burns moved to Seguin from Austin, he began performing with his own country band, called the Burns Family Trio. Actually, it wasn't a trio at all, but a solo act. The trio consisted of another costume Burns made. In the outfit, Burns was flanked by a couple of female mannequins — his made-up sisters Powder Burns and Heart Burns.

One of Burns' jokes was that, without him, his sisters wouldn't have a leg to stand on. His was never a big-time act, but Burns and his "sisters" would perform country songs in nursing homes around town.

The ironic part of all this is that Burns was something of an introvert, quiet, and certainly not showy. He was the kind of man that you really never got to know completely. But everybody loved the guy. He was about as kind and gentle as they come.

Leslie

Paris has can-can girls, New York the Rockettes, and Austin? We had Leslie.

For about a decade, starting in the 1990s, Austin's favorite cross-dresser hung out (literally) in the very vortex of the city, at the corner of Sixth Street and Congress Avenue in downtown Austin. Often he wore only a thong.

Downtown business people would have preferred a different view than Leslie's rear end out their windows. But Austin, being the wack-a-doodle community that it is, adopted Leslie as an icon. After all, he was funny and something different. Word of this man in spike heels and a tiara, wearing a slingshot for pants, circulated about the country. Soon he had followers from beyond the city limits. People would come from other states to get their picture taken with the guy. Sometimes Leslie would charge, say, $20.

Leslie, who ran unsuccessfully for mayor of Austin three times, died in March 2012 at the age of 60. The city, with its motto "Keep Austin Weird," recognized the loss. Mayor Lee

Leffingwell proclaimed March 8 Leslie Cochran Day, issuing an official proclamation that said he had left "an indelible image."

In 2000 Leslie got the attention of Austin Mayor Kirk Watson, when Leslie ran against him in the mayoral race. "My fear is that this will not be an issues-oriented campaign, but (about) who has the best legs, and then I know I'm a dead man," said Watson, who went on to become a Texas state senator. "The only problem I've got is that I've seen freckles where I never really wanted to."

Watson was speaking of Leslie's freckles, not his own. Leslie had really great legs, spotted with freckles. Not that Leslie's legs did much for me. It was the legs/beard combination I found unattractive.

Leslie even made it onto the front page of the *New York Times*, in a tease to his obituary, which ran on Page A9.

How many other Texas men can say they were featured on the front page of the *New York Times* for showing up regularly in public dressed in a miniskirt?

Though Leslie never attained any real political power, he did reprimand me once for showing up late at a press conference he was holding at the Ruta Maya Coffee Shop, to announce he was running for mayor. It's the only time I've ever been scolded by a man who walked around in ladies' duds.

The story goes that Leslie got his start as a cut-up at an early age. Born an identical twin, Leslie survived, while his twin was stillborn. Allegedly while Leslie was growing up in Miami, his mother would torture the boy by telling him she wished he'd died instead of his twin.

So to get back at Mom, Leslie would put on something from, say, women's attire at, say, J.C. Penneys.

Leslie arrived in Austin in the early 1990s with a scrapbook full of photos of his road trip from the East Coast to Austin. I don't remember how he traveled, but I suspect he hitchhiked. I don't know which is scarier: Leslie hitchhiking, or the driver who would actually let him in the car.

It didn't take long for Austin radio deejays to start a morning report of Leslie's whereabouts along North Interstate 35. Legend has it that a big box store in North Austin didn't like a bearded guy in women's fashions hanging around out front, so they blasted him with a water hose.

But Austin had a new eccentric to love, festive in his feathered boa, heels, and tutu.

I wrote about Leslie fairly often, probably too often. People in the newsroom would roll their eyes and think, "Please, not Leslie again." I even gave him a ride in my car once, though I never knew where Leslie went after dark. Leslie, who was often homeless himself, was a homeless advocate. He had a large, heavy cart that he pushed around town, which probably explained his great legs. The cart was decorated with cardboard signs covered with messages addressing the homeless issue, and taunting the cops. He was in and out of jail for vagrancy through the years.

My favorite Leslie moment? He had moved into a brand new toolshed from Home Depot. He had some cash that he'd made by selling Leslie refrigerator magnets. These popular items, which made great stocking stuffers, included a small armadillo likeness, though I'm not sure what the armadillo was doing there.

And don't you go there, either. Anyway, the Wet Salon on South Congress Avenue and Leslie had teamed up on the refrigerator magnet deal, and Leslie got part of the take and he used the money to buy this big toolshed. A friend of his let him put his new shed next to her house on Annie Street in South Austin, and this served as Leslie's new home.

One mid-afternoon I dropped by for a visit. Inside the toolshed, Leslie and a young female companion were drinking wine and watching a video on a big-screen TV. What were they watching? Mel Brooks' *Robin Hood: Men in Tights*. What else?

One good thing you can say about Leslie: until he started drinking heavily late in life, he didn't leave much of a frown footprint on the planet. People always talk about our carbon footprints, but I submit that there's also a frown footprint, the print that measures how much a man has done to make the rest of us miserable.

Leslie was the other way around. Usually, he made us smile. Although he made some of us cringe, or at least blink. Many's the person, who, on first encountering Leslie, wanted to holler, "My Lord, man, you've lost your britches."

But in his favor, Leslie got laughs, or at least quiet grins, from much of the citizenry, and he even handed out helpful what-to-wear advice. High heels in summer, he pointed out, elevated a man a few inches off the pavement, cooling him in the Texas heat. He'd worn those heels at the corner of Sixth and Congress long enough to know what he was talking about. Leslie had an outfit for any occasion. In 1999, Austin held a Congress Avenue parade for Heisman Trophy winner Ricky Williams. Leslie made an appearance while dressed in a Texas Longhorns cheerleader outfit.

Another time involved a bus trip to the fried pickle-eating contest in Houston. Marc Katz, owner of the former Katz's Deli on West Sixth Street, organized the tour. Katz's son Barry had opened his own Katz's Deli in Houston. So to promote the new Katz's, Marc and Barry were having a pickle-eating event.

En route to Houston, you had Austin's two biggest self-promoters — Marc Katz and Leslie — on the same bus. Egos were so inflated by these two that most of the oxygen was sucked out of the bus. We stopped at a convenience store in Smithville, a small town an hour or so east of Austin, and Leslie got off the bus and bought a box of cookies from some Girl Scouts. It was a magic moment. The mother of the girl who sold Leslie the cookies was nonchalant about the event. She said she knew about Leslie, so no big deal. Besides, it was winter, and Leslie was dressed conservatively for the weather.

Leslie was big. He was the only person in Austin I can think of who could be identified with one name. All you had to say was "Leslie" and you got this image in your head that would cross your eyes. He was Austin's Madonna. Did you know there's a Leslie app? Conveniently, there is. I know, because I still have Leslie's app on my iPhone. What this means is that I can still hear from Leslie even though he's left the building. Hit the button and Leslie will share his special brand of wisdom with his "Leslie-isms:"

"It was my favorite tooth, until I lost it."

"You're losing it, you're losing it, aggggh."

"Don't hate the player, hate the game."

"They call me Miss. Miss Appropriate."

During the height of his, um, career, Leslie was everywhere. He was used in local advertisements. In 2001, wearing a pink bikini, he even appeared in a TV Super Bowl ad for an Austin pager company.

For a short time, Leslie was a man of property, though it wasn't his property. A friend of Leslie's, a homeless advocate herself, had moved out of her house in toney West Lake Hills. The home had a pretty serious mold problem, and the homeowner couldn't live with the mold.

However, Leslie, being Leslie, was immune to mold. So the homeowner moved out, and Leslie moved in.

Leslie spent his West Lake Hills days out by the pool. He was allowed to wander the grounds, with one stipulation. The house was for sale, but Leslie was forbidden from showing the place. You've got to draw the line somewhere.

Many Austinites remember the moment we first saw Leslie. If a person didn't have any forewarning, that first peek could be a real surprise.

Twenty years or so ago, I got a phone call from Sam Shanblum, who had a kitchen supply business in downtown Austin. He'd just been out to Northcross Mall in North Central Austin, where he'd seen what he thought was a cute chick with really fantastic legs, sporting a miniskirt.

"And she turned around, *AND SHE HAD A BEARD*," Max said.

Leslie's last few years of life were tough. In 2009 he suffered a head injury on the street in South Austin. He said he was mugged, but doctors suspected he'd had a stroke. In any case, he was never the same after that. It seemed as if he had brain damage. Communicating with him became difficult.

I visited Leslie right before he died, while he was in intensive care at the hospital in South Austin. He couldn't talk, but I could talk to him. I told him he was a good man for making Austin smile. That was the last time I ever spoke to him.

Thumbing My Nose at Growth

If I could be accused of crusading, it would be for thumbing my nose at Austin growth, and the outlanders who created it by moving here. It's not that I mind arugula with my chicken-fried steak, mind you. All right, so I *do* mind arugula with my chicken-fried steak.

But what really chaps me is that when people move here from, say, California, and demand, say, a tangerine wedge as a side with their sliced beef sandwich, it means they don't give a rat's hind end about the local culture. It means they'd just as soon ditch the way we do things around here for the way they did it back there, wherever back there was.

And that's the part that chaps my chaps — that lack of respect for Texas ways. And I'm not even a Texan by birth. (I was born in Oklahoma, which still chaps my behind.)

I've always been fond of regional color, and inclined to preserve it, regardless of region. So I've championed it in my columns.

Notice how I mentioned California a few paragraphs back. I'll admit it. I'm goofing on the wrong people when I single out California. The fact is I should be blaming people from the Panhandle, too. Truth is, more people have moved to Austin from other parts of Texas than have moved here from California with their U-hauls.

But it's more entertaining to make fun of Marin County hot tubs, Hollywood, and those Chardonnay suckers from La La Land than it is to mess with people from Floydada.

So I aimed my pen at Californians. Over and over and over. You know those sharp spikey metal objects that pop up out of the ground at the entrances to rent car places out at the airport? I'm talking about those gnarly devices that pop your tires if you back up.

In one of my columns, I suggested that the way to stop growth would be to install those units in the freeways from here to California. That way when Californians decided to move here, the Michelins on their Beemers would be shredded and they couldn't come here and raise real estate prices to the point where only Mitt Romney can afford to live in the Bouldin Creek Neighborhood.

That's not exactly how I put it, but that was the message. Some people just don't get it. They want Austin to be just the way it is up north. Look at it this way. As I mentioned earlier, I was raised in the state of Maine. So I love a good lobster roll. Yum-yum. But I would never expect somebody to open a lobster pound on South Lamar. But unfortunately, a lot of newcomers don't agree with that philosophy. I remember a colleague named Big Bill who moved here from Cleveland. He once asked me, "Is there a good sit-down restaurant around here?" I thought, *you mean people in Cleveland eat standing up*? Is there a chair shortage in Ohio?

I've written at least one column, maybe more, proposing a mandatory Austin trivia test for new residents. There would be questions such as: the Stallion was known for (a) winning the Preakness (b) chateaubriand (c) its wonderful yeast rolls and fresh baked croissants (d) a really cheap chicken-fried steak. If you got a certain number of questions wrong on this test, you'd have to pack your bags and skedaddle back to wherever you came from.

Years ago, up in Williamson County, there was a class newcomers could take on how to talk Texan. It covered "y'all," "over yonder," "fixin' to" — that sort of thing. I thought that class was an excellent idea. Not that it did any good. Even Texans don't talk Texan nearly as much as they used to. Instead of "y'all" anymore, it's likely to be "you guys."

I knew we were hosed when the Iron Works, a barbecue place in downtown Austin, put in a salad bar. I wrote a column saying that was just wrong, but nobody listened. Since then I've run across barbecued tofu, which I'll admit is probably the best thing you can do with tofu, except take it to the dump. Because barbecued, steamed or baked, it's still tofu.

Back in 2000, I suggested that Austin needed its own William Butler Yeats, a poet of the Emerald Isle who championed Irish nationalism. Yeats "wrote verse that stirred his countrymen to get off their green-wearing behinds, fight back, and preserve their culture," I wrote.

I actually held a poetry contest, in which I asked people to send in their own verse in defense of preserving Austin's cultural soul against the ravages of growth. I said I would name the winning poet Austin's Yeats. First prize would be a trip to the Dr Pepper plant in Dublin, Texas.

Soon I was swamped with a pile of bad poetry. But there were a few gems, among them the work from Bruce McCandless, an insurance lawyer who wrote a poem he called "A Texan Speaks." I named McCandless Austin's Yeats.

``The only thing I have in common with William Butler Yeats is poor eyesight and a hatred of the foreigners infesting my native land," McCandless said when I told him he'd been named Austin's Yeats. ``I stand ready to fight these foreigners by any means necessary. I'll probably just get contact lenses to take care of the eye thing, though."

Incidentally, we never made the trip to the Dr Pepper plant in Dublin, although I don't recall why. I'm suspecting it was a lack of interest — but not on my part. I wish we'd gone. That Dr Pepper plant is now closed and I never got to see it. Rats.

Anyway, here's part of McCandless's winning entry:

Please don't come here anymore.

That's what the rest of the U.S. is for!

Idaho's my preferred growth corridor.

I'm telling you, fellas, I wish you'd skedaddle,

And leave us alone with our Shiner and cattle.

It's good here now. It was better before.

Please don't come here anymore.

It was a nice suggestion, but too few people took it. Every time you turned around, some magazine was naming Austin the best place in the nation to pick up chicks, start your own garage band, or land a job for a start-up in tech support.

And each time one of these polls was announced, the traffic jam got fifteen or twenty minutes longer, and rents jumped, say, $55 a month.

It got so bad that even the locals were making jokes about it. A guy who worked at the state Attorney General's office had a T-shirt made up that said:

"AUSTIN SUCKS: Go Back to California & Tell Your Friends."

The letter "L" in California was shaped like the state of California. The guy sent me one of these shirts, and I started wearing it to the gym. And no, I never got punched out by a weightlifter from San Clemente.

Incidentally, the guy who made up the T-shirt wanted to remain anonymous, because he was afraid he'd get in trouble at work. Heck, if his boss had been from Austin, the guy probably would have gotten a raise.

I was all over growth so frequently that I got into a lighthearted column battle with my friend Ben Wear, the *American-Statesman*'s transportation writer. Ben is an engineer, and he has an engineer's studious way of looking at things. But he regularly crosses over to the funny side, even in his writing. For example, when I came out against growth in my Yeats column, Ben countered with a column saying how Austin was boring when he was a kid growing up here. "Austin was pretty much Omaha with trees," he wrote.

Certainly it's true that in the old days Austin was easier on your wallet. "Sure, it was cheap, but so is Odessa," Ben wrote.

Unlike me, Ben is an Austin native, which gives him some street cred. He added that in the 1970s, when he was attending the University of Texas, there were only five recreational options: "(a) smoke pot, (b) get a tan, (c) watch the Horns, (d) go bowling, or (e) take a nap, hopefully with company."

But the coup de ridiculous popped up when Ben admitted that as a young man he had moved to Oklahoma City to escape Austin's boredom. I pointed out that moving to Oklahoma City to escape boredom was "like going to North Korea to find a comedy club."

I didn't miss a chance to poke fun at the new, swank apartments and condos going up all over town. Therefore, when the Austonian, a swank 55-story luxury condo tower on Congress Avenue at Second Street, announced it was going to have a dog toilet on the tenth floor, I was all over it like, well, like a dog on a dog toilet on the tenth floor.

Yet in a way, the dog toilet seemed to fit. Or, as I pointed out, when you charge between $550,000 and $3.8 million per unit, you've got to have something for the guy who has everything.

Besides, it was the perfect amenity for rich people who were too lazy to take their poodles outside. Sadly, though, the Austonian dropped its plan to put in the dog toilet, a metal unit that would have been built flush to the floor with a wiper blade to get rid of the dog poop. It also was to have come with a scent that would attract the dogs.

I was curious what scent they would have used to attract dogs. I figured Eau de FiFi in Heat would get the job done.

There were times when I blew it. I should have done more to

try to save the local iconic Las Manitas, a charming little downtown Mexican food diner run by the Perez sisters. Las Manitas was run off by plans to build an upscale 33-story, $275 million Marriott convention hotel. Las Manitas was much beloved by Austin's liberal crowd. You could find flyers supporting the arts or saving the warblers up by the cash register. I should have taken that into account. And sometimes I did write columns defending the place and telling the hotel to buzz off.

But on one occasion I turned into a wise guy, and pointed out that the food at Las Manitas wasn't all that great. I look at that as a blunder on my part. For one thing, it was probably better than hotel food, right? And the quality of the cuisine really wasn't the point. It was the unique, laid back ambience, the little details that Austinites loved. Anyone who had been there a few times could point out that you had to walk through the kitchen to get to the bathroom.

Sometimes I may have leaned too far in the other direction, though. Perhaps I was too hard on the developers every so often. When the Transwestern development company decided to fix the broken windows on an old country music band tour bus parked at the Broken Spoke, I made fun of the company.

That may have been a bit picky. Especially since they did go to some trouble to save the big oak tree out front by the road. Transwestern is the company putting in swank apartments on both sides of the Spoke. But in the process, they've left the Spoke pretty much as it's always been.

Thank you for that, Transwestern. And thanks for not making the Spoke serve its chicken-fried steak with a side of baby spinach.

As time has passed, I've mellowed a little on Austin growth. For one thing, crabbing about it is a waste of hot air. It's here. Austin is now a big screaming city, so I lost. Besides, it's nice to have so many dining choices, even if you can't find a place to park, and even if you have to stand in line for forty-five minutes before being seated. And even if the guy sitting at the next table keeps checking his iPhone for Facebook messages from his friends back in Pismo Beach.

Still, every once in a while, like say, Sunday, I'll write a column going after the latest growth insult — like those apartments I mentioned that are being built next to the Spoke. Really. These apartments will have street-level retail. I wonder if Ann Taylor can dance backwards? I guess we're fixing to find out.

Messing With Those Okies

There is an irony behind my sometimes-annual column insulting the University of Oklahoma Sooners: I'm an Okie myself. A reluctant Okie, to be sure. But an Okie by birth. I was born in Lawton, Oklahoma, on June 30, 1944. So send me a birthday card, but not a red one with the word "Boomer" on it. It was not my fault that I was born in Oklahoma. It was Hitler's.

See, when I jumped out into the world, my father Elmer G. Kelso was training for World War II at Fort Sill, an Army base in Lawton, Oklahoma. My dad was an artillery officer. So you can blame Hitler for the name "Oklahoma" appearing on my passport. Which ticks me off.

In my favor, I got out of there as fast as I could. I only lived in Oklahoma for the first six months of my life. But nearly every October for many years, right before the big OU-Texas football game at the Cotton Bowl, I've made a habit of savaging everything Sooner.

I've called the state of Oklahoma a series of degrading names that I invented: Yokelhoma, Jokelahoma, Croaklahoma,

Brokelahoma, and Mobilehoma come to mind. I've pointed out there's no reason to spend time in Oklahoma. "Of course I haven't spent much time in Oklahoma. I've never run out of gas there," I explained.

I've made tasteless dental work jokes. "I can understand why Oklahoma never talks much about its academic programs. If you need a good set of teeth, your priority isn't your grade-point average," I wrote.

In the same column, I claimed that there really isn't a University of Oklahoma anyway. The collection of buildings and the occasional egghead professor in Norman is just a front for a college football team. NCAA rules say you can't play college football unless you've got a college.

So O.U. went out and bought a bunch of blocking dummies, threw up a few classrooms, and faked it.

"Could it be that O.U. is really just a façade, a convenient front created so Oklahoma can field a college football team?" I asked. "I never hear anyone talking about O.U. academic programs. You never meet anyone at a party who says, 'Hi there, I have an English degree from O.U.'"

No rude observation has gone unused in these Okie columns. No cheap shot was left in the chamber. I've penned far too many Oklahoma trailer park jokes. "At most schools, the outstanding students graduate *summa cum laude*," I wrote. "At O.U. they have a special designation — summa cum trailer."

Let's step back in time and examine why my trashing O.U. is so ludicrous, and such a switch from the way things used to be. In the middle-1950s, when I was a little kid growing up in

Winslow, Maine, I was the only kid in the neighborhood who had come from out west, sort of. At least that's how I saw it at the age of about ten.

I had started life in Oklahoma, in the land of cowboys and Indians, and I played it up big with the other children, many of whom had never been out of the state of Maine.

My mother, Dorothy Kelso, who excelled at sewing and looking out for her kids, made me a special little boy flowered-y cowboy shirt. And yes, flowered-y is a word. It means a shirt has flowers sewn all over it.

So I paraded about the neighborhood in this colorful western shirt, like I was a tiny Gene Autry or something. At the same time, I was a serious Oklahoma football fan. Yes, folks, right there in Central Maine, on the banks of the Kennebec River, in the 1950s, you had one child O.U. football fan.

This was back when Oklahoma was coached by Bud Wilkinson, and O.U. was winning everything.

I remember when a friend of my father's came over to the house on a Saturday afternoon. We were watching O.U. play Maryland on TV in the den. I was rooting it up big for the Sooners. So when Maryland went ahead in the game, my father's friend started teasing me. Being a sensitive child, or a spoiled wimp (take your pick), I burst into tears. My father's friend, realizing the little kid was taking this to heart, backed off and started saying he was sorry.

As I got older, I lost interest in O.U. and replaced that sort of wasted activity with more useful pursuits, such as chasing girls. When I went off to college at the University of Missouri, I got used to Oklahoma beating the Missouri Tigers. But I didn't spend a lot of time worrying about it.

Then, in 1976, when I moved to Austin to become a newspaper columnist, I had a real motive to turn on the Okies: Readership. University of Texas fans despise O.U. Plus, it was easy to do these columns, and fun to boot.

And there was one more factor. In 1990, I started buying season tickets to Longhorn football games, and I began adopting the Longhorns as my hometown team. In Austin, U.T. football is THE big game in town. We'd had a minor league baseball team, the Austin Senators, in the 1950s. There was a minor league hockey team, the Austin Ice Bats. And these days, nearby Round Rock has the Round Rock Express, another minor league baseball team.

But Austin is the biggest city in America without a major pro sports franchise.

So, after living in Austin for fourteen years, I finally became a real Longhorn fan and actually began to cringe whenever O.U. would stomp the Longhorns, which happened way too frequently. It's galling to Texas fans how good Oklahoma's football teams are.

Besides, it was just plain giggles to write these O.U. diatribes. I mentioned in one column that it wasn't unusual in Oklahoma for the kids to get mixed in with the adults, since it was common for an 18-year-old to still be in elementary school. And that explained why some of the people at the children's table at Thanksgiving dinner needed a shave.

Granted, I was tacky. I made fun of Oklahoma's famous people, including OU coach Barry Switzer, for trying to board a plane in Dallas with a gun, and New York Yankee legend Mickey Mantle. I wrote that Mantle was the inspiration for the Paul Simon classic, "Fifty Ways to Lose Your Liver."

In 2001, I wrote about my visit to my birth town of Lawton. At the time I was working on a news story up in Wichita Falls, about an hour from Lawton. So I figured I might as well drive up to Oklahoma and see where it all began.

When I got to the exit for Lawton, I saw an establishment called Big Bob's Lease-a-John, a major player in Lawton's portable toilet business wars. How can you beat that? At that point I figured I'd seen the city's highlight. So I never bothered to go into town. I just turned around and headed back to Texas.

On the way back, I stopped in at an under-stocked discount cigarette store just north of the Red River, the river that separates Texas from Oklahoma. The store was about half empty, with a lot of shelf space. A man in his twenties, the proprietor, who said his mother didn't let him out much, came out from the back.

Shortly after, a large dog with pale eyes came out from the back, too, and sat at my feet. At least I thought it was a dog.

"Nice dog," I said.

"He's not a dog," the man said.

"Oh yeah? What is he?"

"He's a wolf."

"Does he like people?" I asked.

"No. You want to buy something?" the guy said.

Yeah, you got any dog biscuits? I was thinking.

What a sales strategy. Have the wolf come out and sit at the customer's feet, tell the customer the wolf is not fond of people, then ask him if he wants to buy something. At that point, to keep from getting mauled by this guy's pet wolf, I would have been willing to buy the store. But I bought a soda and got the heck out of there.

I also pointed out, in the same column, that the first word you see in Oklahoma as you gaze across the Red River from Texas is BINGO, which is painted on a barn. I explained that the word BINGO had been put there because the Oklahoma bureau of tourism wanted something that would paint an accurate picture of the state. And I added that during the selection process it came down to BINGO or CHAW.

I could have said that they put BINGO on the barn because some Okie misspelled BIMBO. But I didn't think of it at the time.

In my Okie columns, I've done what I could to promote tourism up there by mentioning the top attractions, such as the bowling ball fence and shed in the Oklahoma town of Nowata. That's right, there's a fence made of 108 bowling balls, part of a display that contains 1,400 bowling balls.

Makes you want to jump in the car and head on up there, doesn't it?

I also pointed out that the reason Oklahoma made mistletoe the state flower is that most people up there are too ugly to get kissed without some enticement.

When I first started writing these columns, readers from Oklahoma saw their school color — red. I'd get all sorts of e-mails and phone calls from people who were about eight kinds of put out. Over the years, though, it came to seem that the people in Oklahoma had come to look forward to the annual dissing. Then again, maybe they'd just gotten sick of me and weren't paying attention. Who knows? But the funny thing is that, although most Texans would be loathe to admit it, Texas and Oklahoma have many similarities.

"Tell me," I asked my wife, Kay, who grew up in Spearman, Texas, a small Panhandle town not that far from the Oklahoma line, "Is there really that much difference between Texas and Oklahoma?"

"Watch it," she said.

The Meat Lady

For about a decade I did a lot of columns messing with the Meat Lady. That was the honorary title I gave to Jeanne Daniels, owner of the Tarrytown Shopping Center, an open-air mall in Tarrytown, a hoity-toity neighborhood in upscale West Austin.

To call Daniels an animal rights activist would be equivalent to calling Ted Nugent a redneck. Daniels pretty much brought her own mall to its knees by driving out every business that had anything to do with meat products. She'd rather save the whales than save her own mall, apparently.

The moves the Meat Lady made were borderline spectacular. She got after Steve's Liquor & Fine Wines for putting caviar in its Christmas baskets. She told them to stop doing that. Caviar, you see, is fish eggs. And fish eggs have rights. At least in Jeanne Daniels' world they do. Balderdash. Have you ever tried to teach a fish egg to bring in the newspaper?

Daniels became owner of the mall when her mother died in 1999, and as soon as she took over, things began to change. One of her first moves was to tell the Austin Shoe Hospital to hide the leather shoelaces in the back where nobody would see them. That way people would be more likely to buy the fabric laces.

Daniels even wanted to save the bugs. She had the maintenance man tell the owner of Alegra's Bridal and Invitations that she wanted the ants in the store relocated, not exterminated. Instead of a cattle drive there would be an ant drive, I guess.

The owner of the bridal shop had simply wanted to spray. After all, the ants were so prolific that they were walking all over her order forms. So she moved her shop to another part of town.

Daniels told the hardware store to stop selling mousetraps. But worst of all, she ran off every restaurant in the mall that sold meat. She would do that by not extending their leases.

The exodus began when Daniels attacked The Grocery, a popular little mom-and-pop store that sold fine wine, cheeses, and USDA Choice beef at the meat counter.

Daniels told the owner, Harvey Tack, that she wouldn't renew his lease unless he stopped selling meat. Either the meat counter would have to go or The Grocery would have to go.

Tack figured he couldn't make it without his meat counter, so, much to his misery, he closed the store. He'd hoped to make it a lifelong business, and one day sell the place.

The next victim? Texas French Bread, which carried chicken, turkey, tuna, and ham sandwiches. Daniels told Texas French Bread it could stay if it would lose the sandwiches. Texas French Bread lost the sandwiches, but it lost its lease later anyway. After that, Daniels homed in on Formosa, an Asian restaurant. I asked the owner of the place if he was leaving because Daniels wouldn't renew his lease unless he stopped serving meat. He said the reason he was leaving was that his wife was not well and was too tired to work.

Then he told me the mall's lawyer had told him to say that, if the press asked. Maybe Formosa's fortune cookie said, "You will lose your lease because you have meat in your egg rolls." The last straw came when Daniels axed the Holiday House, a cheeseburger hangout that was much beloved by Tarrytown neighbors. The place had been around forever. Ralph Moreland, a legend in Austin's cuisine history and the Holiday House owner, said he'd give me his take on what Daniels had done to the mall after he closed the Holiday House. By then he figured it would be safe to chat about her.

But he never did open up about the situation. I'm just guessing she cut some kind of deal with him to keep his mouth shut.

After all the meat-serving eateries had been sent packing, the only restaurant left standing was a pricey veghead place called the NuAge Cafe. The place bit the dust fairly quickly, because of family problems, I heard. But while it was open it served two kind of tenders, but not your usual cafe favorites — chicken and beef tenders. Instead they had broccoli-soy and sweet and sour tenders. That's the wrong kind of tenders. They also had soy everything: soy nuggets, garden soy kebobs, rainbow soy wraps, sizzling soy, and soy spinach rolls.

"I guarantee you, none of this is going to catch on as the last meal at Huntsville (the state prison)," said my friend, Edd O'Donnell, as he picked at his plate of shrubbery. We went to lunch there together — but only because I was writing about the place.

The neighbors never had any luck trying to talk to Daniels face to face. The neighborhood association, the West Austin Neighborhood Group, (with the unfortunate acronym WANG) tried to get Daniels to meet with them. She wouldn't do it. She would only send word of what she was up to through her property manager.

Meanwhile, the neighbors did little to fight back and just took it on the chin. They didn't appreciate her ravaging the mall, but they weren't about to make waves. Which isn't surprising. You don't see folks marching and carrying protest signs in your fancy neighborhoods. If it had been me, I might have chained myself to a ham.

There was some action brought in from outside the 'hood, though. Bama Brown, a popular Austin radio DJ, got some laughs when he showed up at the mall with a sausage cart. And when Daniels put up a sign at the mall that said "Support Austin's Animal Shelters," some undercover friends of meat in the dark of night covered Daniels' sign up with their own message.

"Eat More Poodle!" it read.

The whole time I was doing columns about this, Daniels wouldn't talk to me. She avoided me as if I had rabies. I left probably a half-dozen notes at her office in the mall. She was never in the office. I called her home in Houston and left a message. She didn't respond.

I even sent her a friendly registered letter. I was nice, polite, and endearing in the letter. Really. But I had wasted my time. The Queen of Green Cuisine sent it back unopened. I still have the letter in my desk drawer at work.

I tried to make a deal with the Meat Lady in one of my columns. Actually, it was more of a tongue-in-cheek threat than a deal. I said I would eat a different kind of meat every day until she called me.

In other words, talk to me or the pig gets it.

I can't remember all the sorts of meat I ate. I remember that I did draw the line at skunk.

"Since this quest began," I wrote, "if it's walked or wiggled, there's a good chance I've tried it, unless it was wearing a collar or was let up on the bed. Frankly, I'm running out of new menu choices — of the meat kind."

So when French scientists uncovered a mammoth carcass in Siberia, I said I hoped the members of the expedition didn't just pitch it. "So it was frozen over 20,000 years. I can deal with a little freezer burn," I said.

In 2007, the Meat Lady went public for a little publicity by teaming up with the People for the Ethical Treatment of Animals (PETA). To make a statement, she had the leather seats ripped out of her 2001 model black Mercedes-Benz CL 500 — a $92,000 car. I called a car dealership and found out it would have cost her about $5,000 to get the leather seats removed and replaced with faux leather seats.

Well, this had publicity stunt written all over it. Daniels mailed the leather seat remains to PETA. Then PETA sent two people dressed as cows to hand-deliver the seat remains to Daimler/Chrysler in both Michigan and Stuttgart, Germany.

The Meat Lady could have avoided all that trouble by buying a VW Bug instead, and giving the $92,000 she paid for her Mercedes to the dog pound.

A little irony here: in 1975, Daniels appeared in a photo in *People Weekly* magazine wearing what appears to be fur around her neck. The occasion was a fashion photo shoot in the small town of Salado, about an hour north of Austin. You can't tell for sure from the photo if what she had draped around her neck is real fur, or fake. But I'm betting it was real, since the women in the photo were Austin society dames. And the wealthy don't wear plastic.

It's not that I don't like animals. I've had dogs since I was a kid. I've got a picture on my desk at work of Bubba and Rufus, a couple of wonderful dogs I had back in the 1980s. We've currently got a Yorkie at home named Ziggy, and my daughter's dog, Zelda, a blue heeler, comes by and visits frequently.

But what got me is that Daniels didn't take into consideration the damage she was doing to people's lives by shutting down their businesses. Hey, people are animals, too, lady.

The end result is that the Tarrytown Mall is a lot deader than it used to be. Oh, the U.S. Post Office is still in the mall. I guess Daniels couldn't run off the federal government. And there's a barbershop, a coffee shop, and some other businesses. But ten or so years ago you'd see a lot more people running around the mall than you do today.

In 2010 the last mainstay of the mall, the Tarrytown Pharmacy, which opened in 1941, moved to a new spot up the street. Mark Newbury, the owner, left because he couldn't tell which way Daniels would jump when his lease came due. After all, a lot of the drugs he sells are the result of animal testing.

Would Daniels object to that and kick him out? He didn't want to be left holding the bag. So now not only can you not find a burger at the mall — you can't find an aspirin, either.

The Big C

There was some amusing irony to the diagnosis of cancer in my mouth.

The doctor found the tumor not long after I'd taken part in a taco-eating contest at Threadgill's World Headquarters home cookin' place in South Austin. This was the only see-how-much-food-you-can-cram-down-your-piehole event I'd ever entered.

And a couple weeks later, I found out my mouth had a cancer in it, hiding toward the back of my mouth, right side, under the tongue.

To my surprise, I hadn't done very well in the taco-eating contest. At the time I thought I'd just wimped out. I'd only downed about two and a half tacos. Maybe it was the annoying little pain from that thingy under my tongue that kept me from eating more. I don't know if that was a factor.

But after going through six weeks of radiation in the summer of 2009, I couldn't have eaten two and a half tacos if you'd put a chile relleno to my head.

I can't say I exactly freaked out when I found out I had the big C. Sure, it scared hell out of me. Anybody who isn't worried when they hear they've got cancer is from a different planet than the one I'm living on. But what concerned me even more than the cancer was the treatment. The diagnosis was good. The radiation doctor I spoke with, Dr. Shannon Cox, said that the survival rate for this one was in the 90%-plus range. No, what had me on edge was the treatment I'd be going through. I've heard for years that the treatments for cancer — radiation, chemotherapy, or both — are worse than the disease itself.

It just stands to reason that anything that can kill cancer has to be some bad-ass stuff.

I began my six weeks of radiation in late June that year. Monday through Friday, I'd travel up MoPac Boulevard to the hospital in far northwest Austin. Various people took turns driving me up there. A guy who had been a patient of Dr. Cox drove me several times. Cancer people help each other out, I discovered. Ed Crowell and Arnold Garcia from the newspaper also drove me up there. My wife Kay drove. So thanks to all you folks who served as my tumor chauffeur, so to speak.

For each zapping, I had to wear this hideous protective mask that looks like a squishy tennis racket. There's an evil look about this mask. It has a serial killer's swagger to it. If you went to somebody's door wearing this mask, the guy who lived there probably wouldn't open up.

A former boss of mine from the newspaper, who went through treatment before I did, kept his mask as a souvenir. The silly bastard, and I use that as a term of endearment here, sent me a photo of himself wearing his mask. He probably uses it on his Christmas card.

However, I couldn't deal with it. I left my mask at the hospital. The staff in the radiation room offered it to me, but I said no thanks. I don't need it; I'll see it in my nightmares.

Ah, radiation. So you're wearing this awful mask that snaps tightly over your face, which makes escaping problematic. You're stretched out, face up, on a bed that looks like a death row gurney. A big machine with a flashing green light makes beeping noises. The tech puts a flat stick in your mouth to protect your tongue. (The techs call this stick a "lollipop." Hey, I'm glad somebody's having a good time, right?) Each treatment takes only about fifteen minutes.

What takes a long time is the recovery. One of the nurses at the cancer treatment center on Martin Luther King, Jr., Boulevard, a great guy named Jimmy, told me they have certain patients whom they refer to as "radiation freaks."

Being a radiation freak is a good thing. A radiation freak is a fortunate soul who can go through radiation with little or no side effects. He's the lucky one who can hop up and mow the lawn right after radiation, as if nothing had happened.

I was not that guy. Not even close. I was on the other end of the spectrum. Radiation made me feel like a popped balloon. Really. It took me a good year to completely get my energy back. There were weeks on end when I would wake up in the morning feeling so listless that I dreaded the sun's coming up. I'd see sunlight peeking through the shades and think, *Aw, hell, another day of misery*. Another long, miserable day feeling like hammered poop. How long can this go on? And I looked as bad as I felt.

A friend of mine, Ben Wear, the *American-Statesman*'s transportation writer, took a look at me one day and said to himself, "Is this Kelso? Is this what's left for him?"

Still, the whole time I figured I'd make it through and come out fine at the other end. I just didn't know how far away the other end was. But brother, did I want to know! I'd ask Dr. Cox about it repeatedly. I pestered him with that question. I must have asked him twenty-five times how much longer it would be before I wouldn't feel like a human piñata. When he heard my questions, Dr. Cox would waffle.

Dr. Shannon Cox is a great guy. We became friends. After I'd completed the treatment, he gave me a framed football action photo from the 2009 Big 12 title game between Texas and Nebraska. I have it hanging on the wall of my office at home. "In honor of his discipline, will, and strength going through treatment of his cancer," the back of the photo reads. Now that's a great doctor, right? I'm honored to have that gift.

But whenever I'd ask Dr. Cox how much longer it would be before I became whole again, he'd fudge. "I would say . . ." he usually began.

But he never really said. How could he? Everybody's different. Some people take six months to bounce back, others a year. He didn't know. He could only guess.

The whole experience was hard on my family. They got as sick of dealing with the disease as I did. There were a couple of weeks when I literally couldn't speak. This is normal with radiation to the mouth. To converse, I carried around a Doodle Pro, one of those kid toys you can write on, then erase your message and start over again.

There was a problem, though: my handwriting is so bad that it caused confusion. The pen that came with the Doodle Pro was shaped like a carrot. So one day I wrote down on the Doodle Pro "The pen is a carrot" and showed the message to my wife, Kay.

She thought I'd written "My penis A carrot." We had a good laugh over that one.

As time went on, though, the laughter stopped, and the situation got old. It's tough being a caregiver. I know. I've done it twice. I spent eight years looking after my mother when she had Alzheimer's. That one was made easier since she was in a nursing home. And I spent another year looking after another family member who had a deadly cancer.

Looking back, what amazes me is that during my radiation experience I kept writing columns for the newspaper. I'm not saying they were any good. But they were good for my mental health. The bright spot of my day was dragging myself down the hall to my office at home, getting on the laptop, and writing. This took my mind off my troubles, at least for a few hours.

They tell me the mouth is the worst place you can have radiation. I believe them. I had a friend who had radiation for prostate cancer. He couldn't understand why I was having so much trouble, since his radiation was a piece of cake.

The difference, of course, is that you don't eat through your nether regions. For some reason, my friend could never grasp the difference.

And yes, eating was a big problem for me. As I write this, I'm munching on an almond croissant from Central Market. While I was going through radiation, eating a croissant would have been a form of torture.

I had a decision to make. Did I want to try to keep eating naturally, or did I want a tummy tube? The idea of a surgeon drilling a hole in my stomach and inserting a tube so that I could pour a little bit of food into the hole every day, well, this didn't sound real cheery. Besides, Dr. Cox explained that you can't put much food in a tummy tube, anyway. So I decided against that route and determined to eat real food the real way.

I couldn't deal with solid food like, say, burgers, chicken, fish — you name it. Radiation dries up your mouth, so I didn't have the saliva to chew up most things.

I survived on a nutrition drink called Ensure, and homemade milkshakes. That was pretty much my menu for several months. I made the milkshakes myself. The key here was to get enough calories down to keep my weight up. When I started this process I weighed 208 pounds, but at the worst point I dropped to a low of 169. Jimmy, the nurse I mentioned earlier, told me the more weight I'd put on, the better I'd feel, and the more I lost, the weaker I'd feel.

Turns out he was right. When I'd drop a few pounds my energy would deteriorate. So I went to the store to find the highest calorie ice cream available on the shelves. The fattest ice cream I could find was Häagen-Dazs®. I loaded up on that stuff. I think Häagen-Dazs® Eggnog was the flavor with the highest calorie count, so I'd buy out the nearby HEB of that flavor. Then I'd stick the ice cream in a blender, along with some protein powder, and let her rip.

I drank as many milkshakes as I could stand nearly every day. Not that I could stand that many. Eating was a chore. Some days I could drink one milkshake, others two.

You'd think by now I couldn't look a milkshake in the face, but I still love milkshakes, although these days I prefer a bowl of Blue Bell Christmas Cookies or Chocolate Chip Cookie Dough.

On the other hand, because of my cancer experience, I could write an article rating Austin's milkshakes. Amy's Ice Cream may have the best one in town, but they're pretty expensive. Steak 'n Shake is just as good as Amy's, and a lot cheaper. The place even had a milkshake happy hour. You could get a milkshake at Steak 'n Shake for $1.99 from 2:00 to 5:00 in the afternoon. Baskin-Robbins was okay, but unpredictable. Quality would depend on who was making the milkshake. I bought one stinker there that tasted like they forgot to add the ice cream. And Sonic has a thick one called a Sonic Blast that you can stand a spoon up in. Remember to add the M&Ms. That really jacks it up.

There were some special moments during my treatment. There was the moment when I really thought I was touched by some supreme power. I'm not a churchgoer. I don't figure a Supreme Being needs my help by my showing up once a week to lend my support, since, after all, the being is supreme, right? But that doesn't mean I count out the possibility of there being some higher authority. I just hope She likes smart-asses.

Anyway, this experience took place a few days before Christmas. The radiation treatment was nearly half a year behind me, but I still felt weak and worn.

Then, in an instant, while I was sitting in the living room, I felt a significant amount of my energy pop back in. In a few seconds, just like that! I can't explain it. But it happened.

The good thing to come from all this? I'm still here, I feel great, and I've only suffered a couple of drawbacks from the radiation.

However, I still can't eat anything spicy. Any pepper in my mouth and my gums feel like they are being stabbed with needles. Really. And that's a shame because I love hot stuff. So now I have to live without chili, wasabi, salsa, horseradish — all the good spicy things. How are you supposed to eat a raw oyster without hot sauce? Have you ever tried sushi without wasabi? And how about tortilla chips? These days I eat the chips dry, right out of the basket. Talk about a letdown.

So, sadly, I'm making no more visits to the Texas Chili Parlor for the 2X. Or any X at all, come to think of it.

When you go into a restaurant, you look up and down the menu for your favorite item, right? Well, I look up and down for something I can actually eat without pain. Radiation leaves you with dry mouth, so I have a hard time with chicken. I can eat it, but I have to gnaw on it for a couple of minutes. Pork ribs are fine, as long as they have some fat on them.

Sure, there are toothpastes and mouthwashes and all sorts of products for dry mouth, and they help, but they don't chase it off.

Still, those inconveniences are a small price to pay, because here's the real kicker that made all of this worthwhile: other cancer patients and survivors wrote me and said the columns about my recovery were a help to them, even an inspiration.

That was the best part of the trip. It was great to be able to give a boost to other people who were suffering through the same ordeal.

Are Newspapers Doomed?

It never occurred to me when I started writing for newspapers in the 1960s that there would come a day when the newspaper business might disappear.

You may remember that earlier in this book I mentioned my grandfather, John Bradford, a master carpenter up in South Portland, Maine, who made spars for clipper ships in his younger days. As he got older, the clipper ships went the way of the buffalo, and my grandfather took a job selling caskets to funeral homes.

The same thing is happening to newspapers. We humans are both the benefactors and the victims of our own technology. We create an advancement of some sort, and then it eats us alive. Around 1440, the printing press was invented. About 570 years later, along came Facebook. So hello, Zuckerberg, and goodbye Guttenberg.

Consequently, the number of people reading the *Austin American-Statesman* is way down, just as newspaper readers are down all over the country. We used to have a circulation of about 220,000 on a Sunday back in the 1990s, and 170,000 or so on a weekday. Now our readership is closer to 140,000 on Sundays and 110,00 on weekdays.

The right-wingers will gloat and tell you this is because newspapers are too liberal, but that's not it. In fact, right-wingers love to read newspapers they think are too liberal because it gives them something to crab about.

Nope, the reason newspapers are in decline is the Internet.

People don't get their news off the driveway anymore. They don't have to. It shows up right in their pockets. Instead of A.P. being the big news source, it's the APP. Simple as that.

Signs of the decline are everywhere. In 2012, the *Statesman* redesigned the newspaper to make it skinnier. I think it's a couple inches narrower than it used to be. That's not enough shrinkage, though. The way to compete in the new world would be to create a front page the size of an iPhone.

You can tell that not as many people are reading newspapers by checking out the newspaper's parking lot. In the good old days, on payday, you'd have a hard time finding a place to park. Now there's so much available parking that on a hot summer day, you might even get a spot under a shade tree.

The newspaper's staff has been trimmed. Back in the good old days, when budgets were loaded, the newsroom had about 170 employees: photographers, copy editors, reporters, and page designers. Now we're down to about 120 staff members in the newsroom. And many of the old hands are long gone now. In 2011, I was one of many *American-Statesman* veterans who took a buy-out of a year's pay. Budgets are being cut. In 2012, the money the paper pays me for freelance work was cut almost in half.

Not that I'm complaining. I'm not. I'm happy they keep me around at all.

And no, I don't think newspapers will disappear. Daily newspapers carry information you can't find anywhere else. As I write this I'm working on a column about Luther Edmonson, a pig-tailed dog groomer in Austin who has probably the world's largest collection of Coca-Cola paraphernalia. He's sold his shop, retired, and he's going to sell his massive collection of Coke stuff — collectible bottles, toy trucks, Barbie dolls, Coke machines, lunch boxes, you name it — at an estate sale.

Where else but in your local newspaper are you going to read about this kind of stuff? The *New York Times* isn't going to cover this. And I doubt you'll be able to find it online, unless some blogger mentions it. And if a blogger mentions it, he'll probably misspell Luther's name, since he doesn't have a managing editor who'll kick his butt if he screws up the story.

And where else but in your local paper are you going to read about the issues your City Council candidates are pushing?

I believe that for as long as the locals care about their town, newspapers will be around. I do think papers will continue to shrink, but they'll keep doing a print edition for the old folks, who prefer a real newspaper over the online substitute. What happens when today's young folks become tomorrow's old folks, though, is anybody's guess.

At the same time, I believe the online edition will keep growing. That's where the future is, and the future is already here. Newspaper reporters will tell you how the online version has changed the way they do business. Now, as the day goes along, thanks to technology, reporters have to plug in information as it changes throughout the day by Tweeting.

That's a change? Reporters used to do the same thing on a pay phone. And when you get right down to it, the way reporters find out what's going on is the same, whether the story appears in print or on a laptop. We still have to talk to people and dig.

So yeah, local newspapers will be around, as long as the citizens remain curious. And with a vice-presidential candidate talking about getting rid of Medicare, they better stay curious.

I Did It For the Laughs

After I landed the humor columnist job in Austin, nothing made me happier than to walk into a place and see somebody reading my column and laughing. That's what I was aiming for. I did win an award from the National Press Club in 2005 for humor writing. The column that sealed up the victory told the story of a redneck in Florida who hit his girlfriend with a live alligator he'd been keeping in the bathtub. The sheriff's deputy showed up in the morning and they had been drinking.

When I say "they" I'm talking about the guy and his girlfriend, not the alligator.

But actually seeing the laughter happen was more important than the award.

I remember one day, probably a quarter century ago, when I walked into the 290 Café out in Manor for breakfast. I had just written a column about the Trojan Enz company coming out with a new super size condom. For the column, I had researched Trojan Enz's audacious size claims on the new condom by taking one of these units over to a University of Texas chemistry professor. He filled it up with a beaker.

I reported the mathematical measurement findings in my column. Another thing I remember about the column was that it included the phrase "the size of a saxophone." Anyway, out at the Manor Café, behind the counter a couple of waitresses were reading the super size Trojan Enz column. They were laughing out loud, and they didn't even know I was there.

Really, that's up there with an Oscar for a humor columnist, seeing someone reading your stuff, and watching them guffaw. It doesn't get any better than that for a guy who tries to write funny stuff.

So that's what I set out to do, pretty much every time I sat down at a typewriter or a computer keyboard.

CPSIA information can be obtained at www.ICGtesting.com
Printed in the USA
LVOW12s2338141013

356825LV00002B/2/P